MY Lovey-Dovey Wife IS A STONE COLD KILLER

story & art by
Donten Kosaka

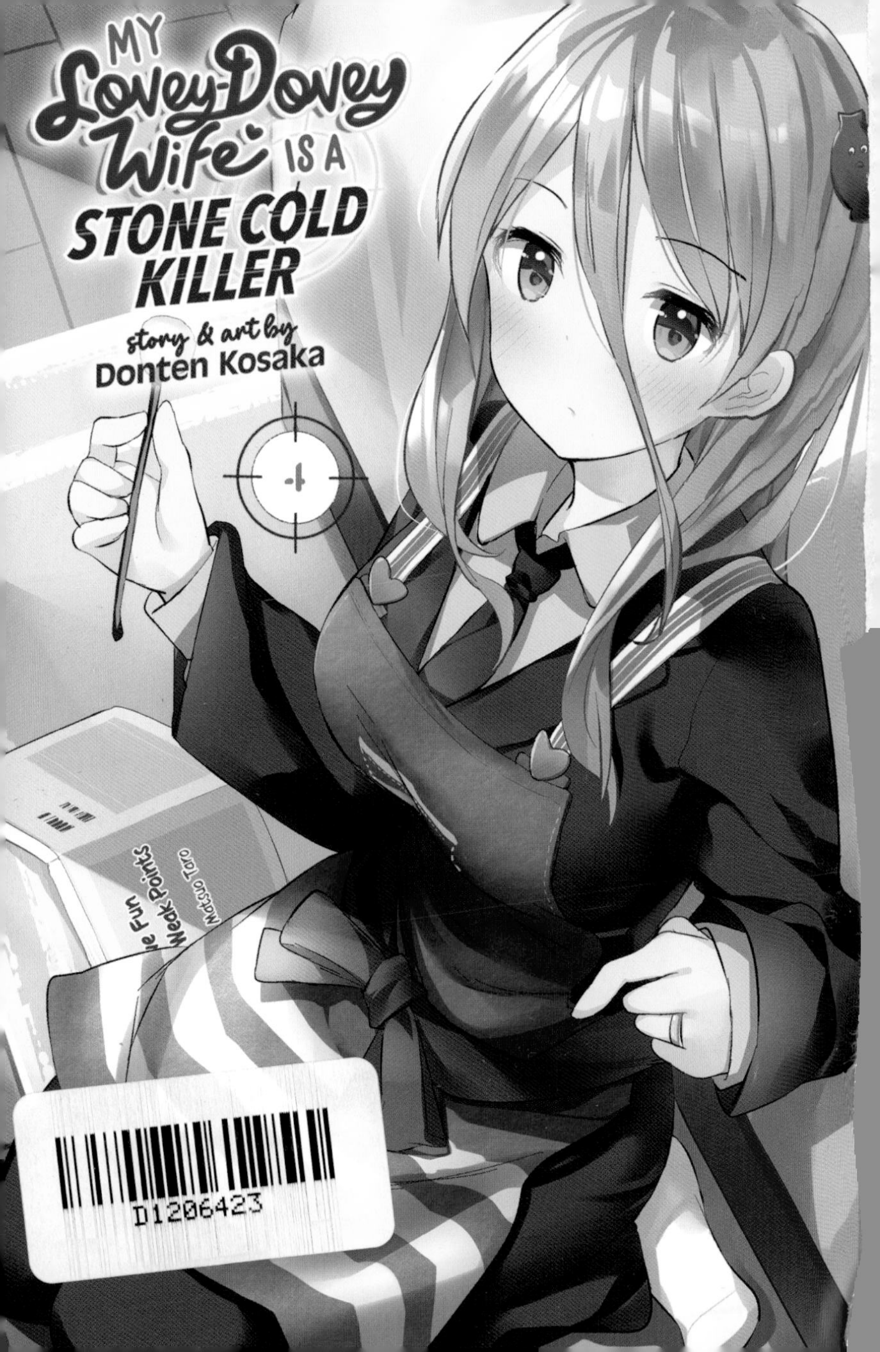
4
Weak Points
Matsuo Taro

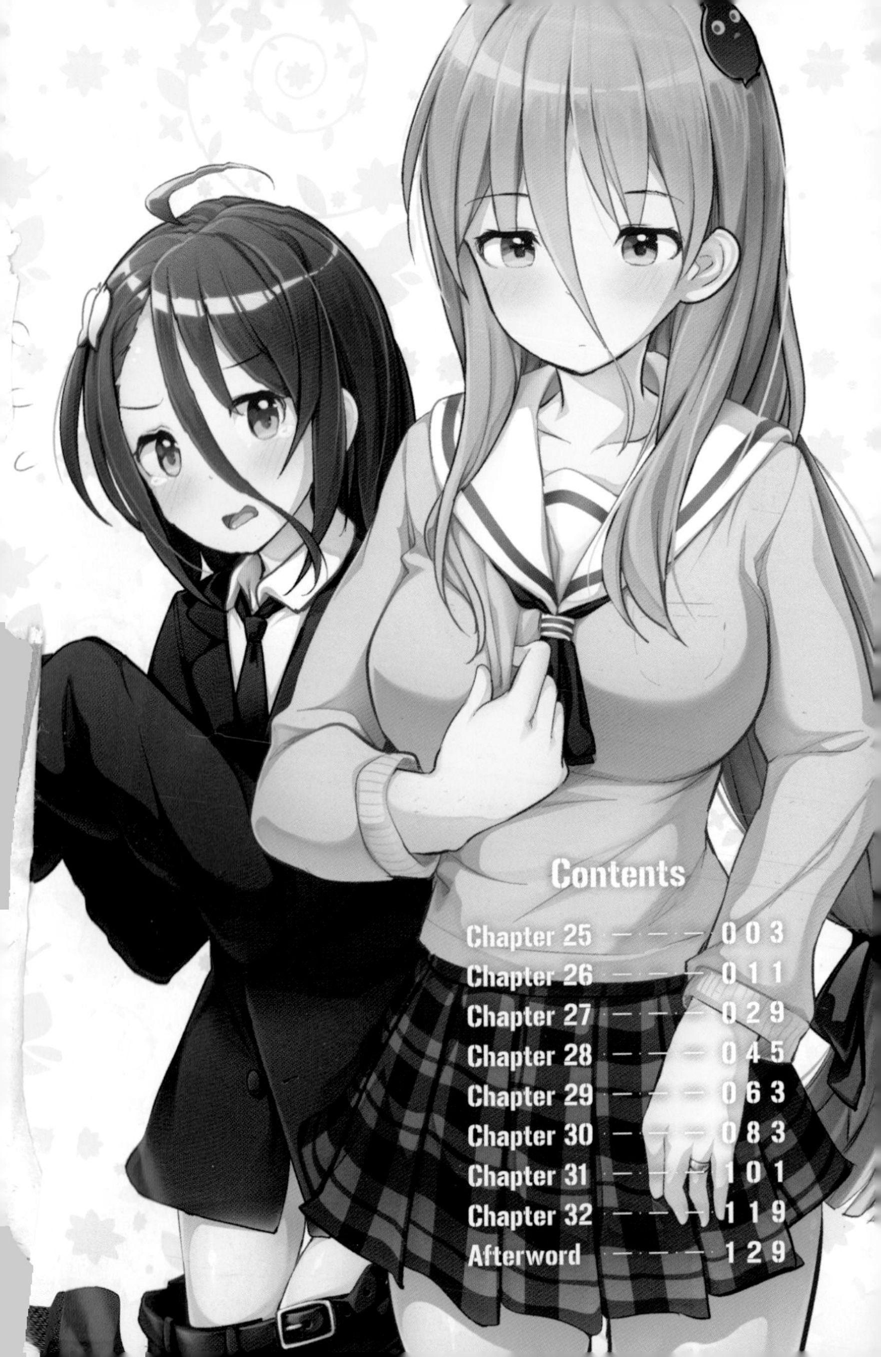

Contents

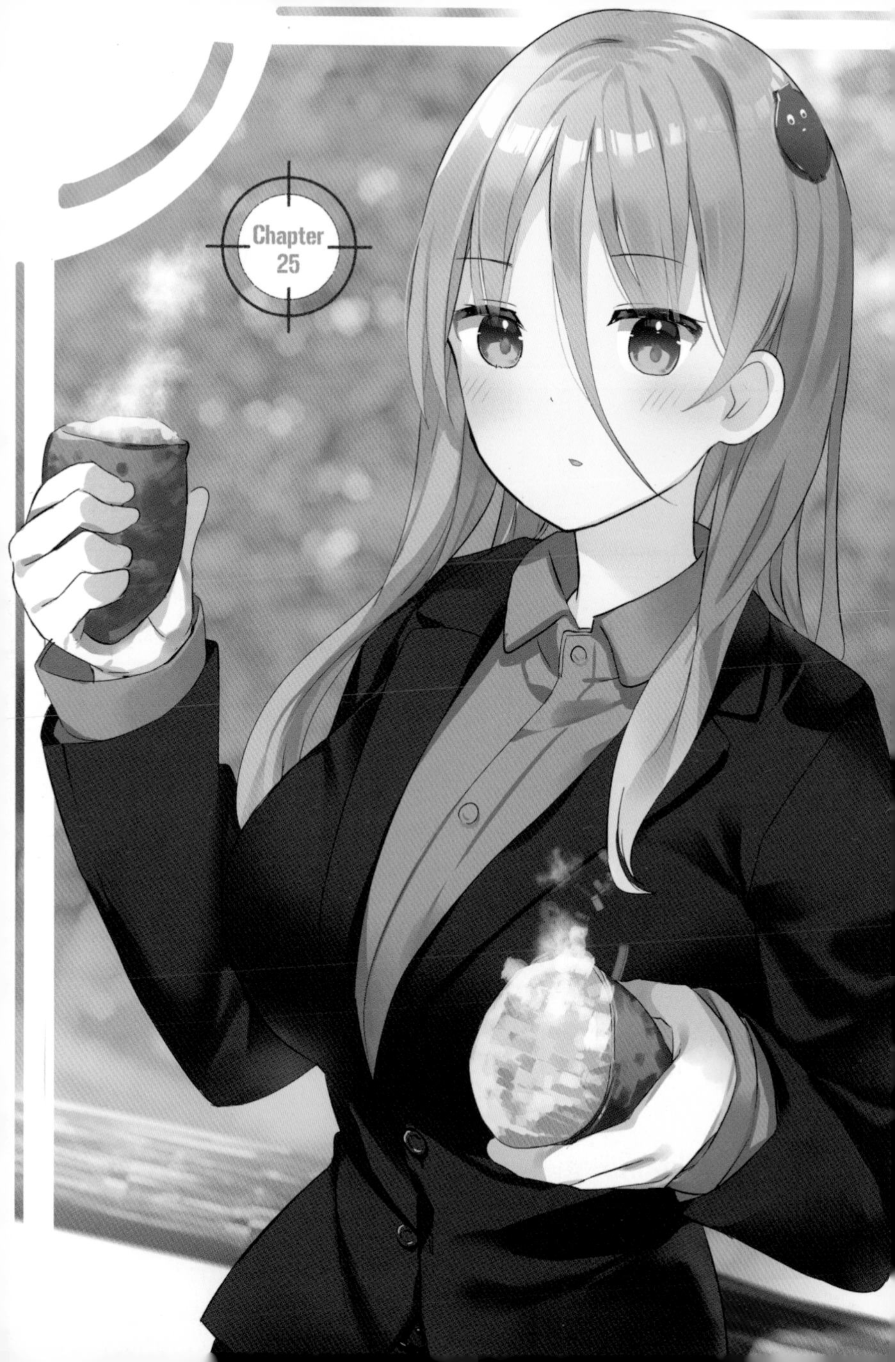
Chapter
25

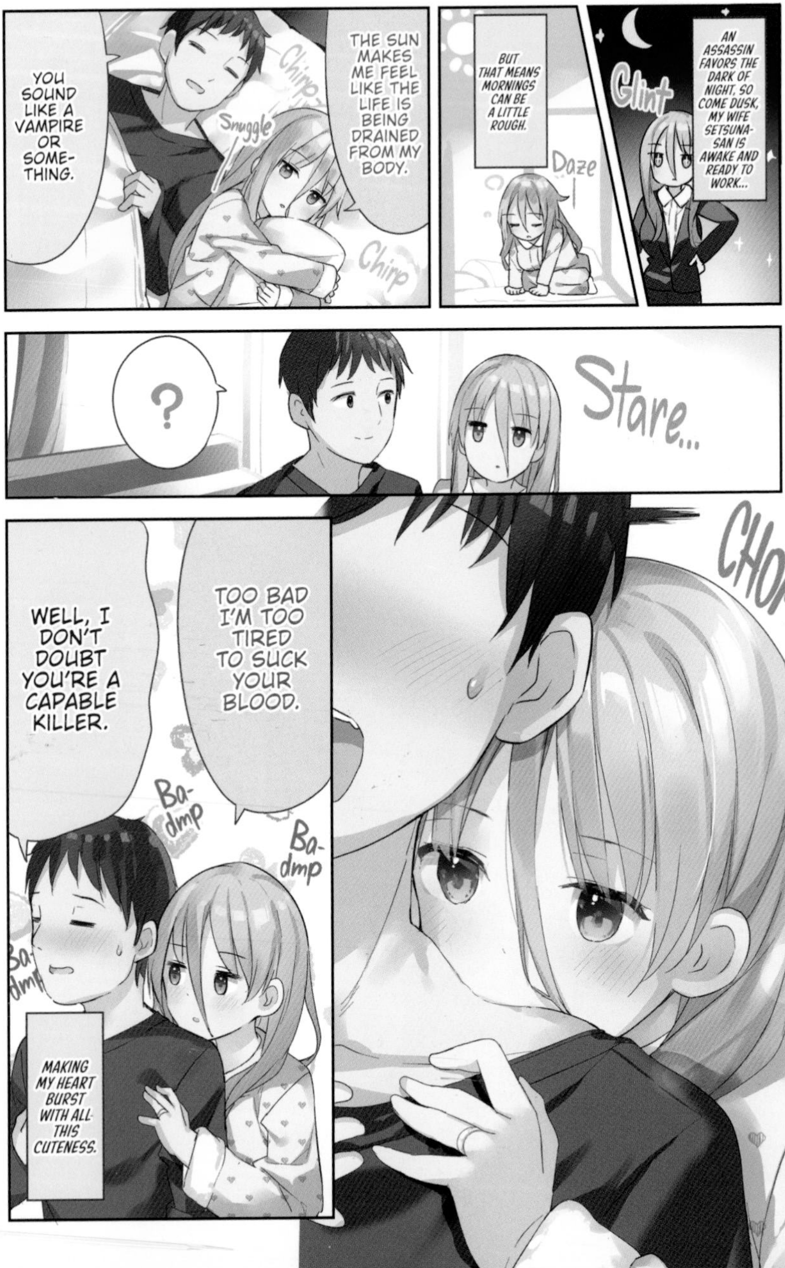
AN ASSASSIN FAVORS THE DARK OF NIGHT, SO COME DUSK, MY WIFE SETSUNA-SAN IS AWAKE AND READY TO WORK...
Glint
BUT THAT MEANS MORNINGS CAN BE A LITTLE ROUGH.
Daze
THE SUN MAKES ME FEEL LIKE THE LIFE IS BEING DRAINED FROM MY BODY.
Chirp
Snuggle
YOU SOUND LIKE A VAMPIRE OR SOME-THING.
Chirp
Stare...
?
CHOMP
TOO BAD I'M TOO TIRED TO SUCK YOUR BLOOD.
WELL, I DON'T DOUBT YOU'RE A CAPABLE KILLER.
Ba-dmp
Ba-dmp
Ba-dmp
MAKING MY HEART BURST WITH ALL THIS CUTENESS.

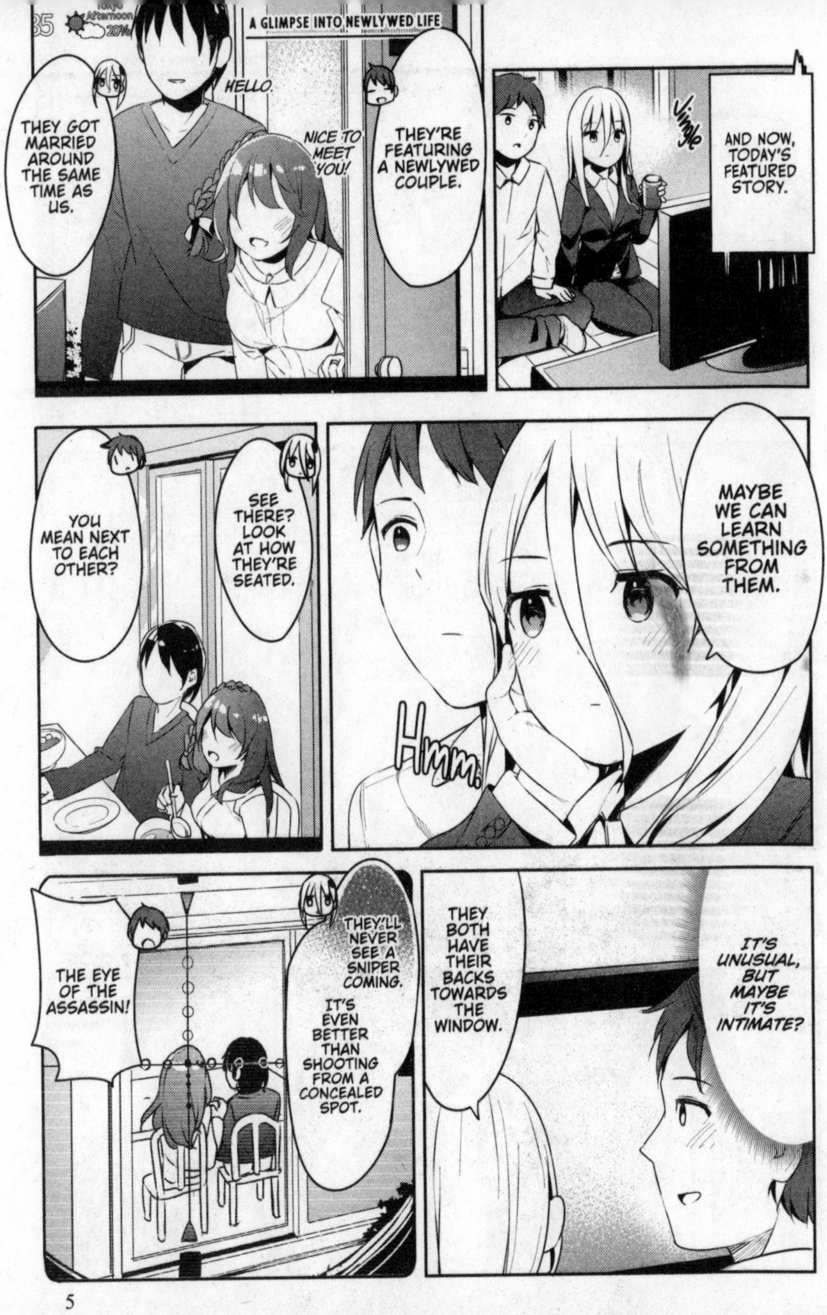
35
Tokyo
Afternoon
20%
A GLIMPSE INTO NEWLYWED LIFE
AND NOW, TODAY'S FEATURED STORY.
Jingle
THEY'RE FEATURING A NEWLYWED COUPLE.
NICE TO MEET YOU!
HELLO.
THEY GOT MARRIED AROUND THE SAME TIME AS US.
MAYBE WE CAN LEARN SOMETHING FROM THEM.
Hmm.
SEE THERE? LOOK AT HOW THEY'RE SEATED.
YOU MEAN NEXT TO EACH OTHER?
IT'S UNUSUAL, BUT MAYBE IT'S INTIMATE?
THEY BOTH HAVE THEIR BACKS TOWARDS THE WINDOW.
THEY'LL NEVER SEE A SNIPER COMING.
IT'S EVEN BETTER THAN SHOOTING FROM A CONCEALED SPOT.
THE EYE OF THE ASSASSIN!

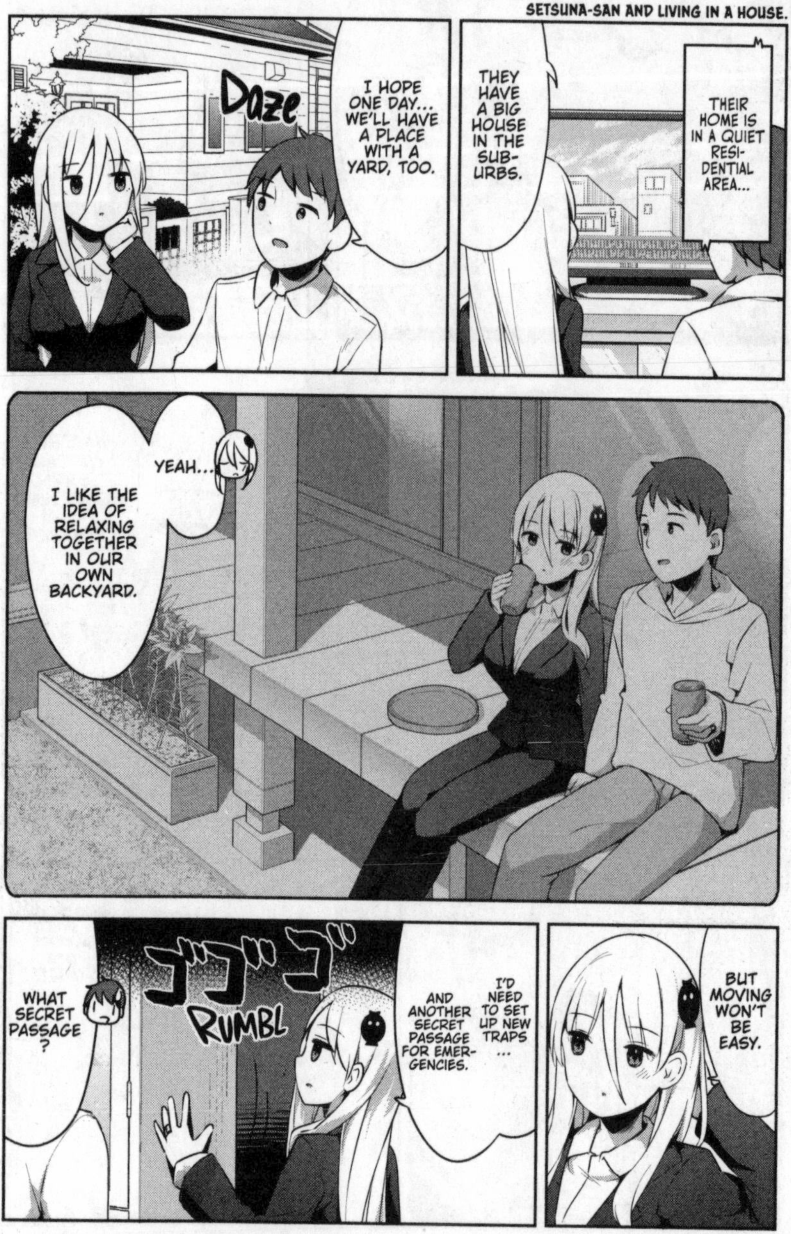
THEIR HOME IS IN A QUIET RESIDENTIAL AREA...
THEY HAVE A BIG HOUSE IN THE SUBURBS.
Daze
I HOPE ONE DAY... WE'LL HAVE A PLACE WITH A YARD, TOO.
YEAH...
I LIKE THE IDEA OF RELAXING TOGETHER IN OUR OWN BACKYARD.
BUT MOVING WON'T BE EASY.
I'D NEED TO SET UP NEW TRAPS...
AND ANOTHER SECRET PASSAGE FOR EMERGENCIES.
ゴゴゴ
RUMBL
WHAT SECRET PASSAGE?

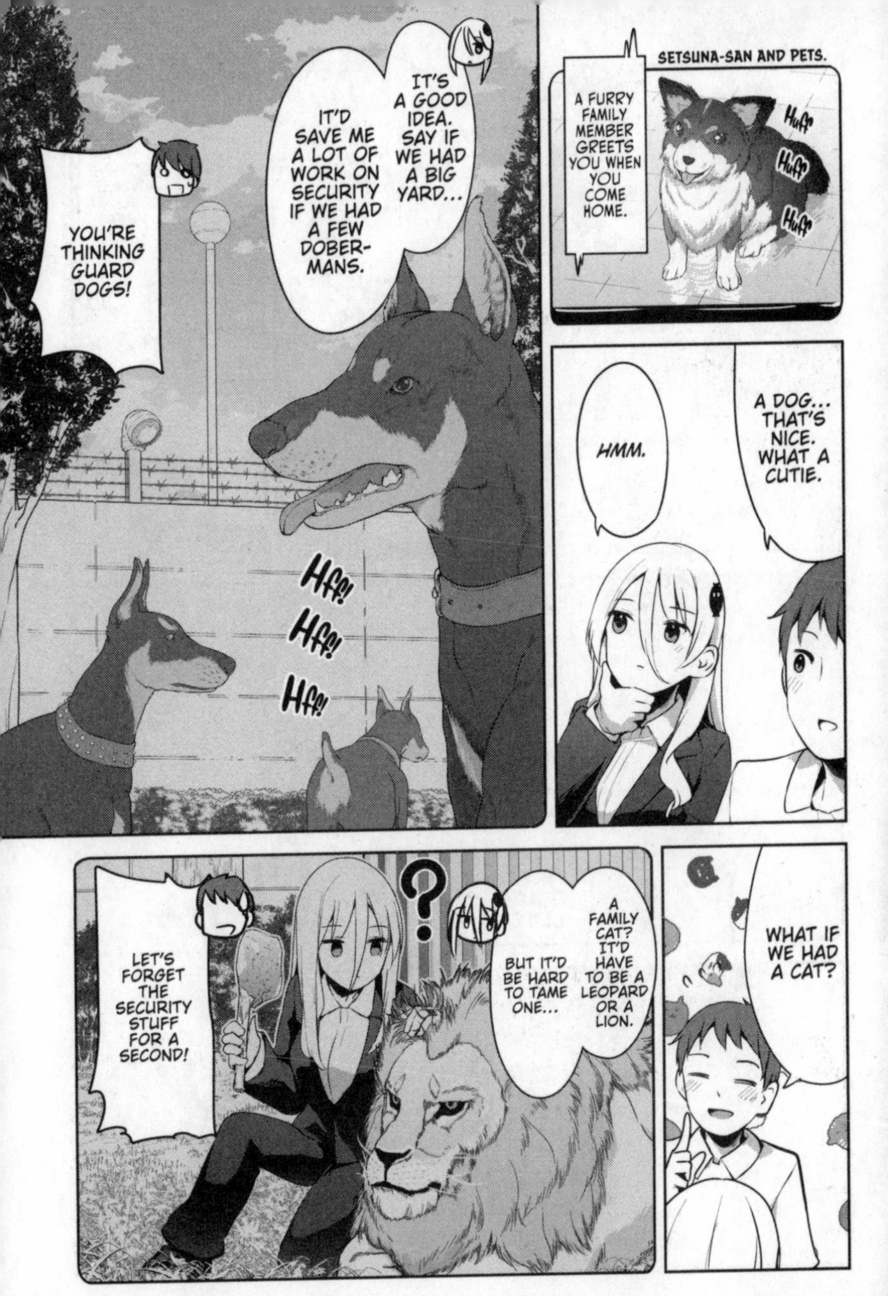
SETSUNA-SAN AND PETS.
A FURRY FAMILY MEMBER GREETS YOU WHEN YOU COME HOME.
Huff
Huff
Huff
A DOG... THAT'S NICE. WHAT A CUTIE.
HMM.
IT'S A GOOD IDEA. SAY IF WE HAD A BIG YARD...
IT'D SAVE ME A LOT OF WORK ON SECURITY IF WE HAD A FEW DOBER-MANS.
YOU'RE THINKING GUARD DOGS!
Hff!
Hff!
Hff!
WHAT IF WE HAD A CAT?
?
A FAMILY CAT? IT'D HAVE TO BE A LEOPARD OR A LION.
BUT IT'D BE HARD TO TAME ONE...
LET'S FORGET THE SECURITY STUFF FOR A SECOND!

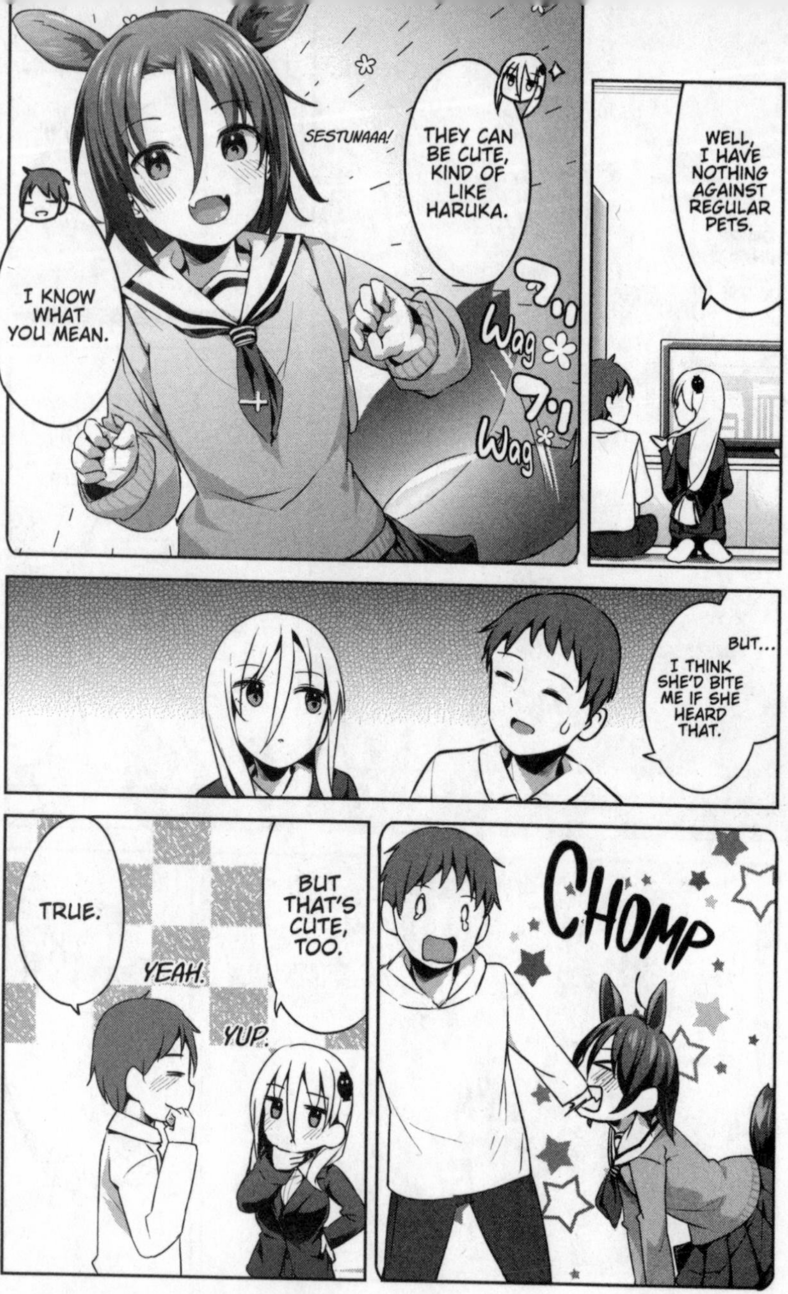
WELL, I HAVE NOTHING AGAINST REGULAR PETS.
THEY CAN BE CUTE, KIND OF LIKE HARUKA.
SESTUNAAA!
Wag
Wag
I KNOW WHAT YOU MEAN.
BUT... I THINK SHE'D BITE ME IF SHE HEARD THAT.
CHOMP
BUT THAT'S CUTE, TOO.
TRUE.
YEAH.
YUP.

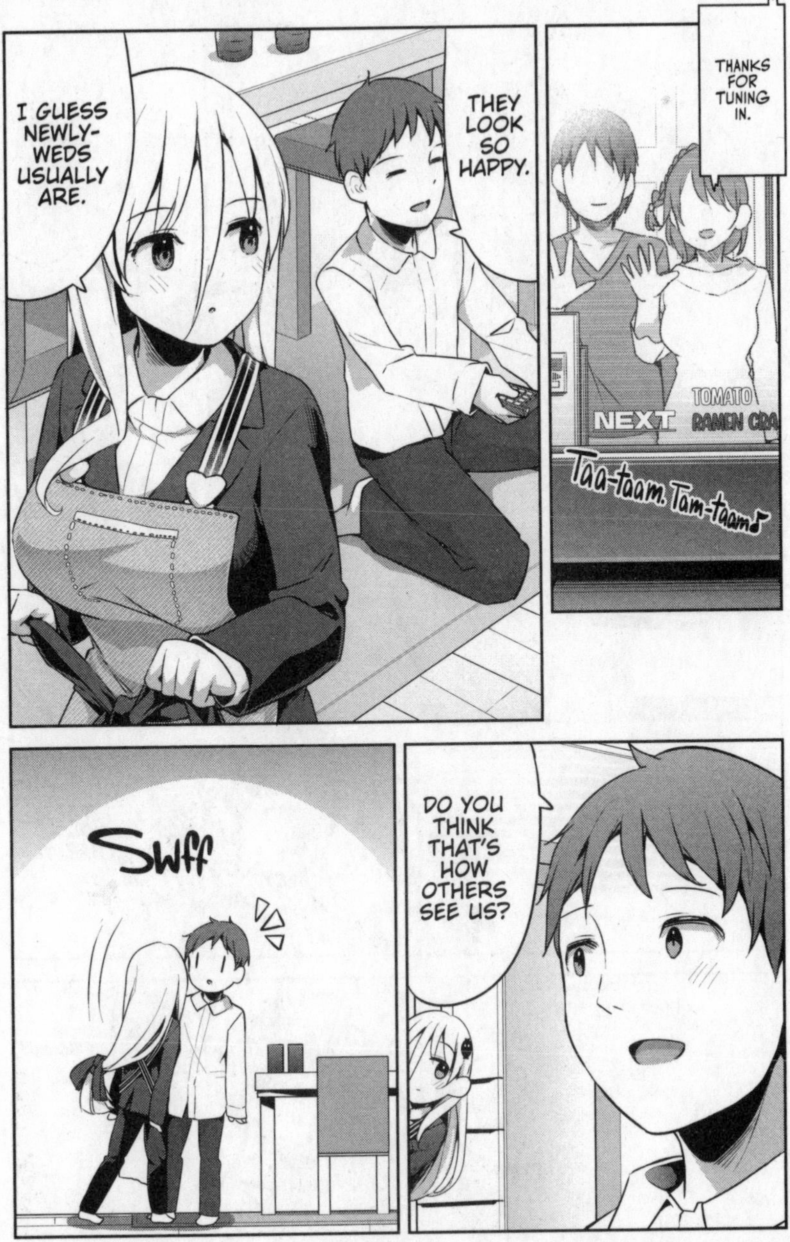
THANKS FOR TUNING IN.
TOMATO
NEXT
RAMEN CRA
Taa-taam. Tam-taam♪
THEY LOOK SO HAPPY.
I GUESS NEWLY-WEDS USUALLY ARE.
DO YOU THINK THAT'S HOW OTHERS SEE US?
Swff

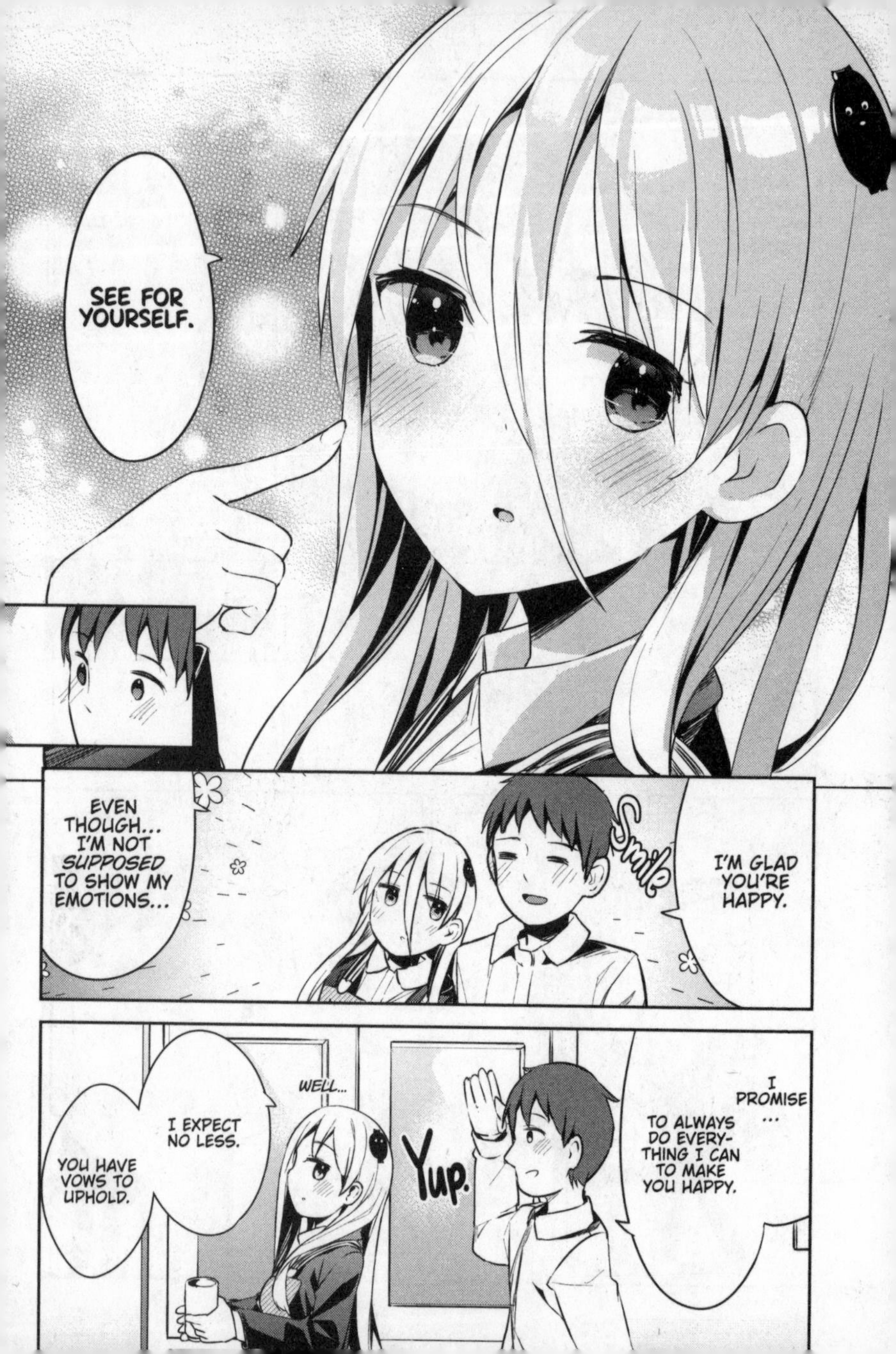
SEE FOR YOURSELF.
I'M GLAD YOU'RE HAPPY.
Smile
EVEN THOUGH... I'M NOT *SUPPOSED* TO SHOW MY EMOTIONS...
I PROMISE ...
TO ALWAYS DO EVERY-THING I CAN TO MAKE YOU HAPPY.
Yup.
WELL...
I EXPECT NO LESS.
YOU HAVE VOWS TO UPHOLD.

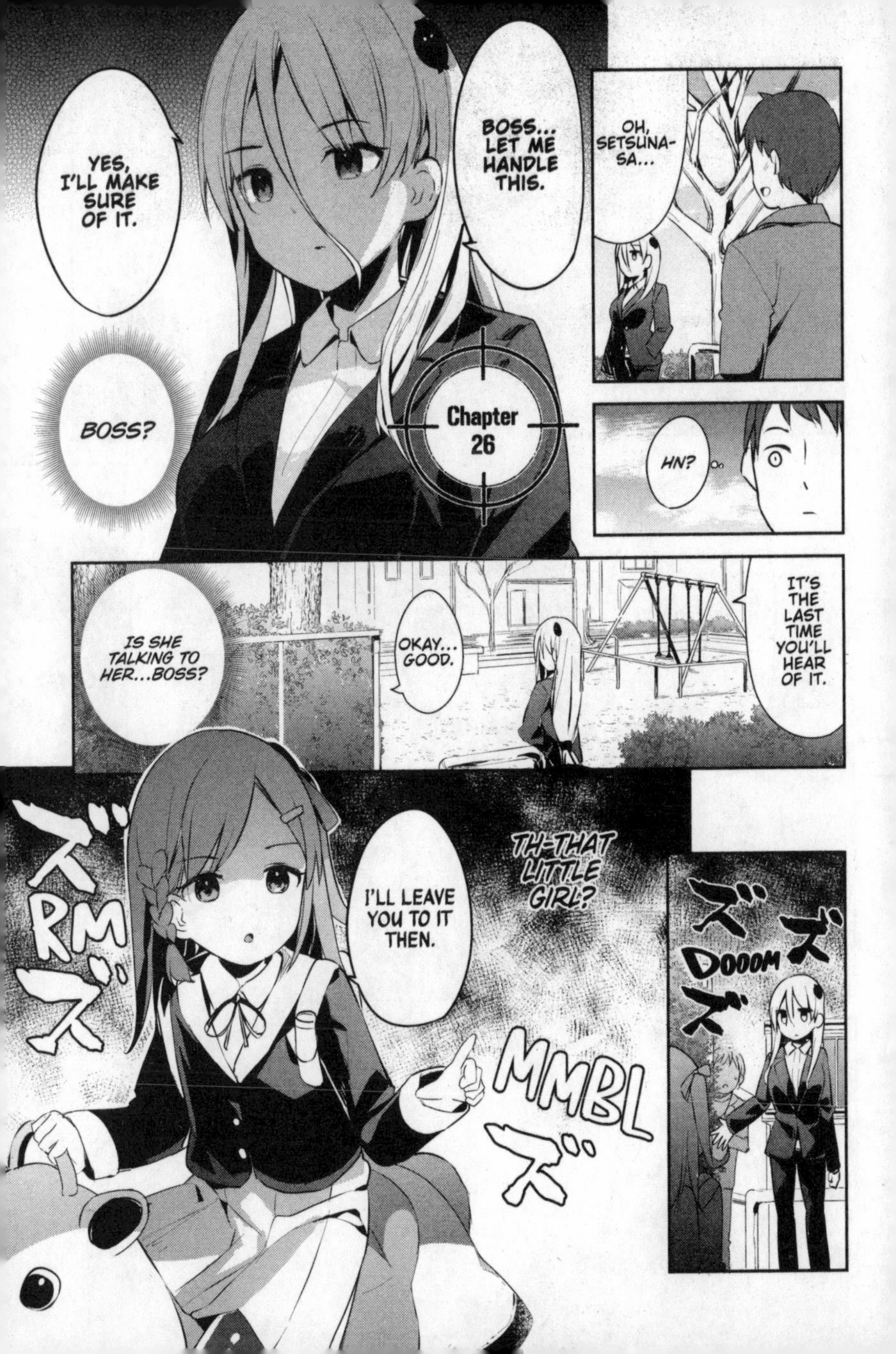
OH, SETSUNA-SA...
HN?
BOSS... LET ME HANDLE THIS.
YES, I'LL MAKE SURE OF IT.
BOSS?
Chapter 26
IT'S THE LAST TIME YOU'LL HEAR OF IT.
OKAY... GOOD.
IS SHE TALKING TO HER...BOSS?
ズズ DOOOM ズズ
TH-THAT LITTLE GIRL?
I'LL LEAVE YOU TO IT THEN.
MMBL ズズ
ズ RM ズズ

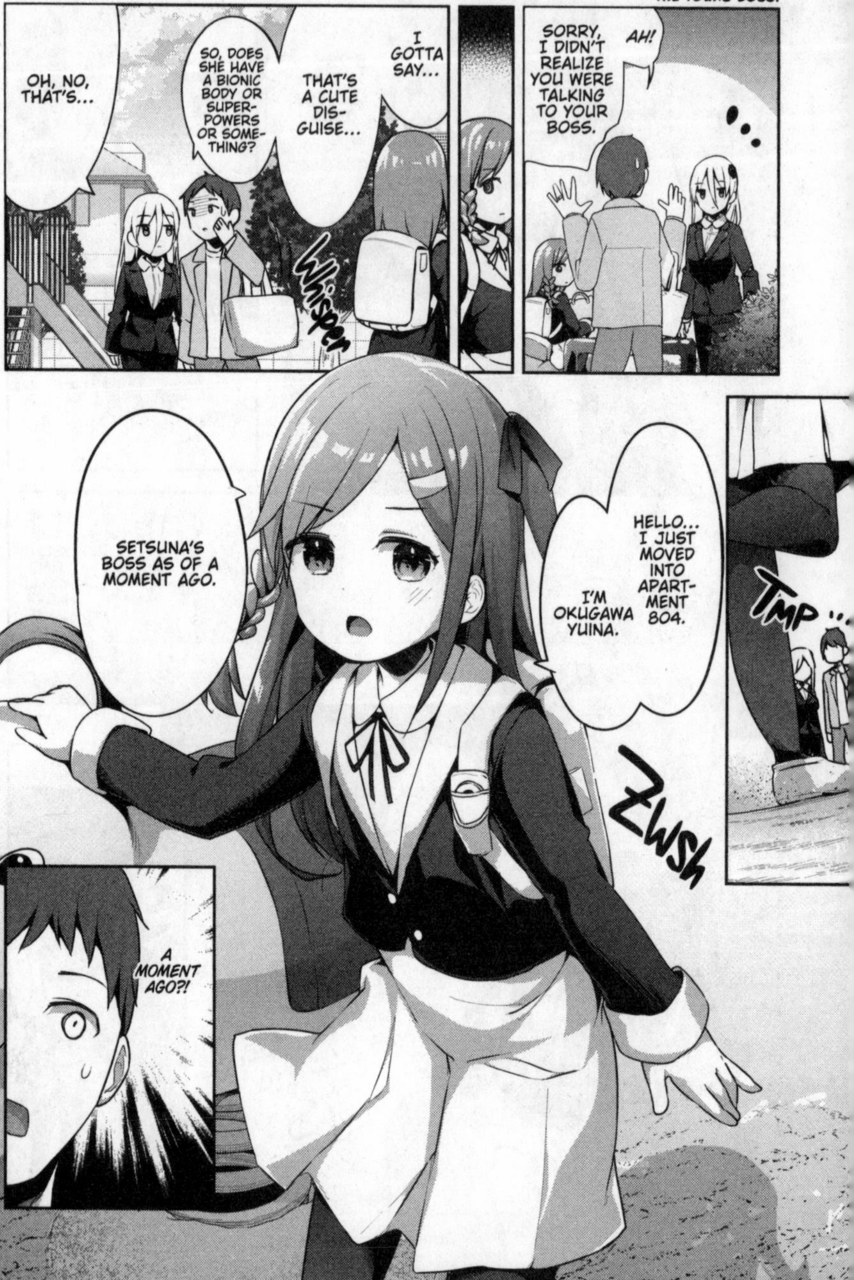
AH!
SORRY, I DIDN'T REALIZE YOU WERE TALKING TO YOUR BOSS.
...
I GOTTA SAY...
THAT'S A CUTE DISGUISE...
SO, DOES SHE HAVE A BIONIC BODY OR SUPERPOWERS OR SOMETHING?
Whisper
OH, NO, THAT'S...
TMP...
HELLO... I JUST MOVED INTO APARTMENT 804.
I'M OKUGAWA YUINA.
ZWSH
SETSUNA'S BOSS AS OF A MOMENT AGO.
A MOMENT AGO?!

SETSUNA-SAN'S NEW BOSS.

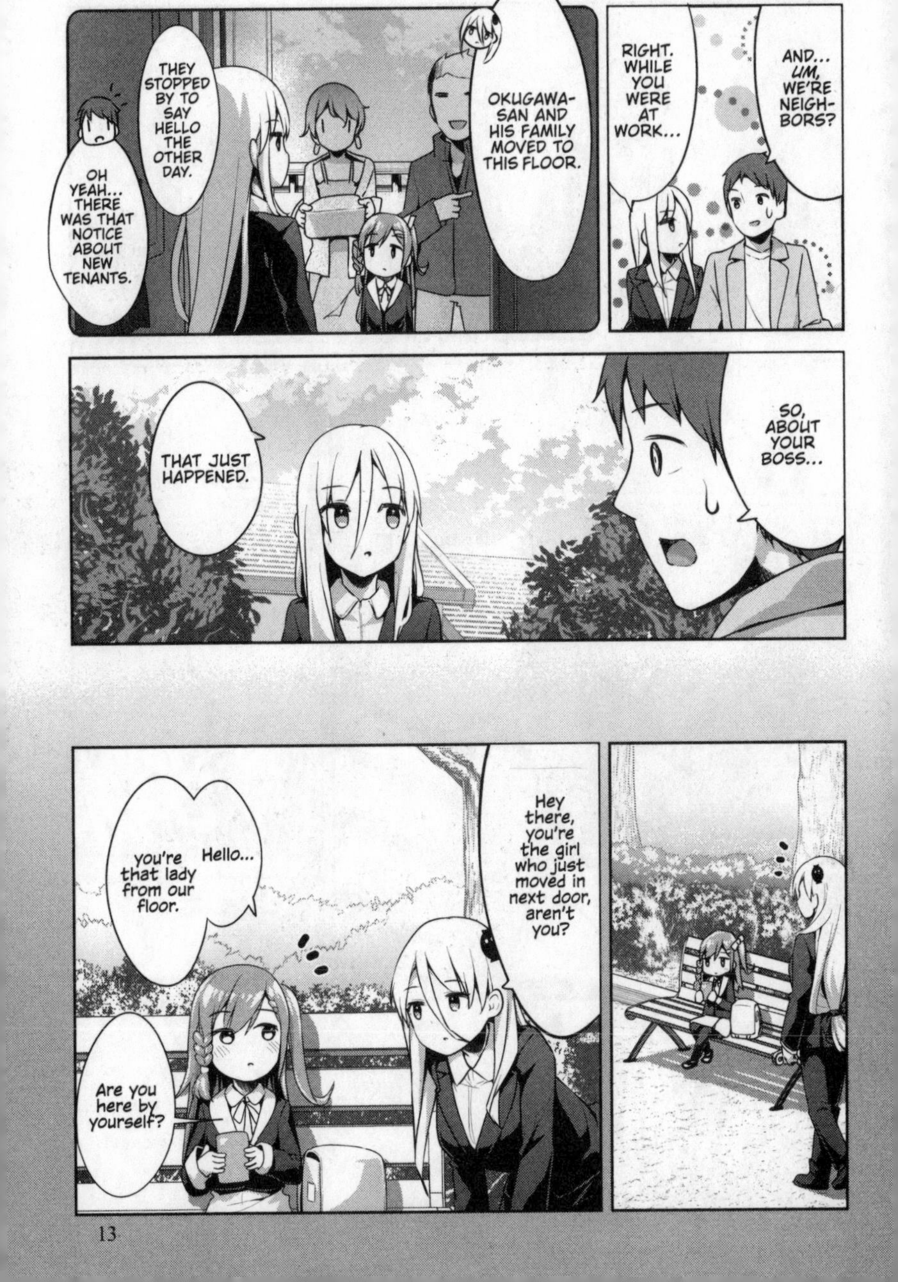
AND... UM, WE'RE NEIGHBORS?
RIGHT. WHILE YOU WERE AT WORK...
OKUGAWA-SAN AND HIS FAMILY MOVED TO THIS FLOOR.
THEY STOPPED BY TO SAY HELLO THE OTHER DAY.
OH YEAH... THERE WAS THAT NOTICE ABOUT NEW TENANTS.
SO, ABOUT YOUR BOSS...
THAT JUST HAPPENED.
Hey there, you're the girl who just moved in next door, aren't you?
Hello... you're that lady from our floor.
Are you here by yourself?

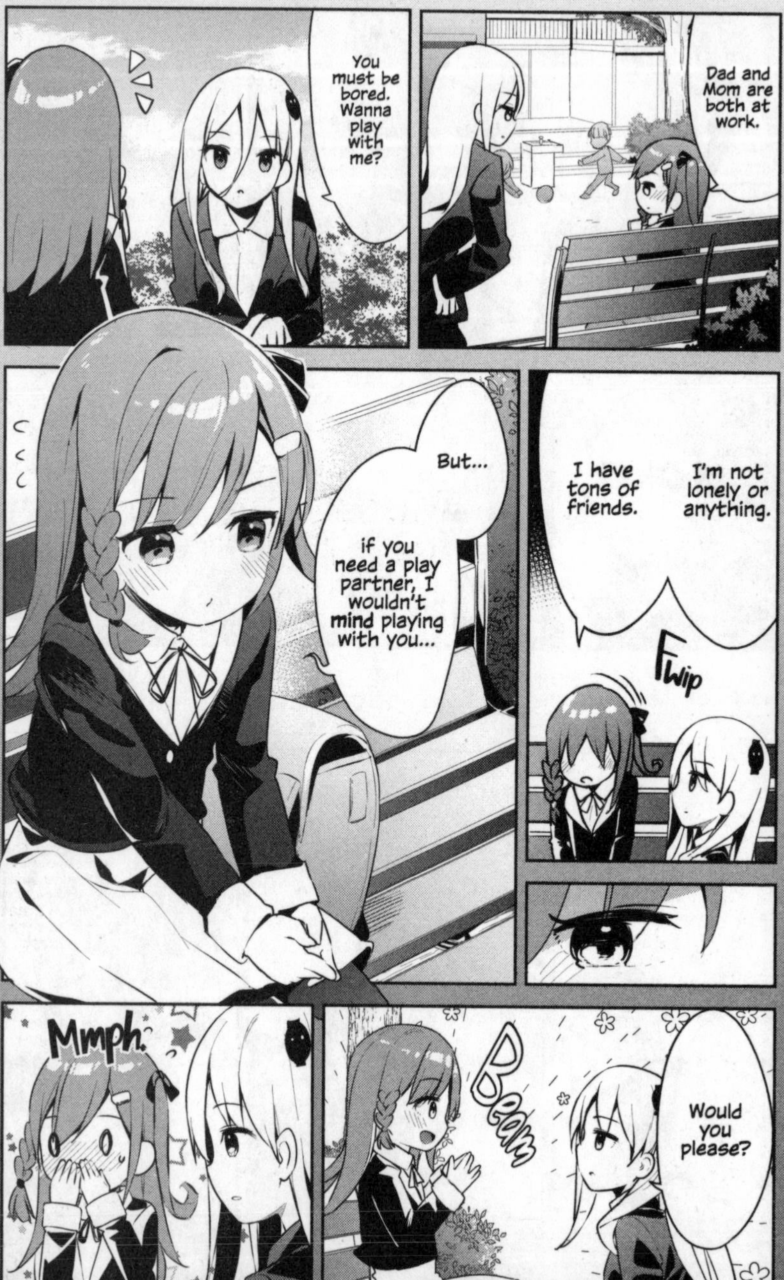
Dad and Mom are both at work.
You must be bored. Wanna play with me?
I'm not lonely or anything.
I have tons of friends.
Fwip
But...
if you need a play partner, I wouldn't mind playing with you...
Would you please?
Beam
Mmph.

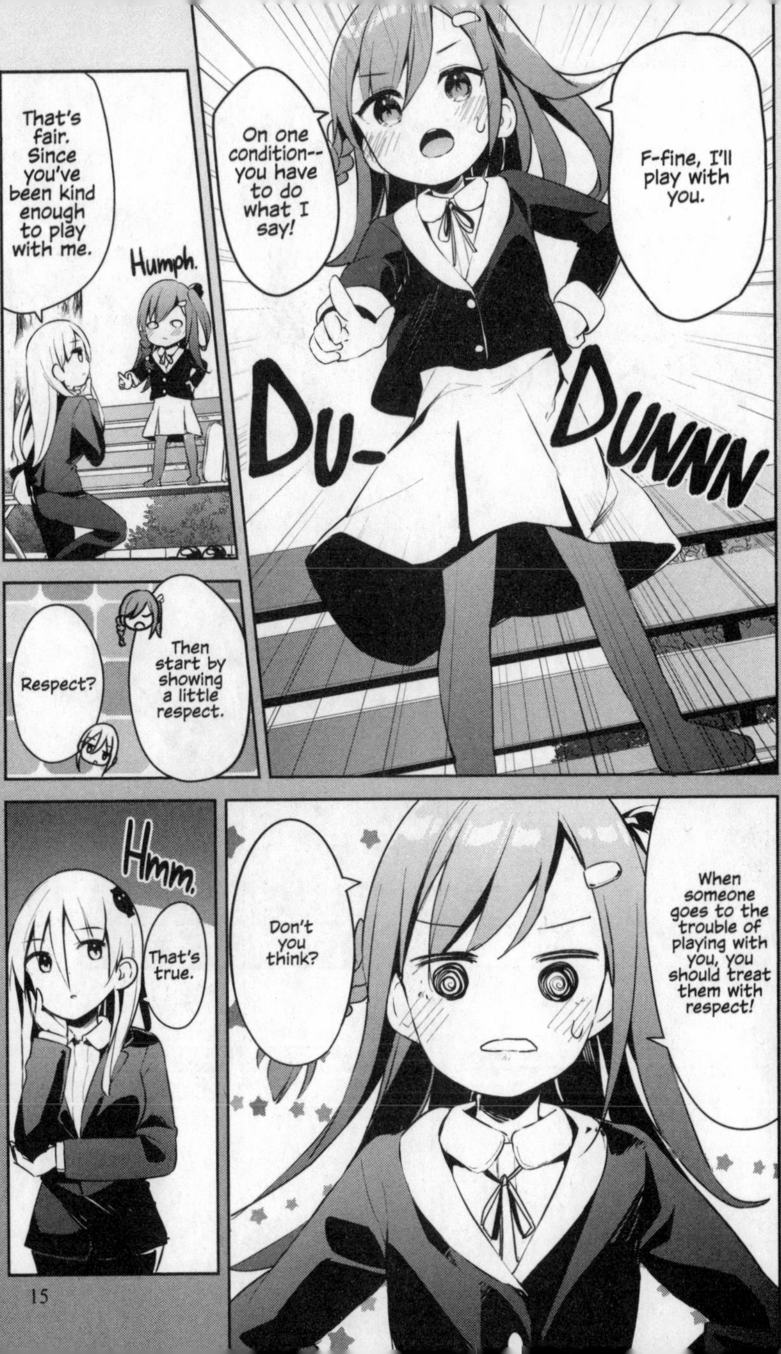
F-fine, I'll play with you.
On one condition--you have to do what I say!
DU-DUNNN
That's fair. Since you've been kind enough to play with me.
Humph.
Then start by showing a little respect.
Respect?
When someone goes to the trouble of playing with you, you should treat them with respect!
Don't you think?
Hmm.
That's true.

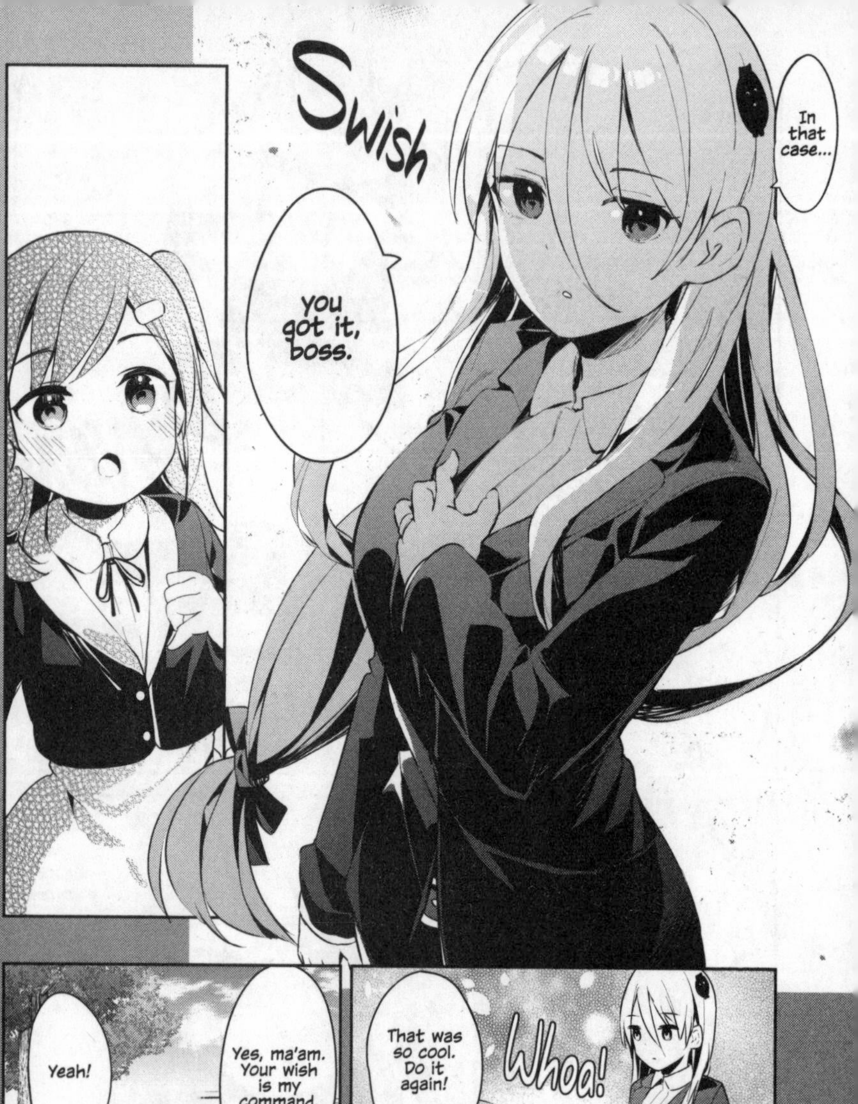
In that case...
Swish
you got it, boss.
Whoa!
That was so cool. Do it again!
Yes, ma'am. Your wish is my command.
Yeah!

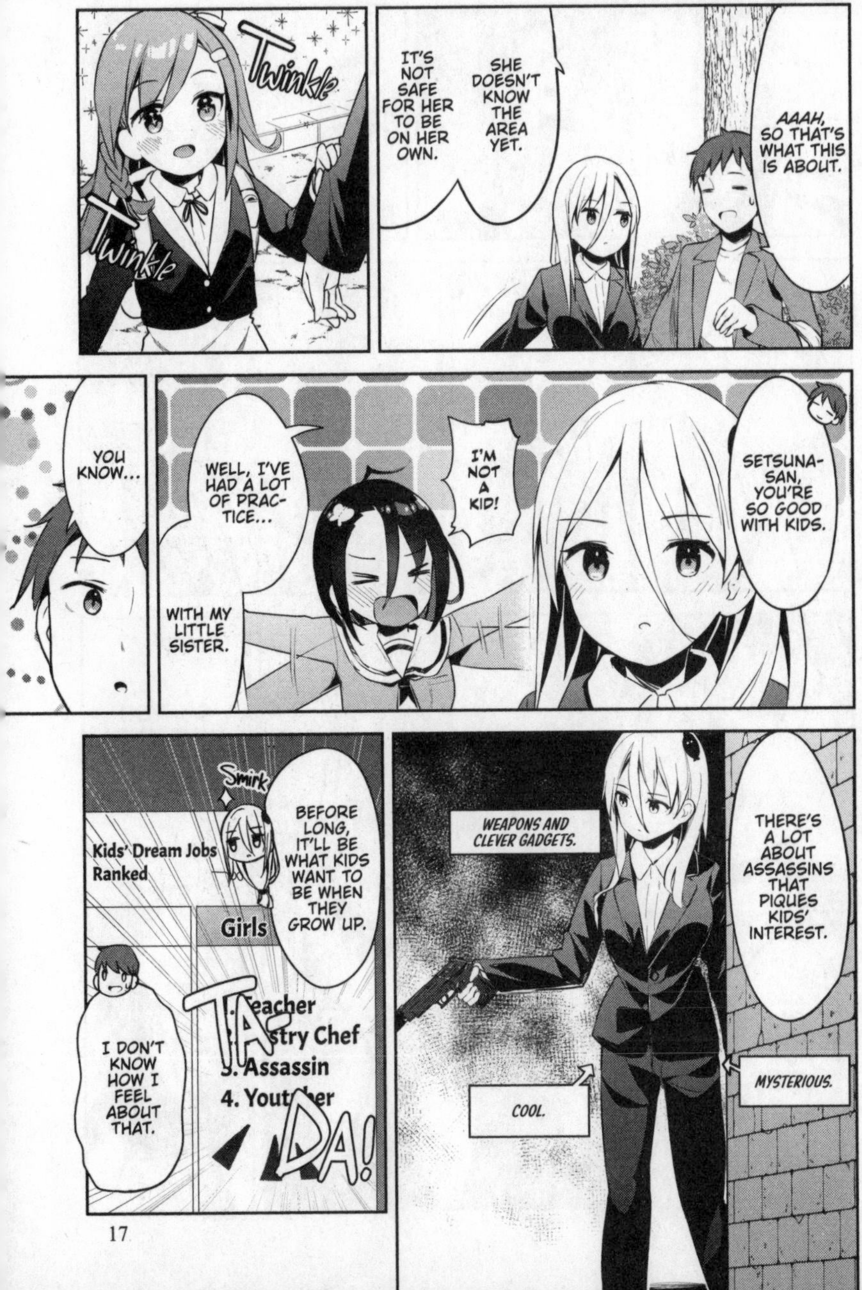
AAAH, SO THAT'S WHAT THIS IS ABOUT.
SHE DOESN'T KNOW THE AREA YET.
IT'S NOT SAFE FOR HER TO BE ON HER OWN.
Twinkle
Twinkle
SETSUNA-SAN, YOU'RE SO GOOD WITH KIDS.
I'M NOT A KID!
WELL, I'VE HAD A LOT OF PRAC-TICE...
WITH MY LITTLE SISTER.
YOU KNOW...
THERE'S A LOT ABOUT ASSASSINS THAT PIQUES KIDS' INTEREST.
MYSTERIOUS.
WEAPONS AND CLEVER GADGETS.
COOL.
Smirk
BEFORE LONG, IT'LL BE WHAT KIDS WANT TO BE WHEN THEY GROW UP.
Kids' Dream Jobs Ranked
Girls
Teacher
stry Chef
3. Assassin
4. Yout ber
TA-DA!
I DON'T KNOW HOW I FEEL ABOUT THAT.

A HAPPY FAMILY.

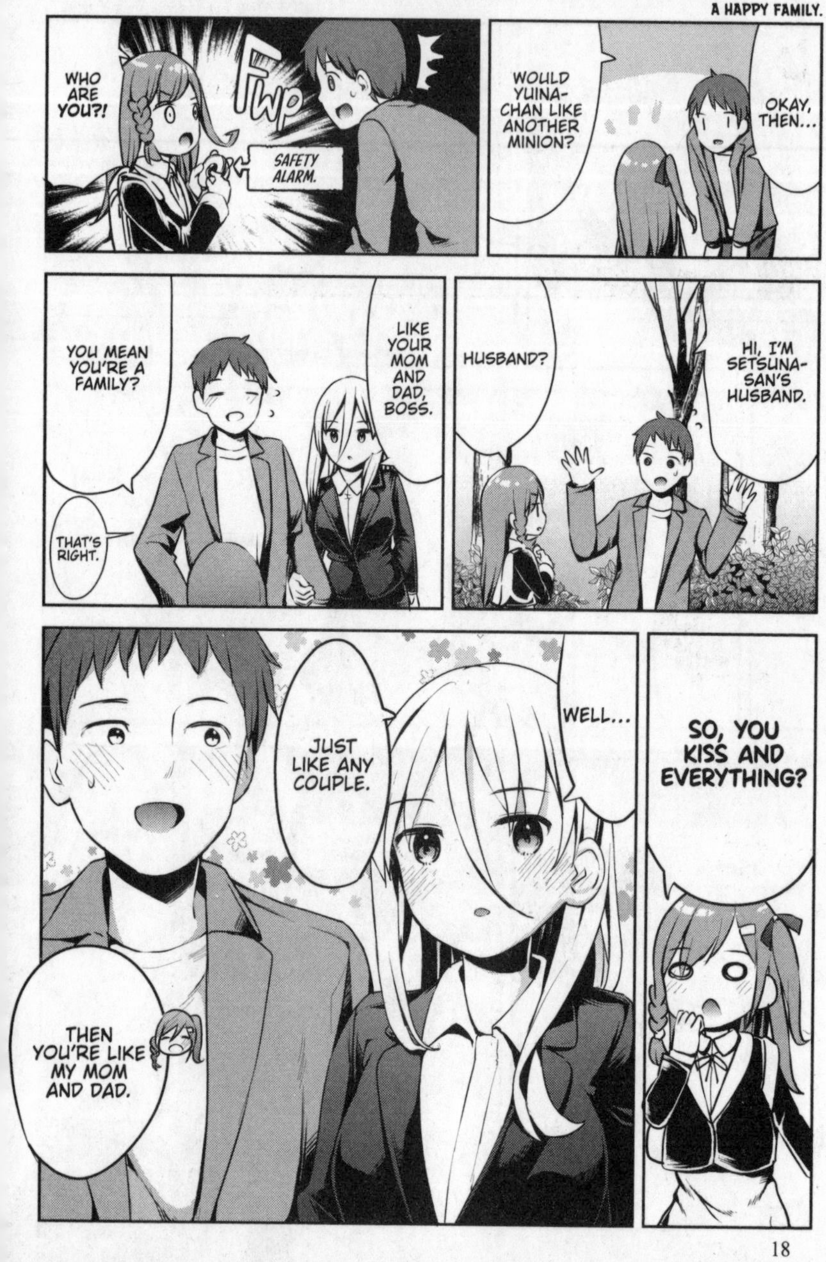
OKAY, THEN...
WOULD YUINA-CHAN LIKE ANOTHER MINION?
WHO ARE YOU?!
FWP
SAFETY ALARM.
HI, I'M SETSUNA-SAN'S HUSBAND.
HUSBAND?
LIKE YOUR MOM AND DAD, BOSS.
YOU MEAN YOU'RE A FAMILY?
THAT'S RIGHT.
SO, YOU KISS AND EVERYTHING?
WELL...
JUST LIKE ANY COUPLE.
THEN YOU'RE LIKE MY MOM AND DAD.

WHAT IT TAKES TO BE A BOSS.

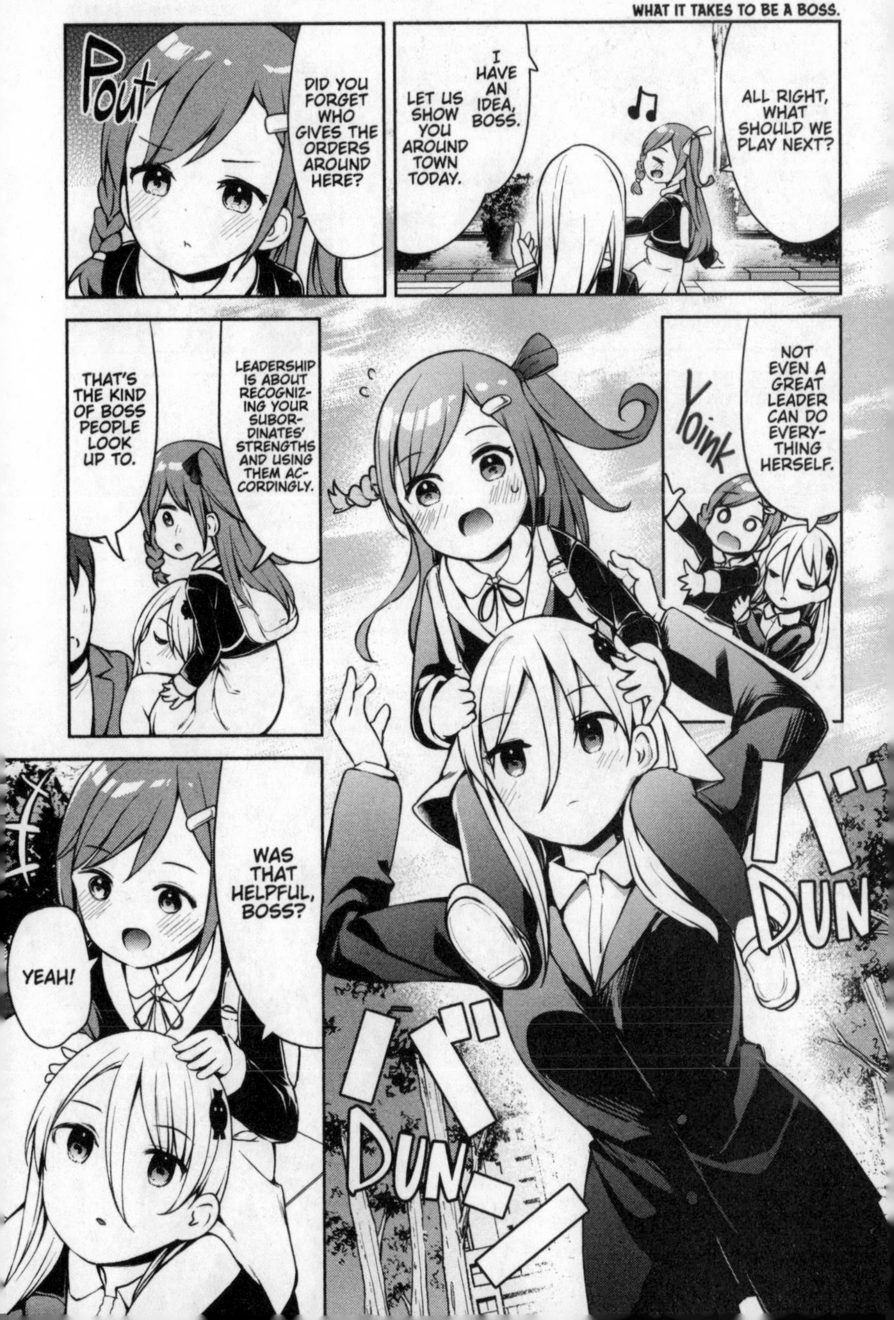

ALL RIGHT, WHAT SHOULD WE PLAY NEXT?
I HAVE AN IDEA, BOSS.
LET US SHOW YOU AROUND TOWN TODAY.
DID YOU FORGET WHO GIVES THE ORDERS AROUND HERE?
Pout
NOT EVEN A GREAT LEADER CAN DO EVERYTHING HERSELF.
Yoink
DUN
DUN...
LEADERSHIP IS ABOUT RECOGNIZING YOUR SUBORDINATES' STRENGTHS AND USING THEM ACCORDINGLY.
THAT'S THE KIND OF BOSS PEOPLE LOOK UP TO.
WAS THAT HELPFUL, BOSS?
YEAH!

KEEPING THE BOSS SAFE.

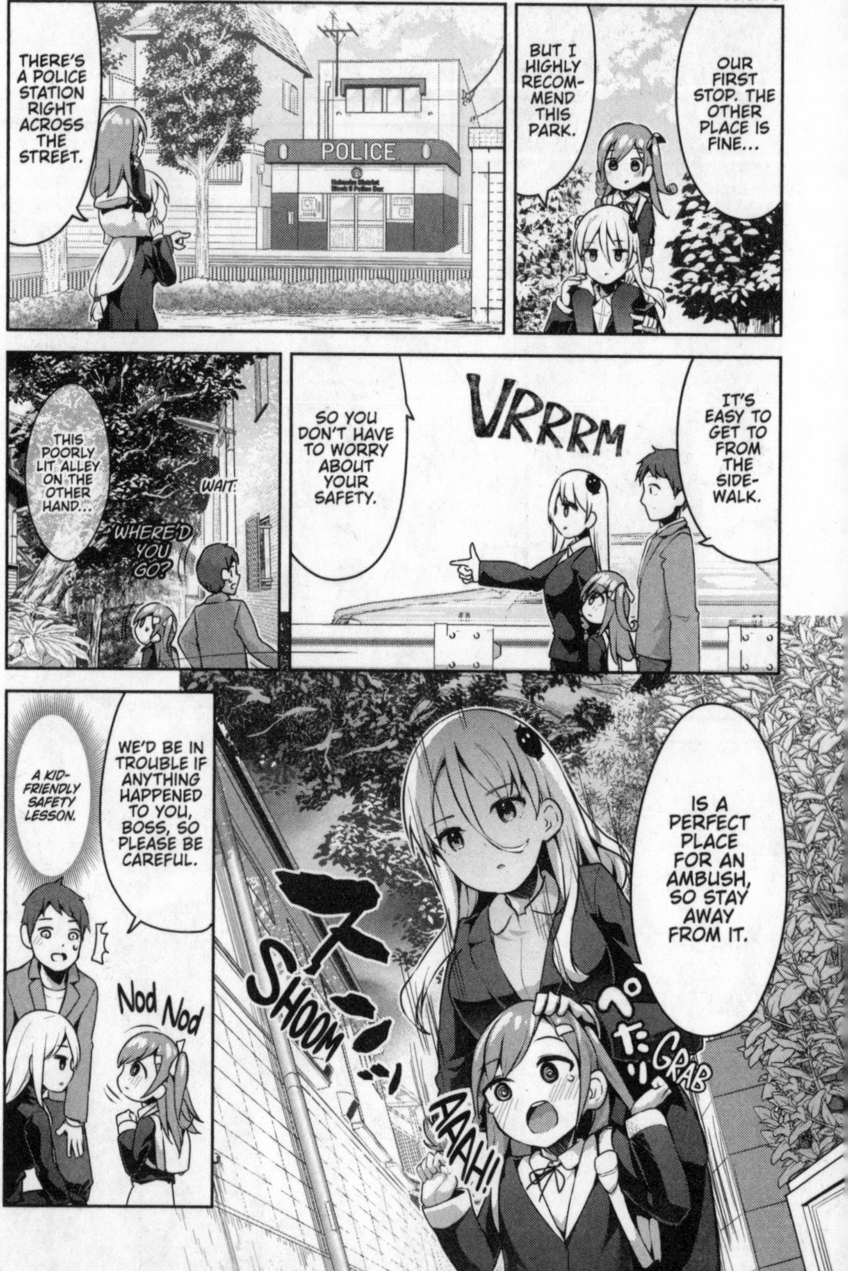
OUR FIRST STOP. THE OTHER PLACE IS FINE...
BUT I HIGHLY RECOMMEND THIS PARK.
POLICE
THERE'S A POLICE STATION RIGHT ACROSS THE STREET.
IT'S EASY TO GET TO FROM THE SIDEWALK.
VRRRM
SO YOU DON'T HAVE TO WORRY ABOUT YOUR SAFETY.
THIS POORLY LIT ALLEY ON THE OTHER HAND...
WAIT.
WHERE'D YOU GO?
IS A PERFECT PLACE FOR AN AMBUSH, SO STAY AWAY FROM IT.
GRAB
SHOOM
AAAH!
WE'D BE IN TROUBLE IF ANYTHING HAPPENED TO YOU, BOSS, SO PLEASE BE CAREFUL.
A KID-FRIENDLY SAFETY LESSON.
Nod Nod

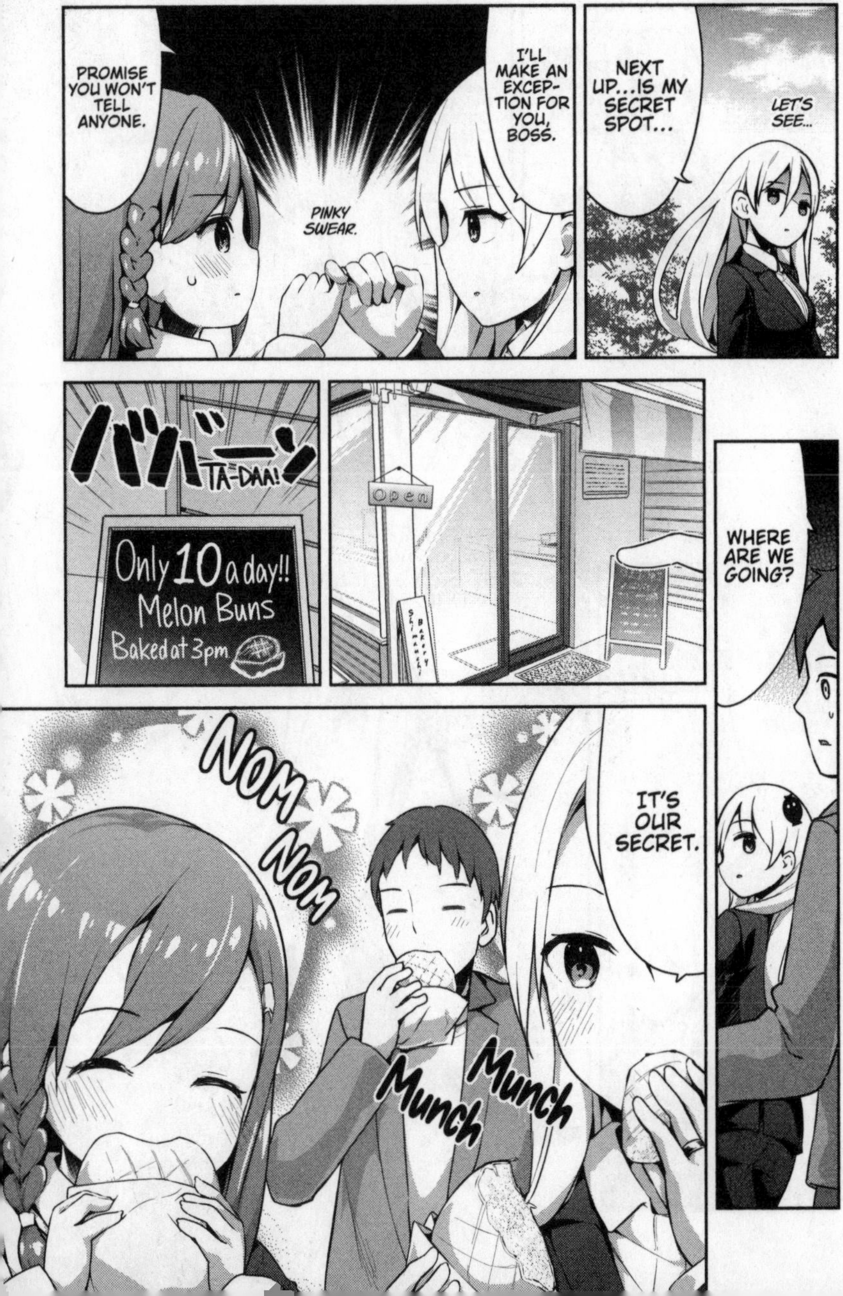
NEXT UP...IS MY SECRET SPOT...
LET'S SEE...
I'LL MAKE AN EXCEPTION FOR YOU, BOSS.
PROMISE YOU WON'T TELL ANYONE.
PINKY SWEAR.
WHERE ARE WE GOING?
IT'S OUR SECRET.
Open
ババーン
TA-DAA!
Only 10 a day!!
Melon Buns
Baked at 3pm
NOM NOM
Munch Munch

A SMIDGE OF JEALOUSY.

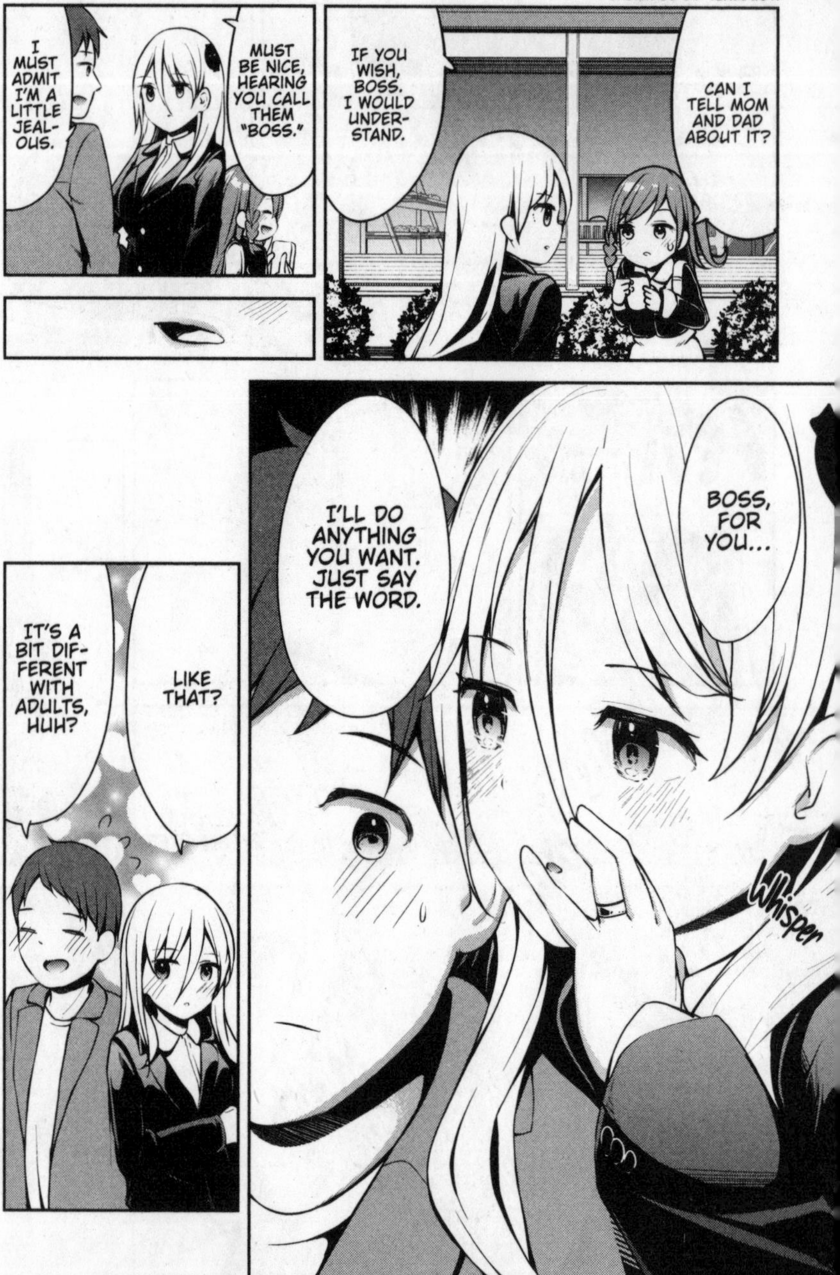
CAN I TELL MOM AND DAD ABOUT IT?
IF YOU WISH, BOSS. I WOULD UNDER-STAND.
MUST BE NICE, HEARING YOU CALL THEM "BOSS."
I MUST ADMIT I'M A LITTLE JEAL-OUS.
BOSS, FOR YOU...
I'LL DO ANYTHING YOU WANT. JUST SAY THE WORD.
Whisper
LIKE THAT?
IT'S A BIT DIF-FERENT WITH ADULTS, HUH?

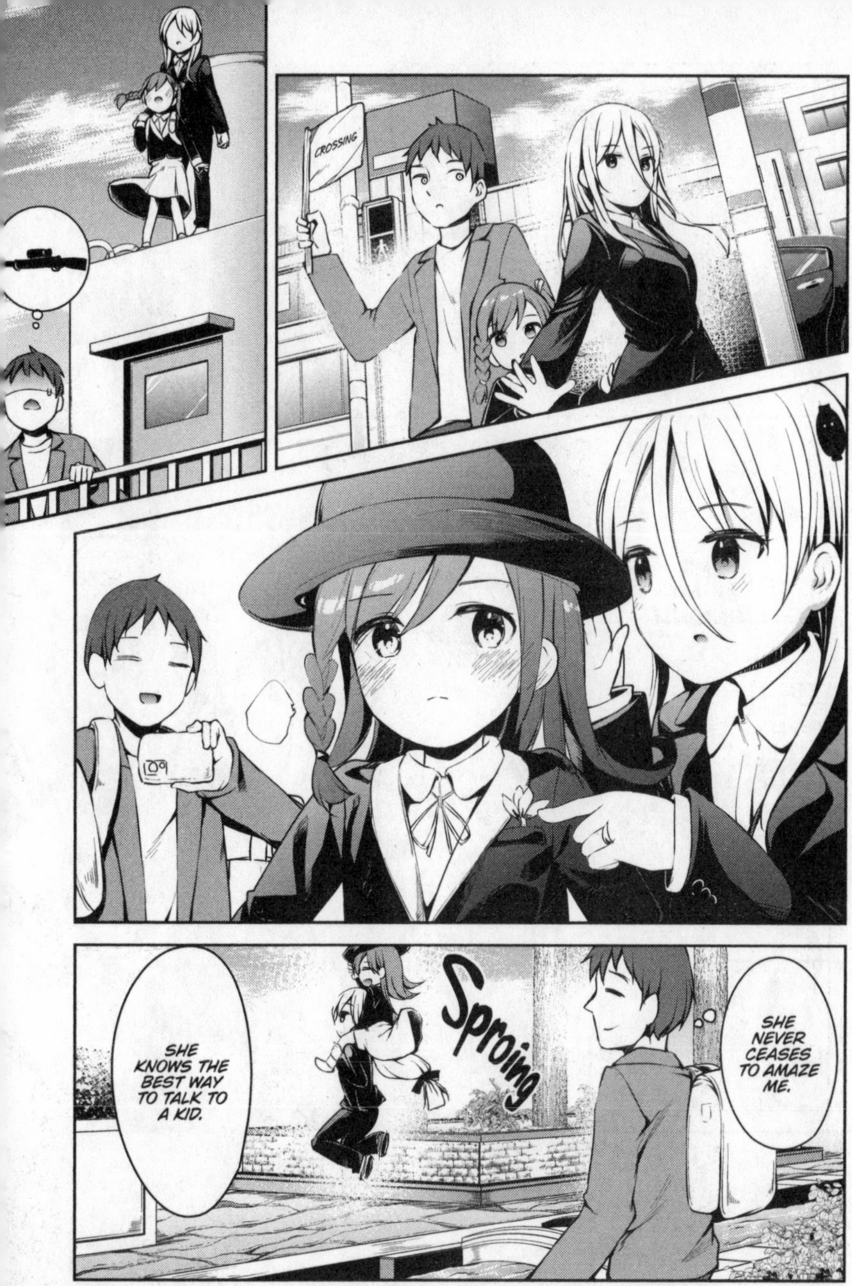
CROSSING
SHE NEVER CEASES TO AMAZE ME.
Sproing
SHE KNOWS THE BEST WAY TO TALK TO A KID.

ONE LAST ORDER.

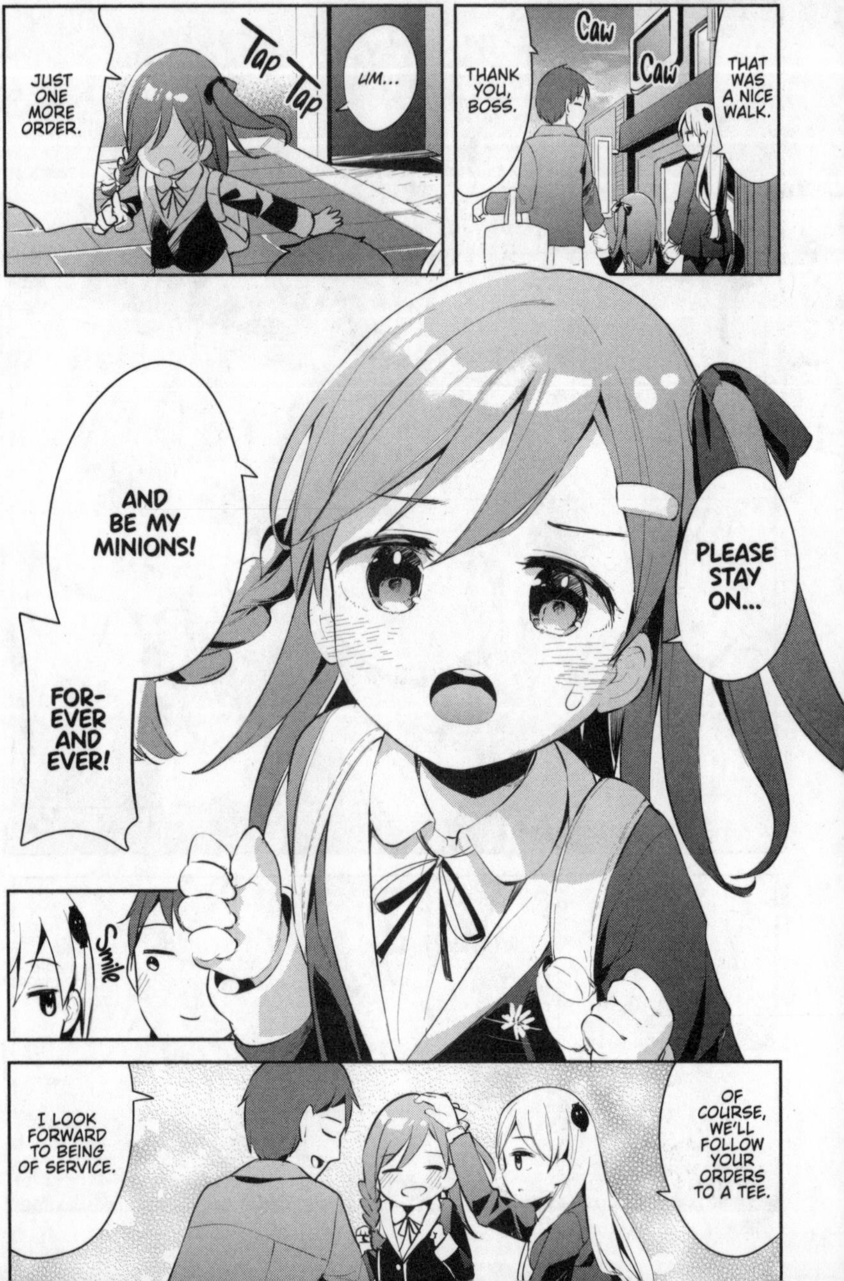
Caw
Caw
THAT WAS A NICE WALK.
THANK YOU, BOSS.
UM...
Tap Tap
JUST ONE MORE ORDER.
PLEASE STAY ON...
AND BE MY MINIONS!
FOR-EVER AND EVER!
Smile
OF COURSE, WE'LL FOLLOW YOUR ORDERS TO A TEE.
I LOOK FORWARD TO BEING OF SERVICE.

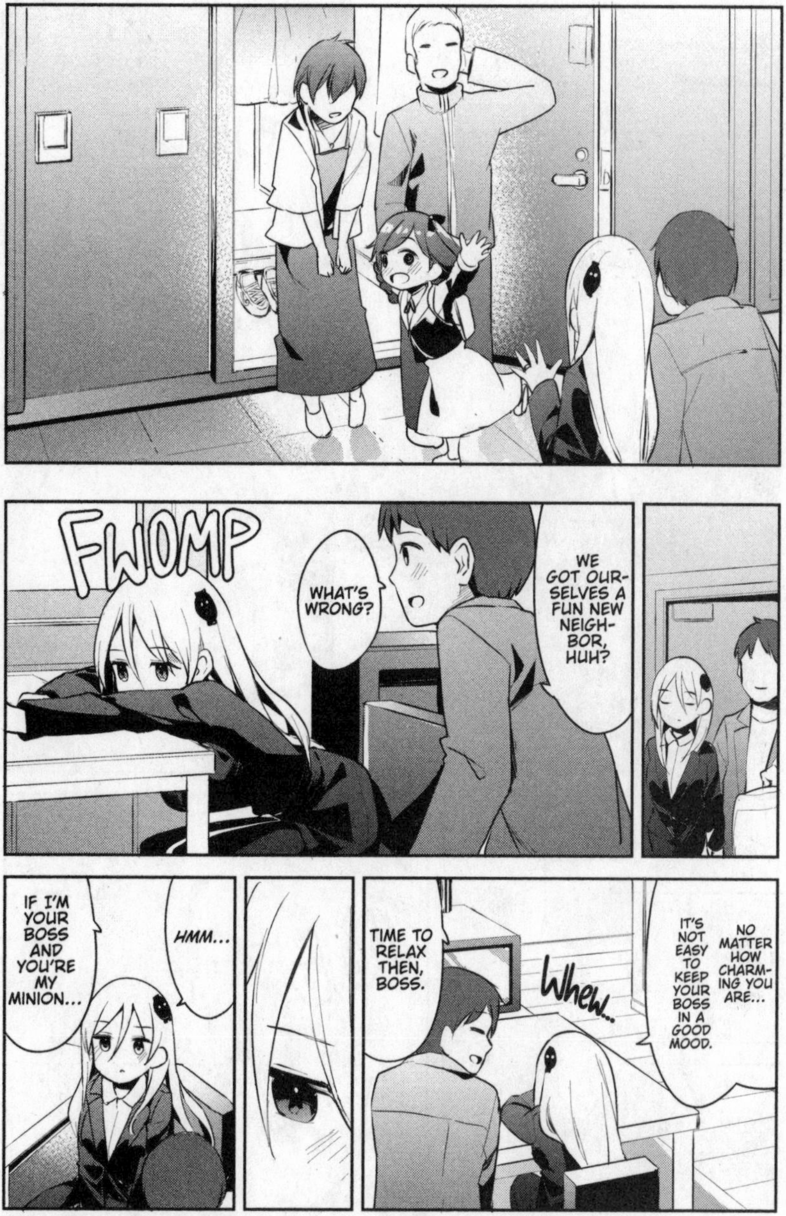
WE GOT OURSELVES A FUN NEW NEIGHBOR, HUH?
WHAT'S WRONG?
FWOMP
NO MATTER HOW CHARMING YOU ARE...
IT'S NOT EASY TO KEEP YOUR BOSS IN A GOOD MOOD.
Whew...
TIME TO RELAX THEN, BOSS.
HMM...
IF I'M YOUR BOSS AND YOU'RE MY MINION...

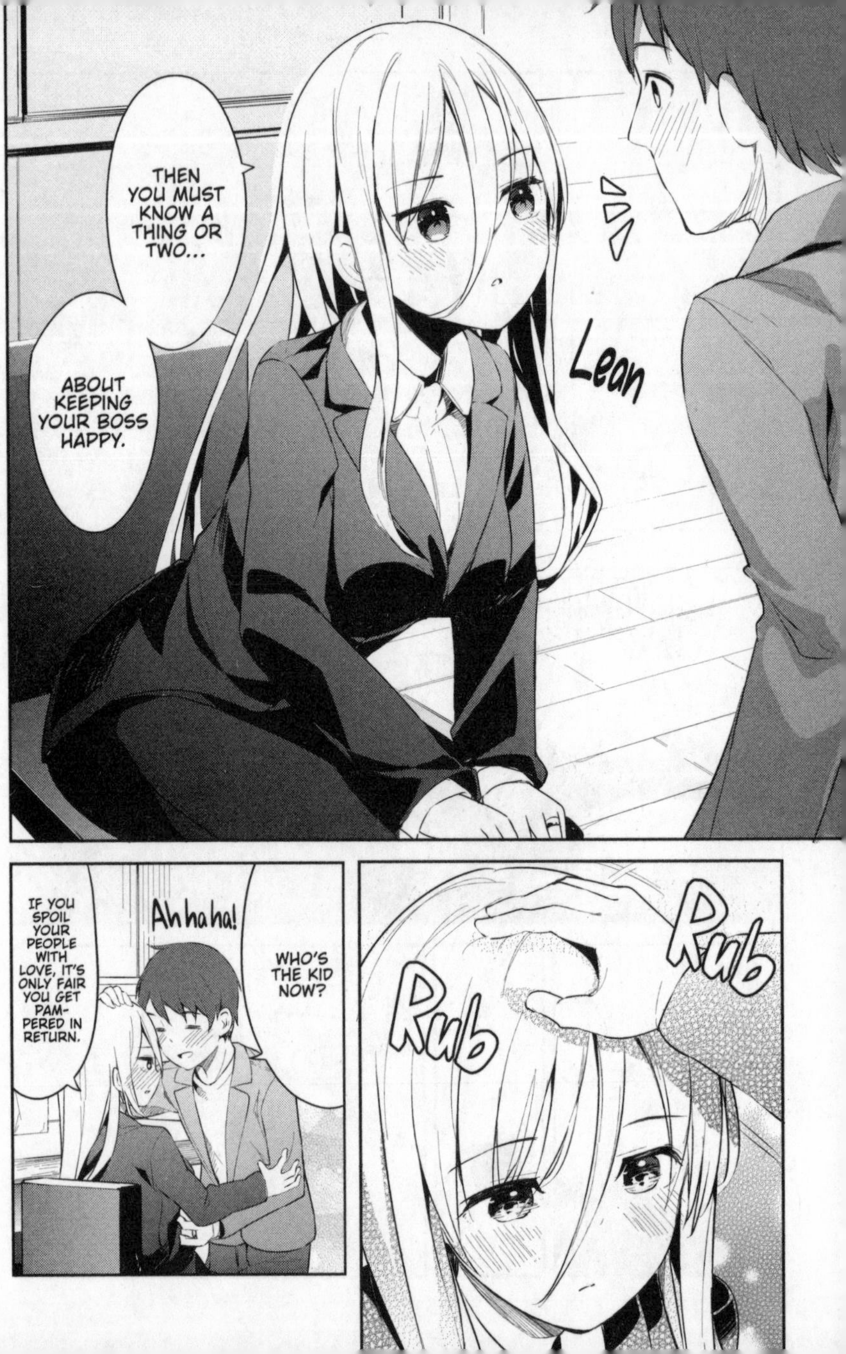
THEN YOU MUST KNOW A THING OR TWO…
ABOUT KEEPING YOUR BOSS HAPPY.
Lean
Rub
Rub
WHO'S THE KID NOW?
Ah ha ha!
IF YOU SPOIL YOUR PEOPLE WITH LOVE, IT'S ONLY FAIR YOU GET PAM-PERED IN RETURN.

FEVERISH SETSUNA-SAN.

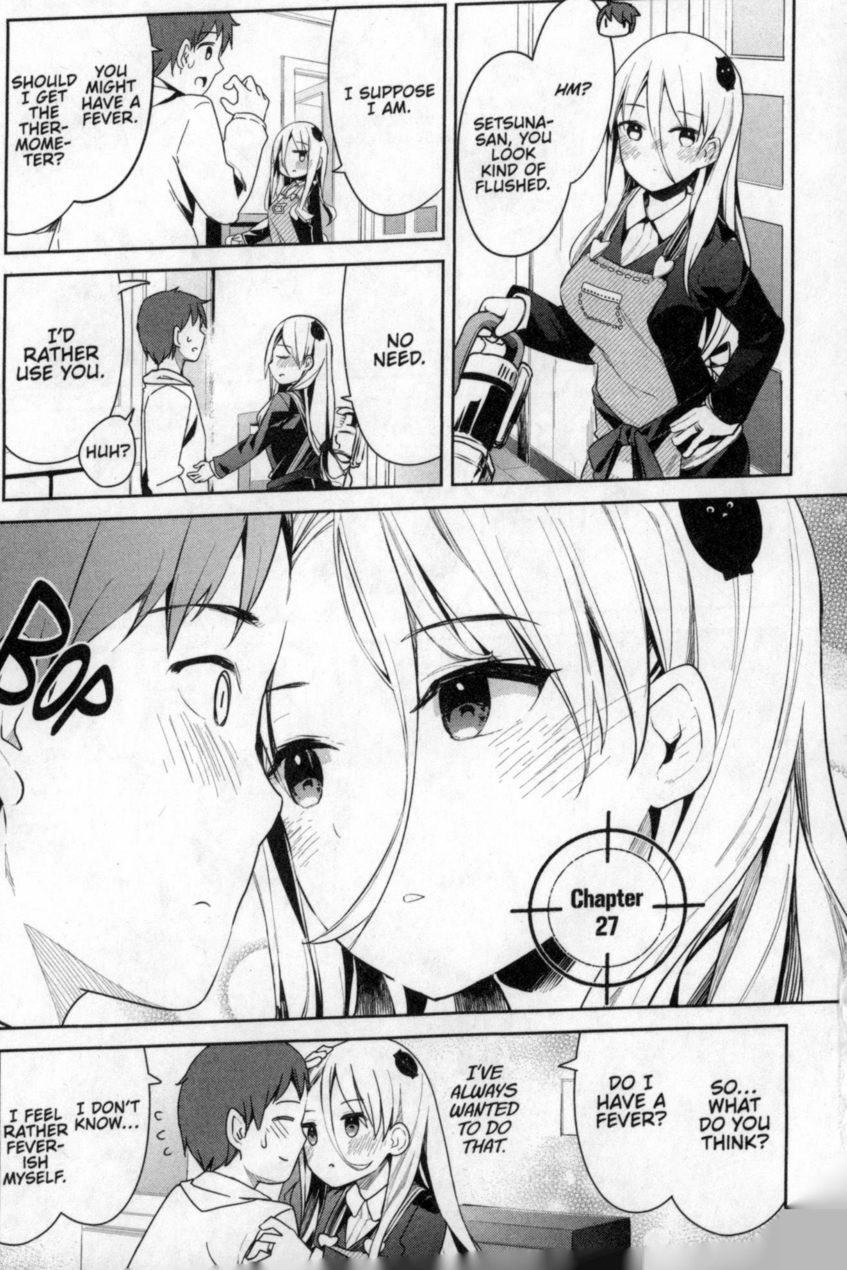
HM?
SETSUNA-SAN, YOU LOOK KIND OF FLUSHED.
I SUPPOSE I AM.
YOU MIGHT HAVE A FEVER.
SHOULD I GET THE THERMOMETER?
NO NEED.
I'D RATHER USE YOU.
HUH?
BOP
Chapter 27
SO... WHAT DO YOU THINK?
DO I HAVE A FEVER?
I'VE ALWAYS WANTED TO DO THAT.
I DON'T KNOW...
I FEEL RATHER FEVERISH MYSELF.

RISKING HER LIFE.

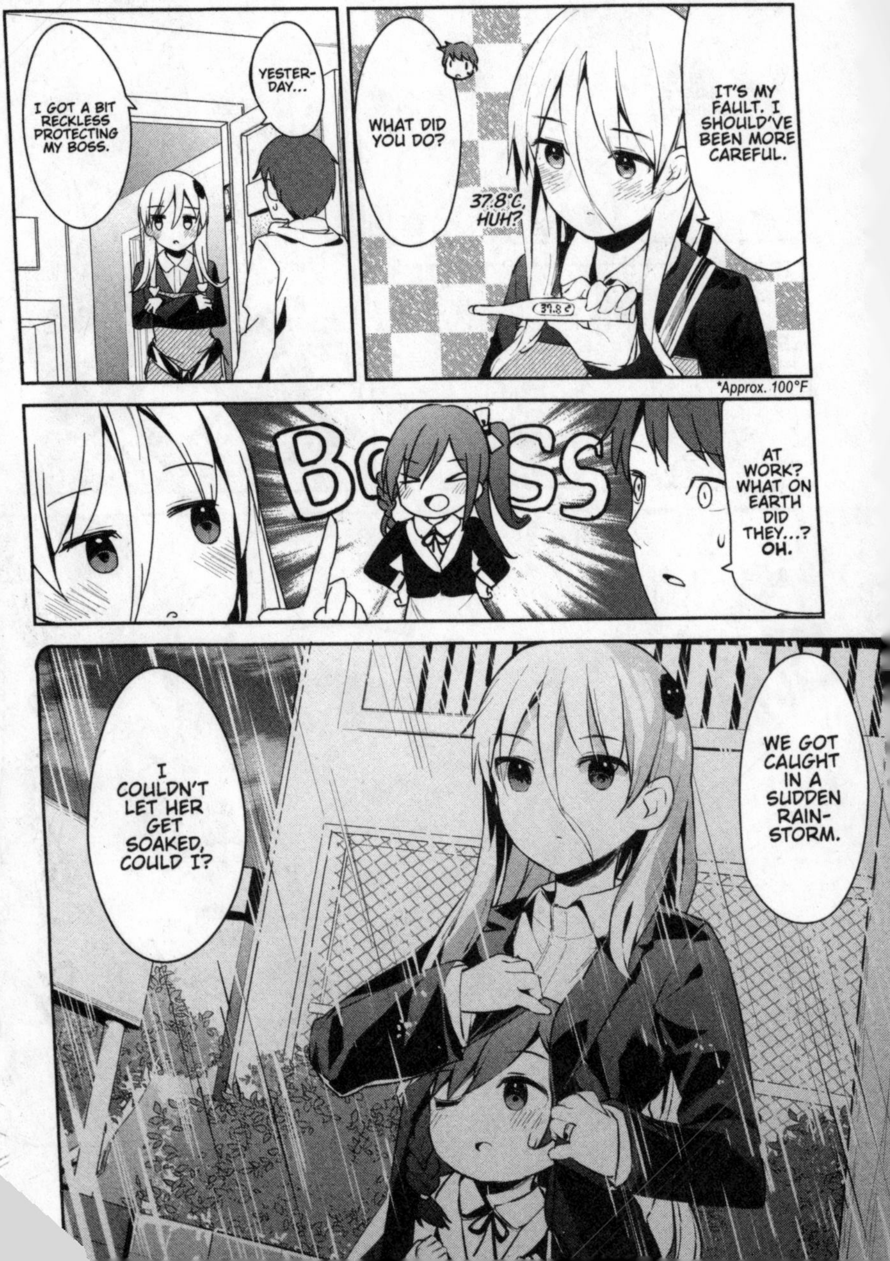
IT'S MY FAULT. I SHOULD'VE BEEN MORE CAREFUL.
37.8°C, HUH?
WHAT DID YOU DO?
37.8°C
YESTER-DAY...
I GOT A BIT RECKLESS PROTECTING MY BOSS.
AT WORK? WHAT ON EARTH DID THEY...? OH.
BOSS
WE GOT CAUGHT IN A SUDDEN RAIN-STORM.
I COULDN'T LET HER GET SOAKED, COULD I?

*Approx. 100°F

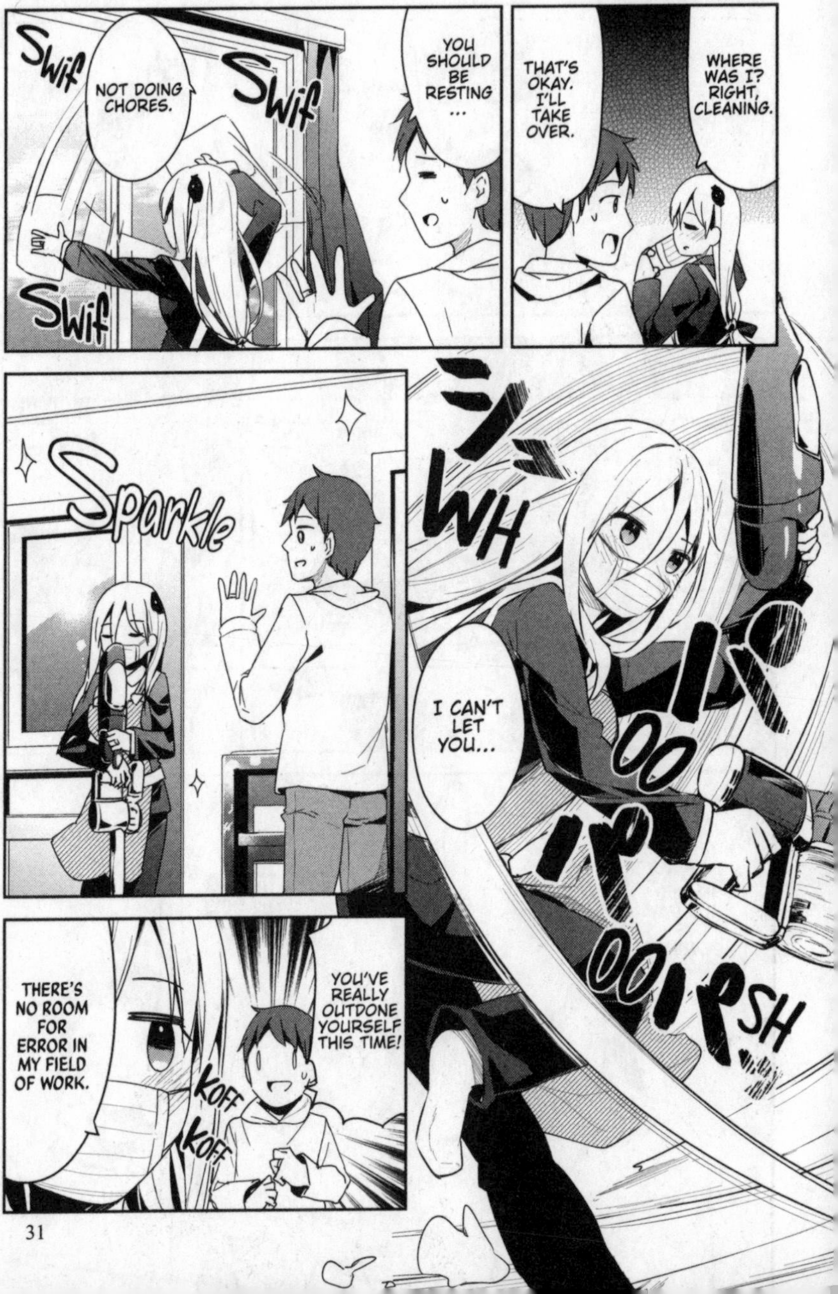
YOU SHOULD BE RESTING ...
NOT DOING CHORES.
Swif
Swif
Swif
THAT'S OKAY. I'LL TAKE OVER.
WHERE WAS I? RIGHT, CLEANING.
WHOOOOOSH
I CAN'T LET YOU...
Sparkle
YOU'VE REALLY OUTDONE YOURSELF THIS TIME!
KOFF
KOFF
THERE'S NO ROOM FOR ERROR IN MY FIELD OF WORK.

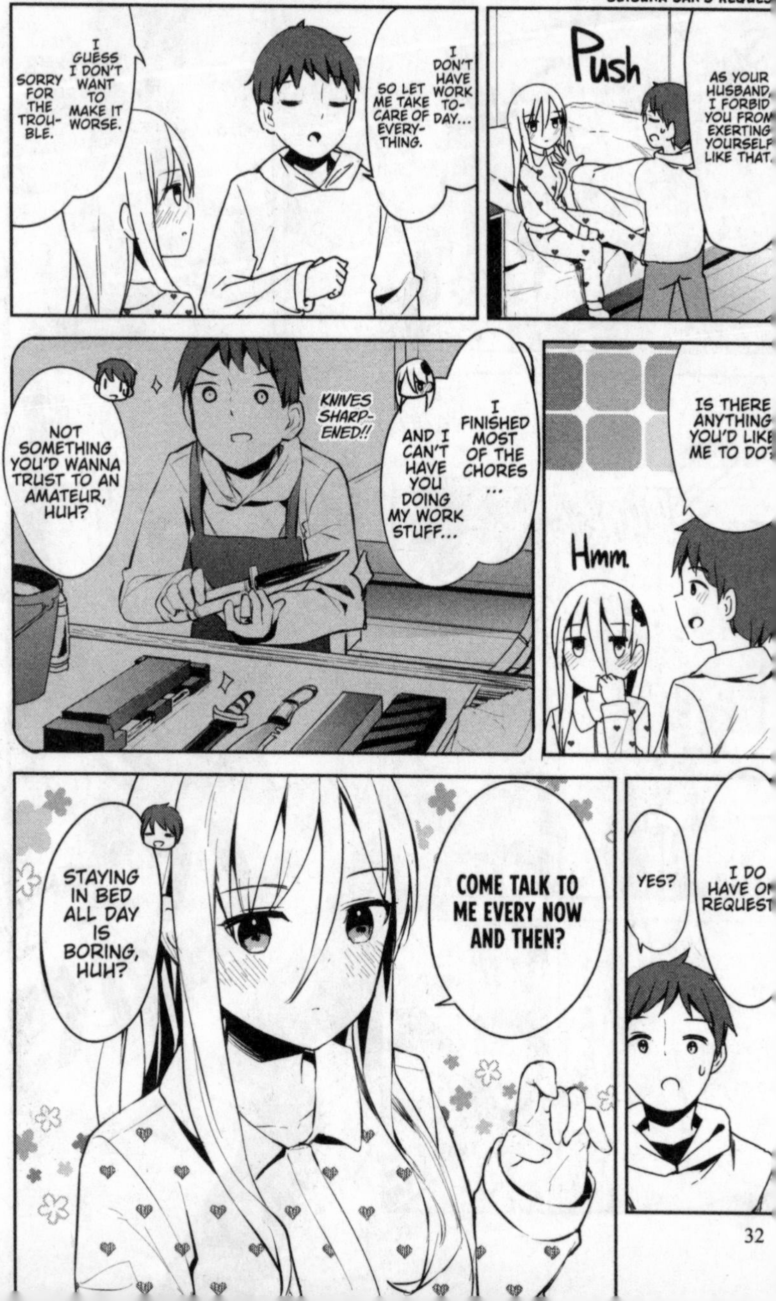
Push
AS YOUR HUSBAND, I FORBID YOU FROM EXERTING YOURSELF LIKE THAT.
I DON'T HAVE WORK TO-DAY...
SO LET ME TAKE CARE OF EVERY-THING.
I GUESS I DON'T WANT TO MAKE IT WORSE.
SORRY FOR THE TROU-BLE.
IS THERE ANYTHING YOU'D LIKE ME TO DO
Hmm.
I FINISHED MOST OF THE CHORES...
AND I CAN'T HAVE YOU DOING MY WORK STUFF...
KNIVES SHARP-ENED!!
NOT SOMETHING YOU'D WANNA TRUST TO AN AMATEUR, HUH?
I DO HAVE O REQUEST
YES?
COME TALK TO ME EVERY NOW AND THEN?
STAYING IN BED ALL DAY IS BORING, HUH?

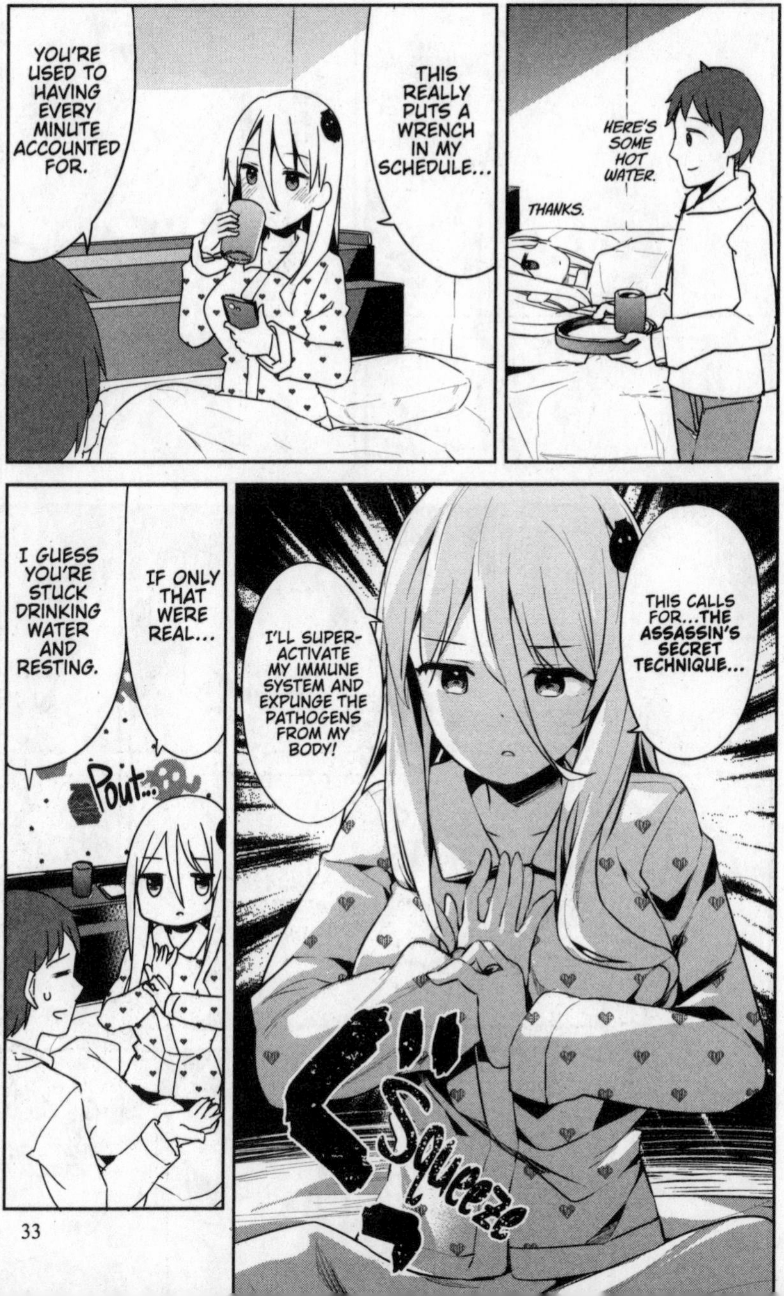
HERE'S SOME HOT WATER.
THANKS.
THIS REALLY PUTS A WRENCH IN MY SCHEDULE...
YOU'RE USED TO HAVING EVERY MINUTE ACCOUNTED FOR.
THIS CALLS FOR...THE ASSASSIN'S SECRET TECHNIQUE...
I'LL SUPER-ACTIVATE MY IMMUNE SYSTEM AND EXPUNGE THE PATHOGENS FROM MY BODY!
Squeeze
I GUESS YOU'RE STUCK DRINKING WATER AND RESTING.
IF ONLY THAT WERE REAL...
Pout...

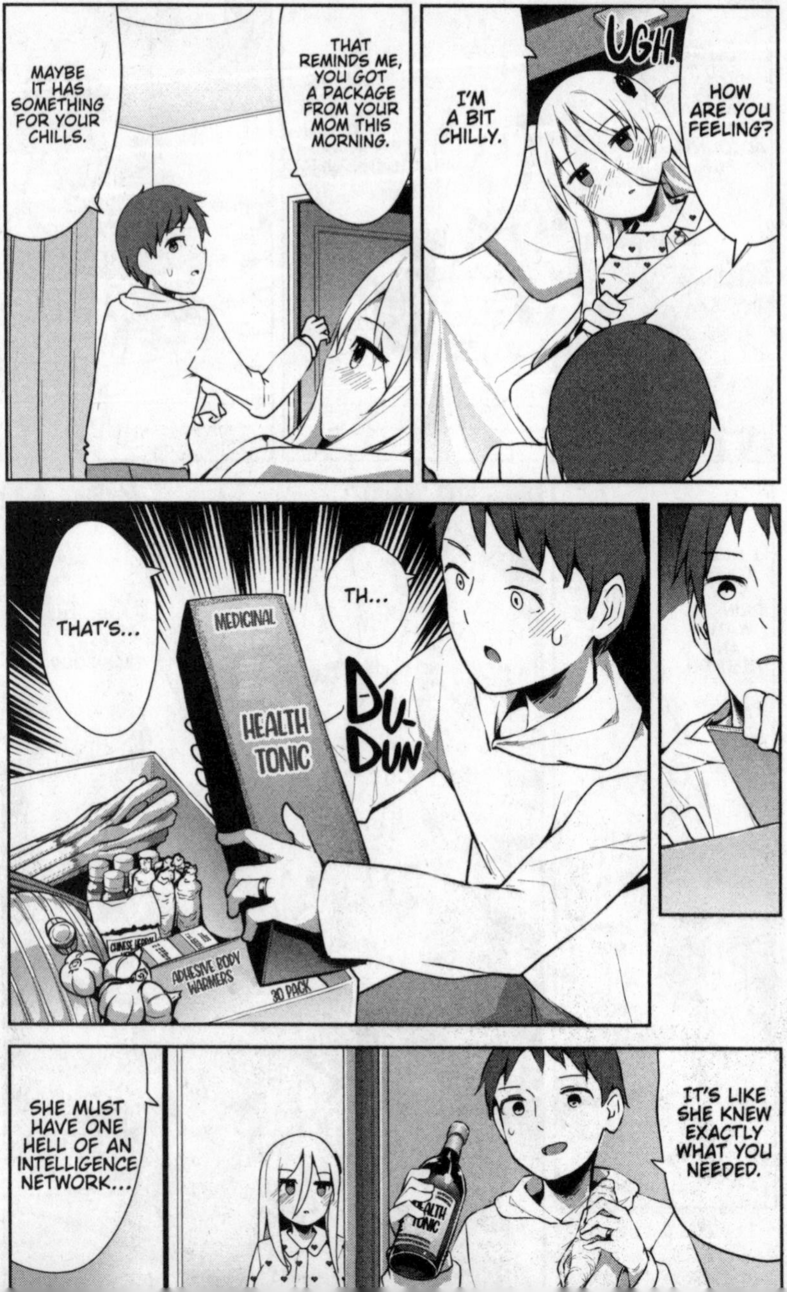
HOW ARE YOU FEELING?
UGH.
I'M A BIT CHILLY.
THAT REMINDS ME, YOU GOT A PACKAGE FROM YOUR MOM THIS MORNING.
MAYBE IT HAS SOMETHING FOR YOUR CHILLS.
TH...
DU-DUN
MEDICINAL
HEALTH TONIC
THAT'S...
ADHESIVE BODY WARMERS
30 PACK
IT'S LIKE SHE KNEW EXACTLY WHAT YOU NEEDED.
HEALTH TONIC
SHE MUST HAVE ONE HELL OF AN INTELLIGENCE NETWORK...

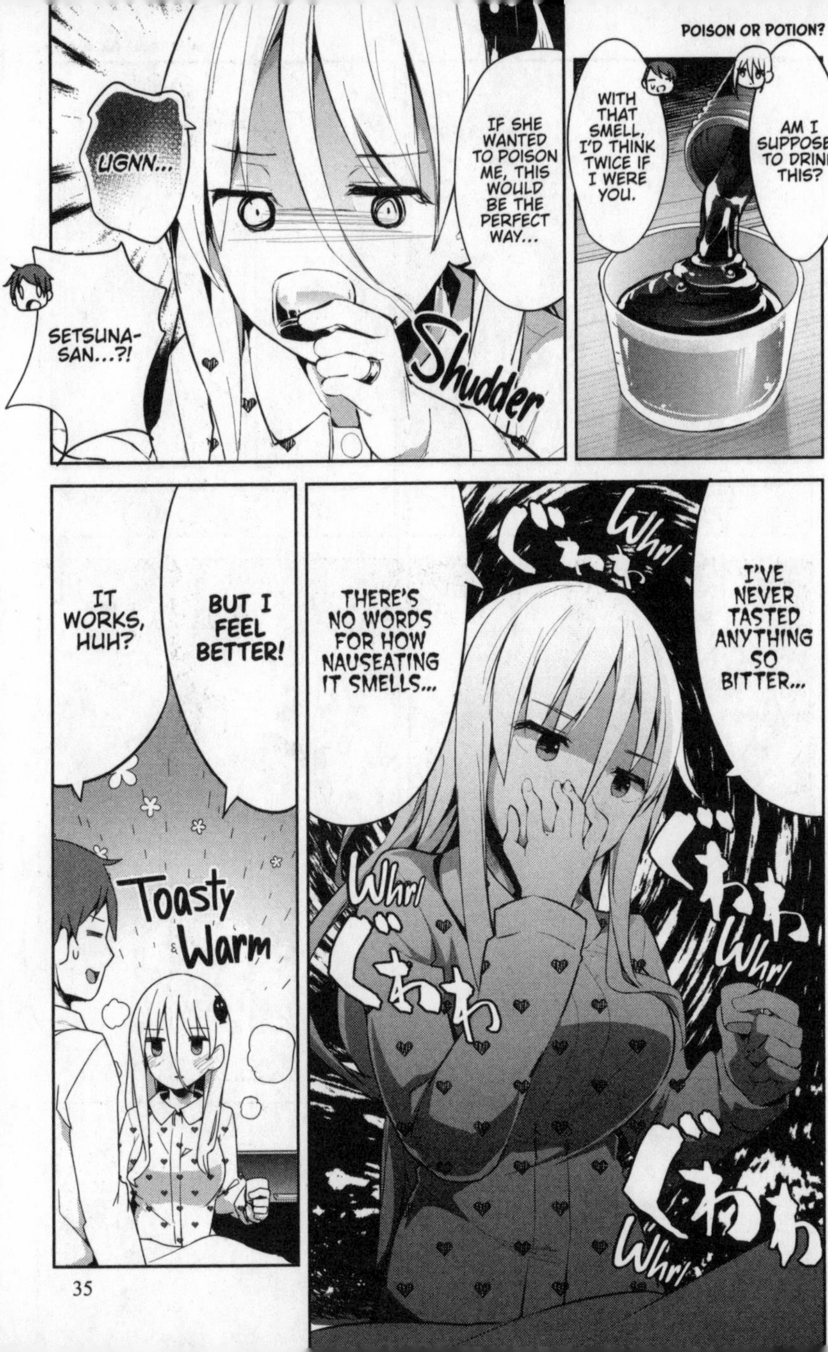
AM I SUPPOSED TO DRINK THIS?
WITH THAT SMELL, I'D THINK TWICE IF I WERE YOU.
IF SHE WANTED TO POISON ME, THIS WOULD BE THE PERFECT WAY...
UGNN...
Shudder
SETSUNA-SAN...?!
I'VE NEVER TASTED ANYTHING SO BITTER...
THERE'S NO WORDS FOR HOW NAUSEATING IT SMELLS...
Whr!
Whr!
Whr!
Whr!
BUT I FEEL BETTER!
IT WORKS, HUH?
Toasty & Warm

A VISIT FROM THE BOSS.

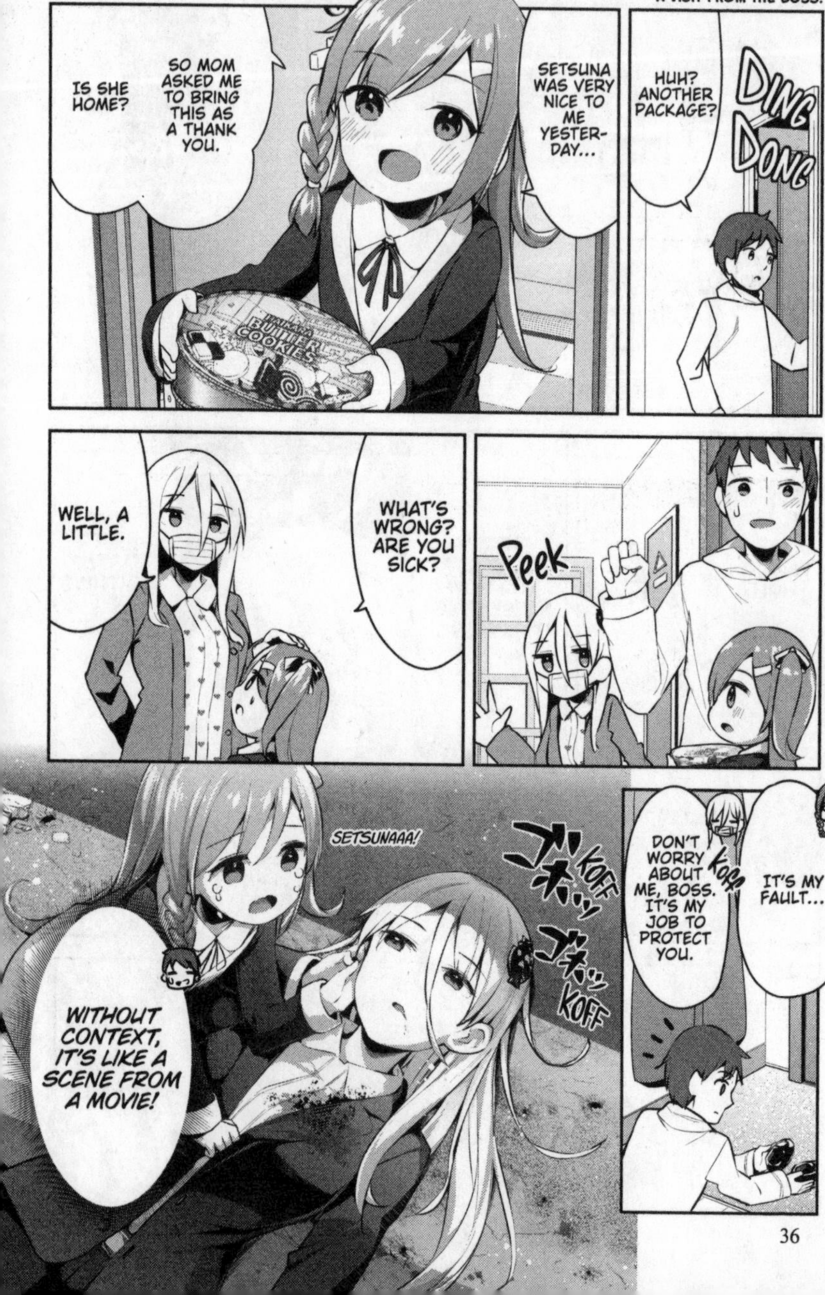
DING DONG
HUH? ANOTHER PACKAGE?
SETSUNA WAS VERY NICE TO ME YESTER-DAY...
SO MOM ASKED ME TO BRING THIS AS A THANK YOU.
IS SHE HOME?
BUTTER COOKIES
PEEK
WHAT'S WRONG? ARE YOU SICK?
WELL, A LITTLE.
IT'S MY FAULT...
DON'T WORRY ABOUT ME, BOSS. IT'S MY JOB TO PROTECT YOU.
KOFF
SETSUNAAA!
KOFF
KOFF
WITHOUT CONTEXT, IT'S LIKE A SCENE FROM A MOVIE!

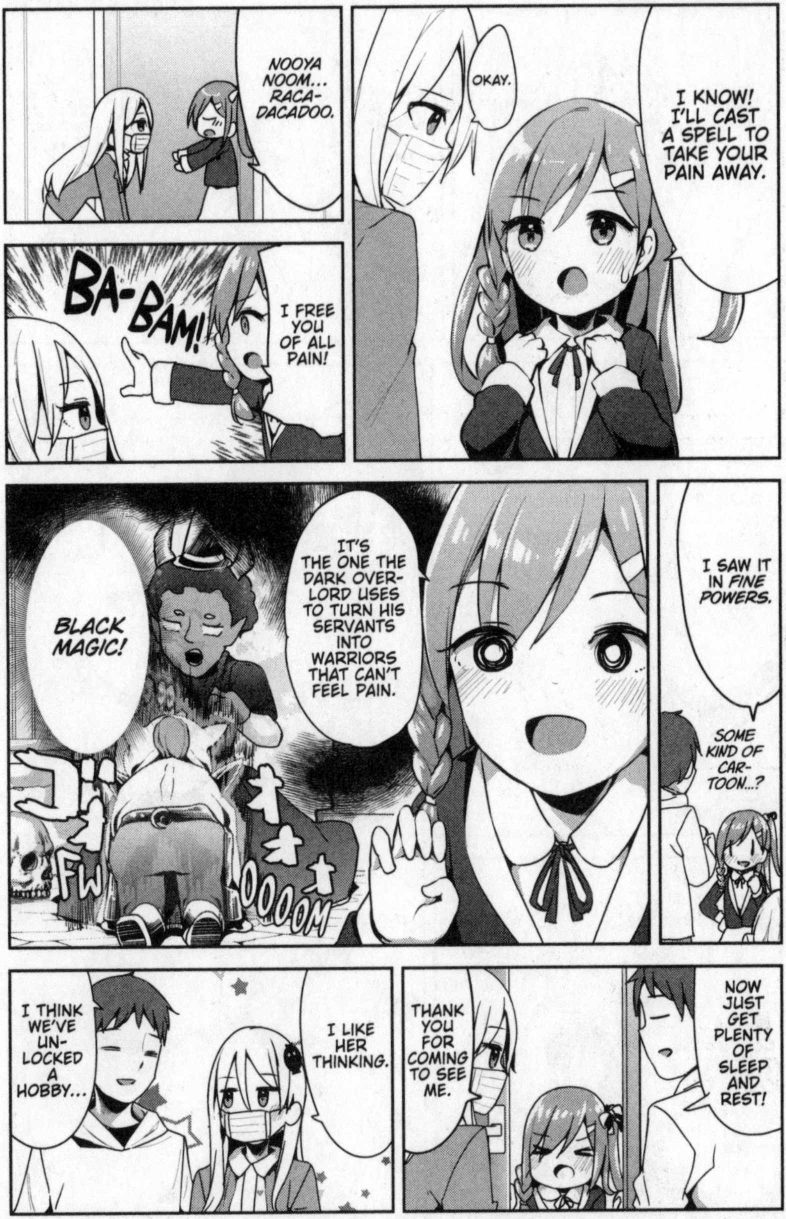
I KNOW! I'LL CAST A SPELL TO TAKE YOUR PAIN AWAY.
OKAY.
NOOYA NOOM... RACA-DACADOO.
I FREE YOU OF ALL PAIN!
BA-BAM!
I SAW IT IN *FINE POWERS*.
SOME KIND OF CAR-TOON...?
IT'S THE ONE THE DARK OVER-LORD USES TO TURN HIS SERVANTS INTO WARRIORS THAT CAN'T FEEL PAIN.
BLACK MAGIC!
FWOOOOM
NOW JUST GET PLENTY OF SLEEP AND REST!
THANK YOU FOR COMING TO SEE ME.
I LIKE HER THINKING.
I THINK WE'VE UN-LOCKED A HOBBY...

PUTTING ON A BRAVE FACE.

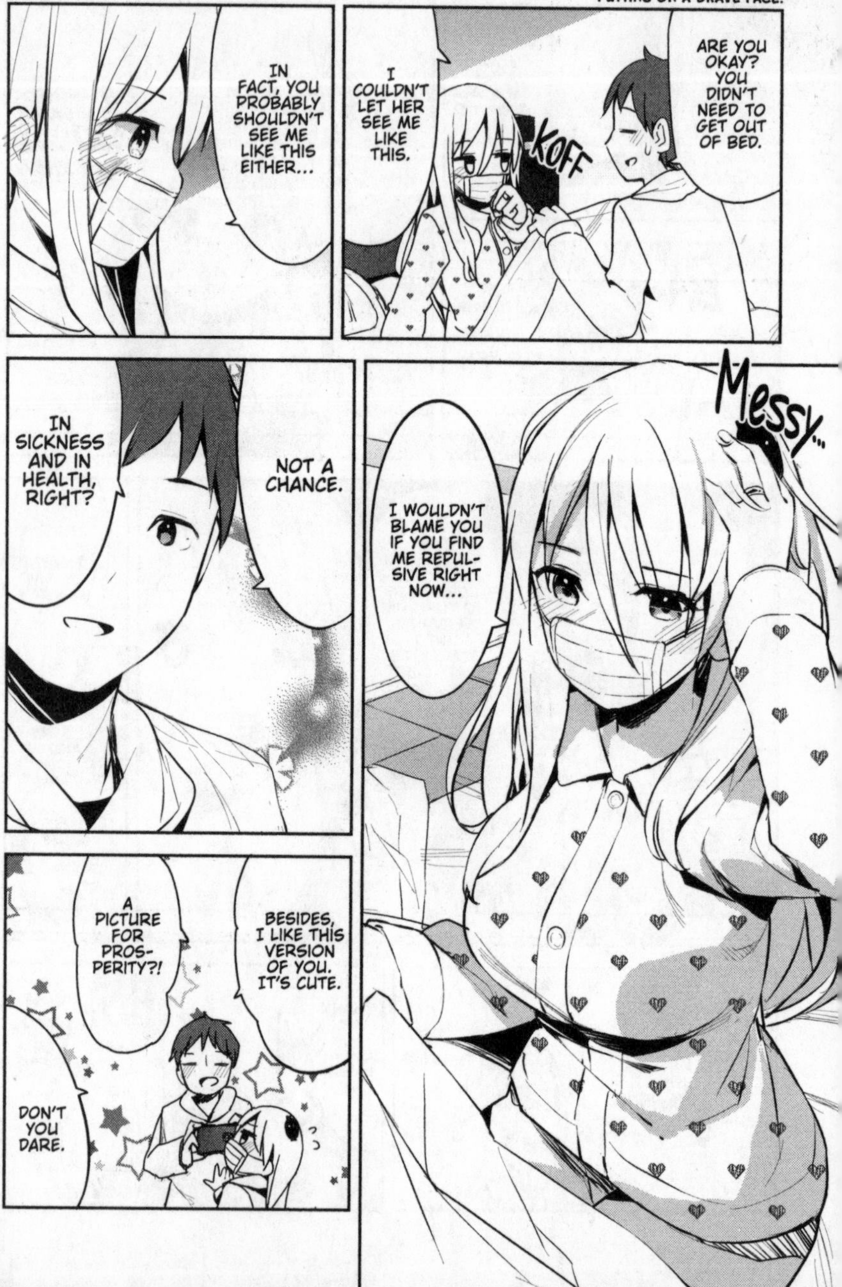
ARE YOU OKAY? YOU DIDN'T NEED TO GET OUT OF BED.
KOFF
I COULDN'T LET HER SEE ME LIKE THIS.
IN FACT, YOU PROBABLY SHOULDN'T SEE ME LIKE THIS EITHER...
Messy...
I WOULDN'T BLAME YOU IF YOU FIND ME REPUL-SIVE RIGHT NOW...
NOT A CHANCE.
IN SICKNESS AND IN HEALTH, RIGHT?
BESIDES, I LIKE THIS VERSION OF YOU. IT'S CUTE.
A PICTURE FOR PROS-PERITY?!
DON'T YOU DARE.

THE SECRET INGREDIENT.

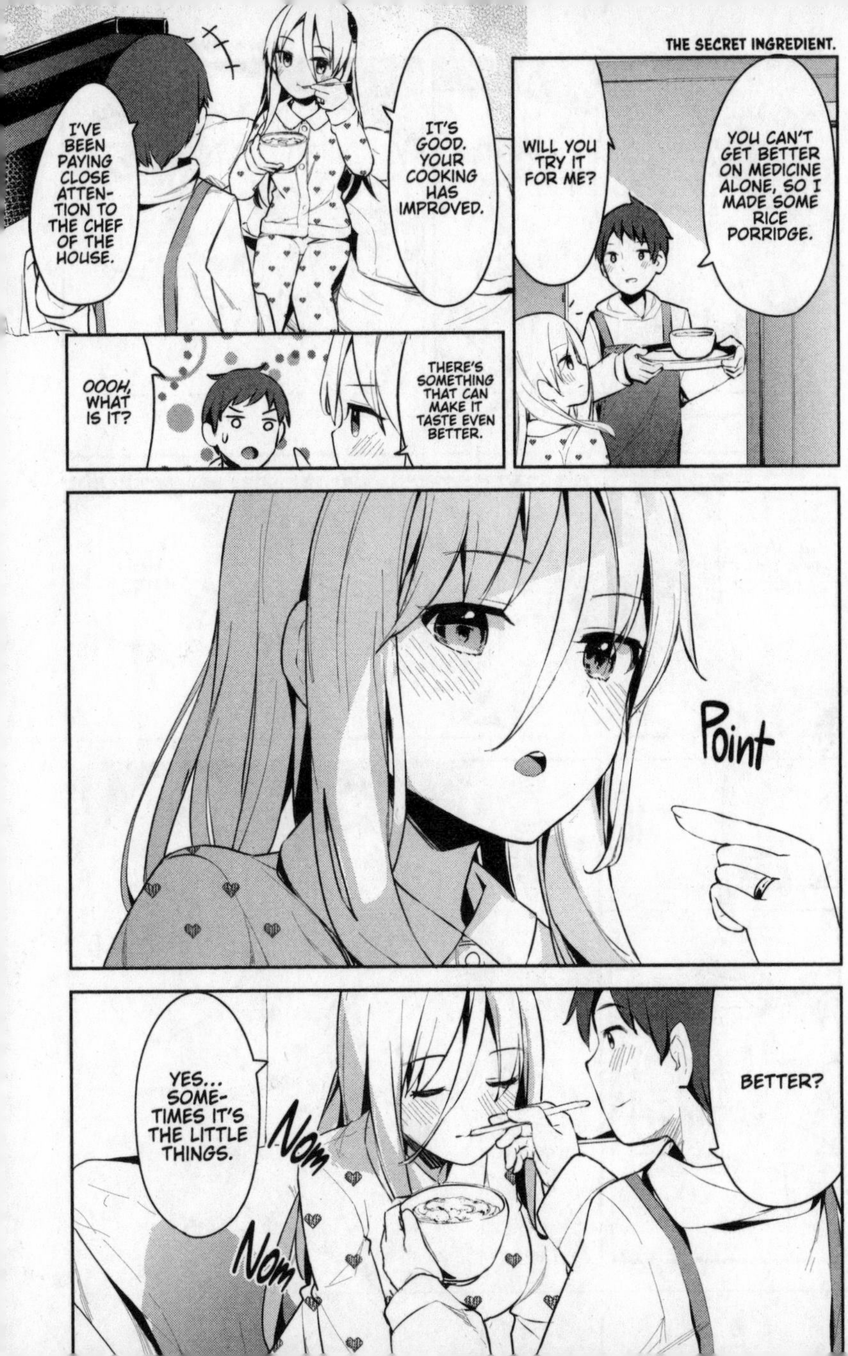

YOU CAN'T GET BETTER ON MEDICINE ALONE, SO I MADE SOME RICE PORRIDGE.
WILL YOU TRY IT FOR ME?
IT'S GOOD. YOUR COOKING HAS IMPROVED.
I'VE BEEN PAYING CLOSE ATTEN-TION TO THE CHEF OF THE HOUSE.
THERE'S SOMETHING THAT CAN MAKE IT TASTE EVEN BETTER.
OOOH, WHAT IS IT?
Point
BETTER?
YES... SOME-TIMES IT'S THE LITTLE THINGS.
Nom
Nom

SETSUNA-SAN AND SLEEP-TALKING.

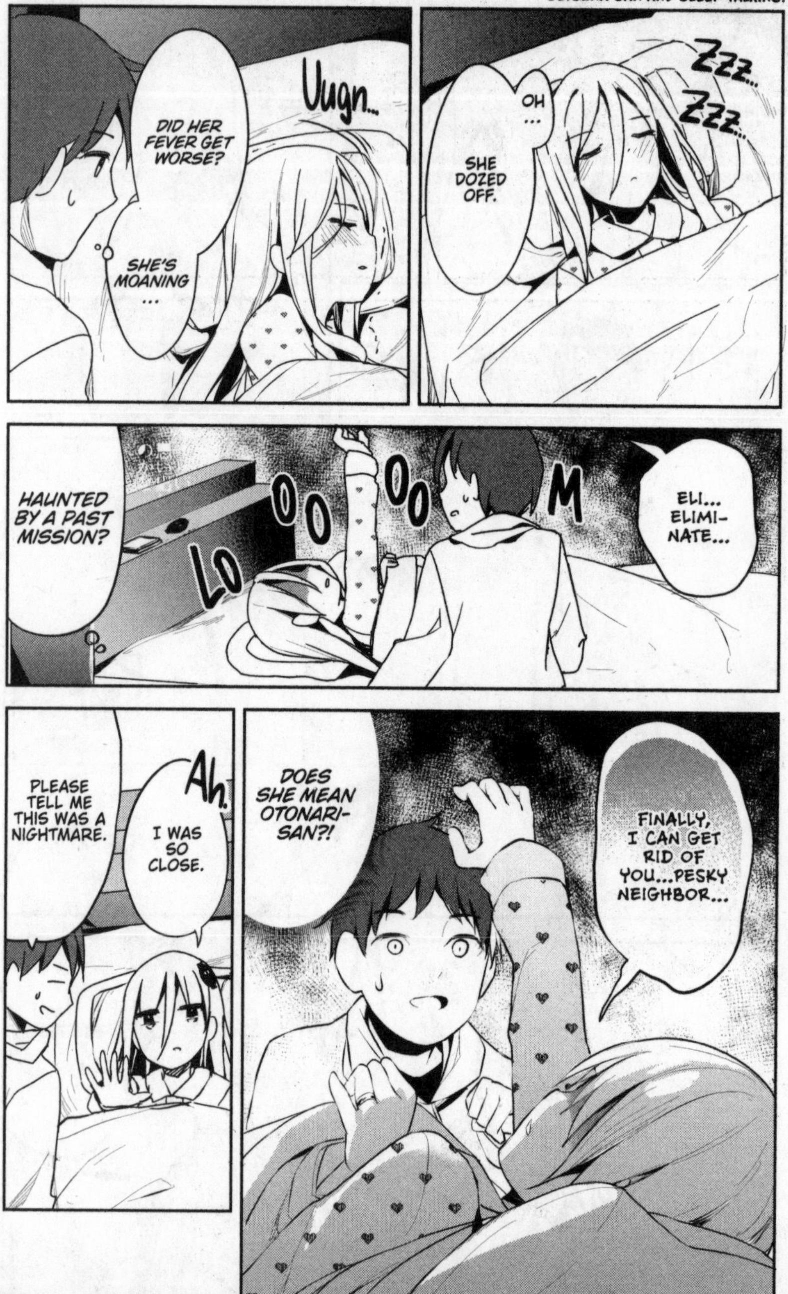
Zzz... Zzz...
OH ...
SHE DOZED OFF.
Uugn...
DID HER FEVER GET WORSE?
SHE'S MOANING ...
ELI... ELIMINATE...
LOOOOOM
HAUNTED BY A PAST MISSION?
FINALLY, I CAN GET RID OF YOU...PESKY NEIGHBOR...
DOES SHE MEAN OTONARI-SAN?!
Ah.
I WAS SO CLOSE.
PLEASE TELL ME THIS WAS A NIGHTMARE.

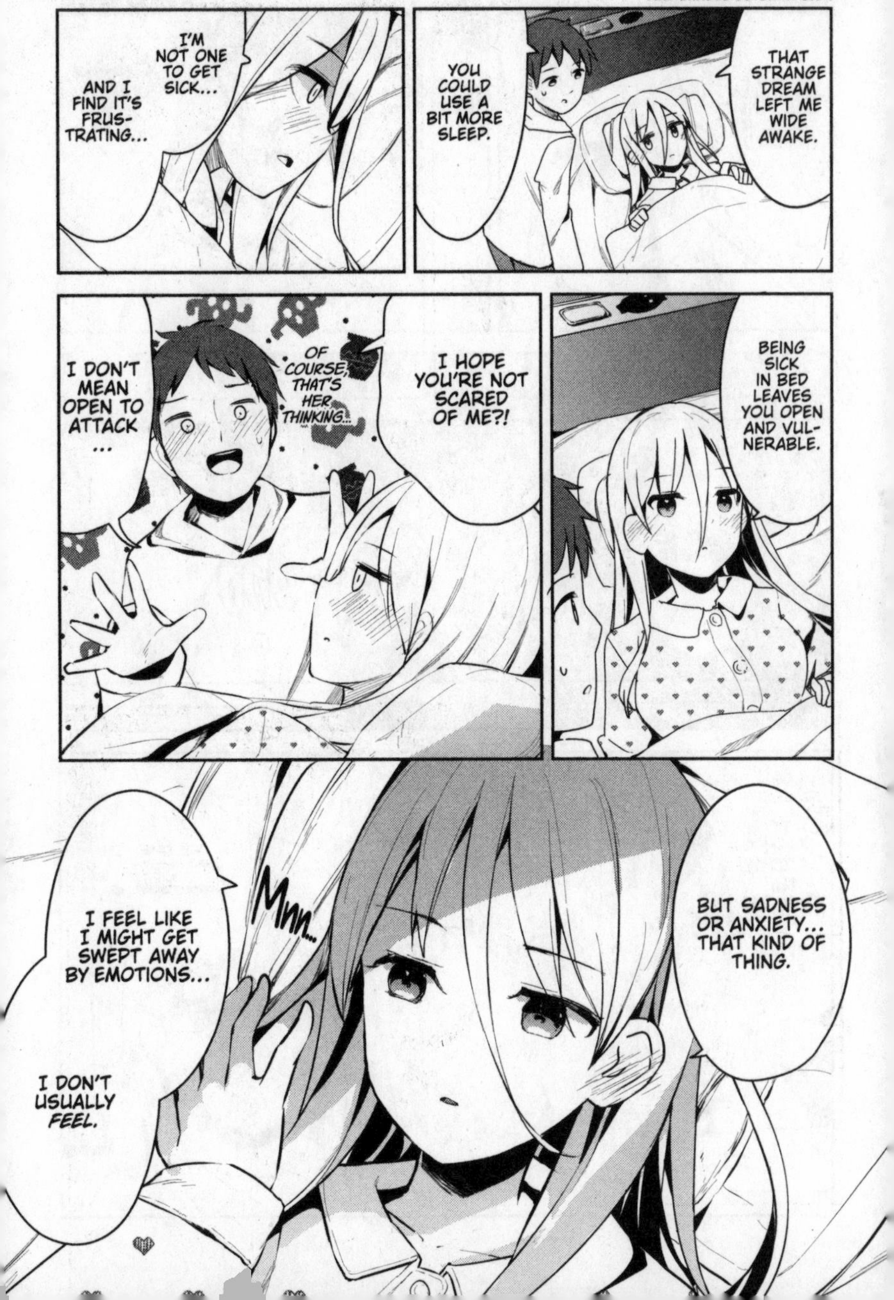
THAT STRANGE DREAM LEFT ME WIDE AWAKE.
YOU COULD USE A BIT MORE SLEEP.
I'M NOT ONE TO GET SICK...
AND I FIND IT'S FRUS-TRATING...
BEING SICK IN BED LEAVES YOU OPEN AND VUL-NERABLE.
I HOPE YOU'RE NOT SCARED OF ME?!
OF COURSE, THAT'S HER THINKING...
I DON'T MEAN OPEN TO ATTACK ...
BUT SADNESS OR ANXIETY... THAT KIND OF THING.
Mnn...
I FEEL LIKE I MIGHT GET SWEPT AWAY BY EMOTIONS...
I DON'T USUALLY FEEL.

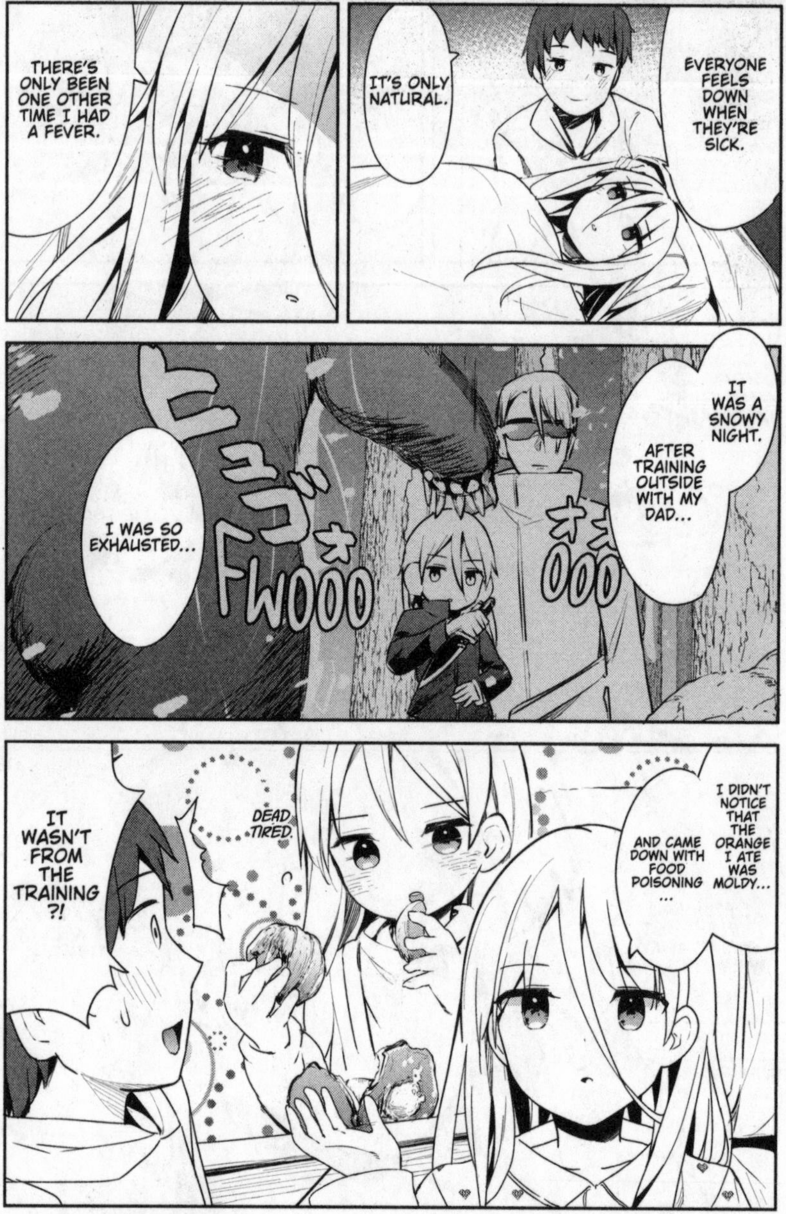
EVERYONE FEELS DOWN WHEN THEY'RE SICK.
IT'S ONLY NATURAL.
THERE'S ONLY BEEN ONE OTHER TIME I HAD A FEVER.
IT WAS A SNOWY NIGHT.
AFTER TRAINING OUTSIDE WITH MY DAD...
FWOOO
OOO
I WAS SO EXHAUSTED...
I DIDN'T NOTICE THAT THE ORANGE I ATE WAS MOLDY...
AND CAME DOWN WITH FOOD POISONING ...
DEAD TIRED.
IT WASN'T FROM THE TRAINING?!

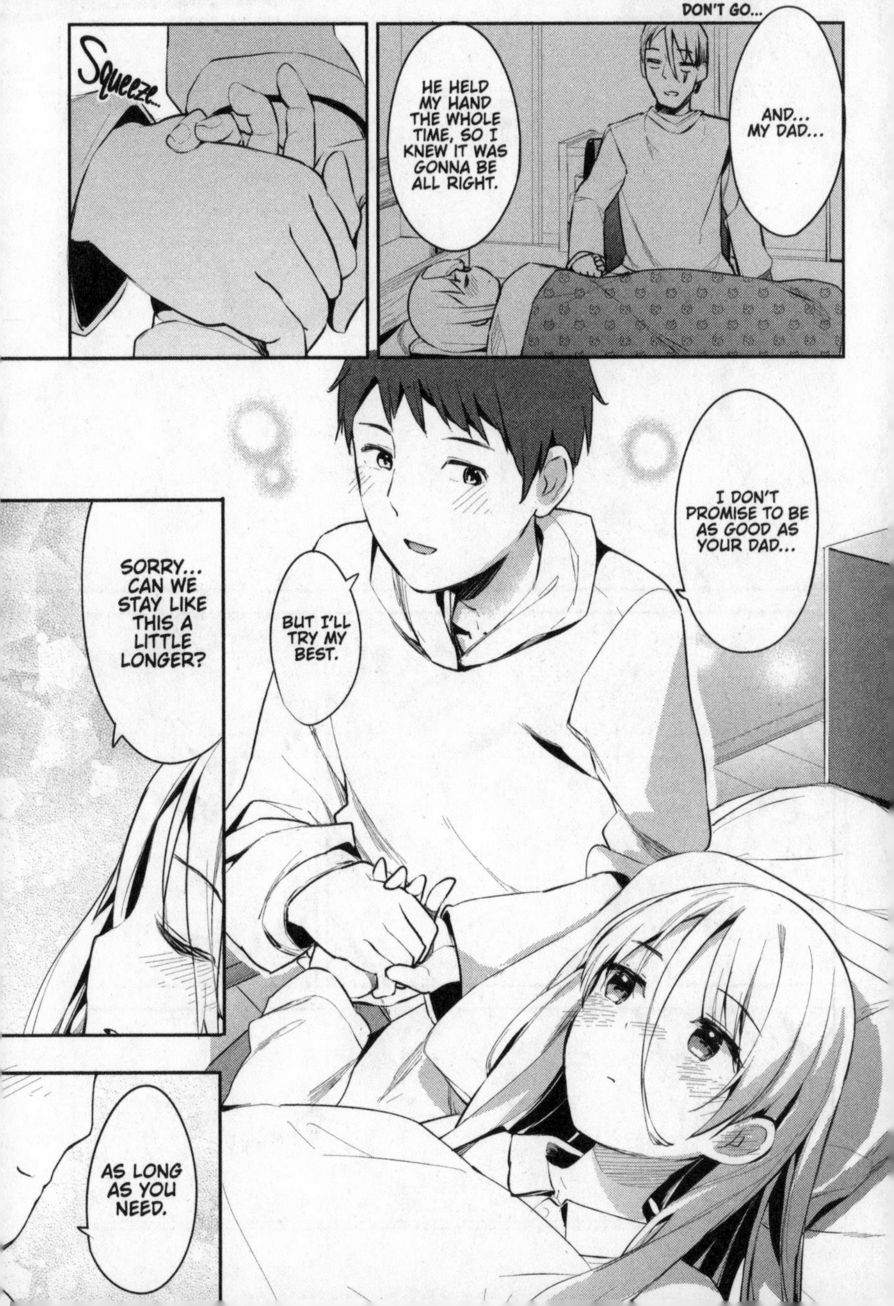
DON'T GO...
AND... MY DAD...
HE HELD MY HAND THE WHOLE TIME, SO I KNEW IT WAS GONNA BE ALL RIGHT.
Squeeze...
I DON'T PROMISE TO BE AS GOOD AS YOUR DAD...
BUT I'LL TRY MY BEST.
SORRY... CAN WE STAY LIKE THIS A LITTLE LONGER?
AS LONG AS YOU NEED.

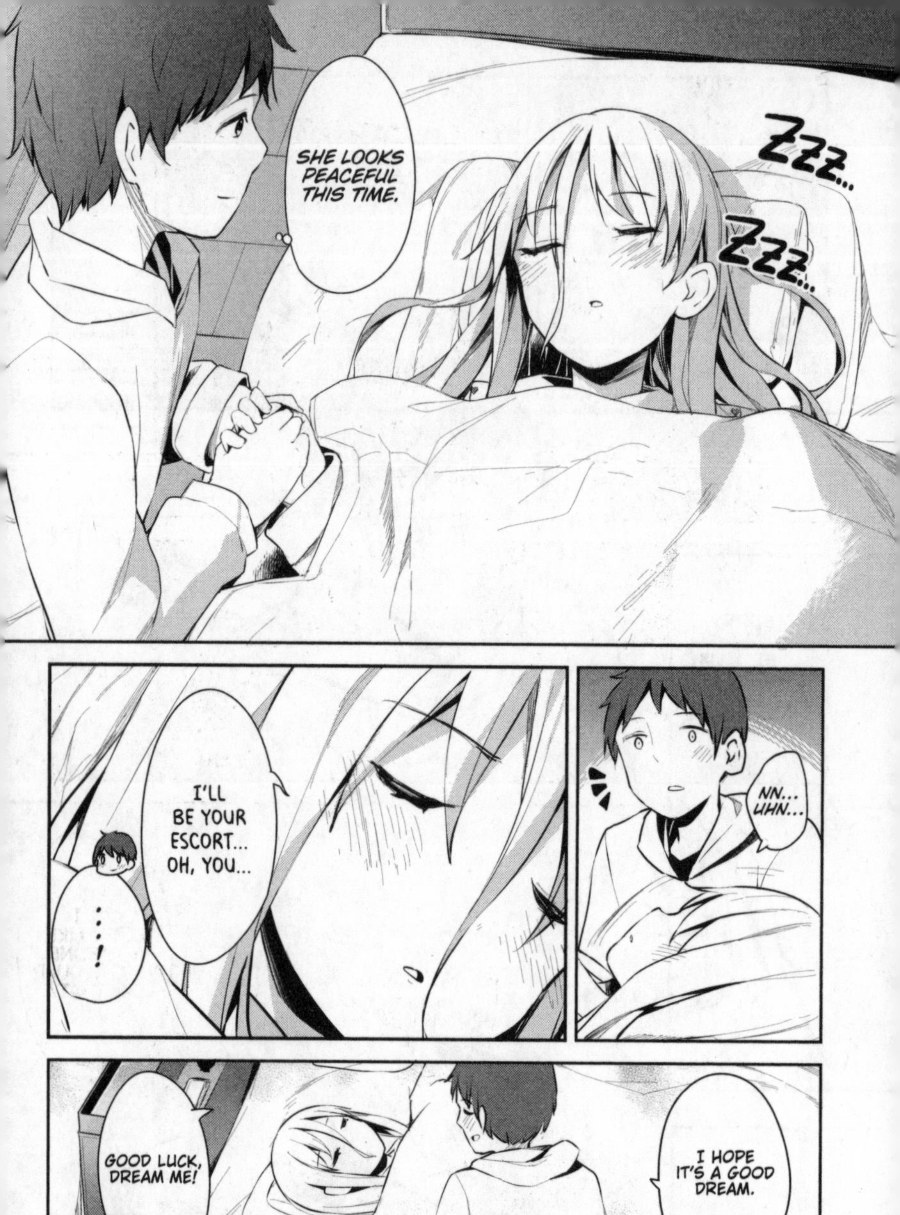
Zzz...
Zzz...
SHE LOOKS PEACEFUL THIS TIME.
NN... UHN...
I'LL BE YOUR ESCORT... OH, YOU...
...!
I HOPE IT'S A GOOD DREAM.
GOOD LUCK, DREAM ME!

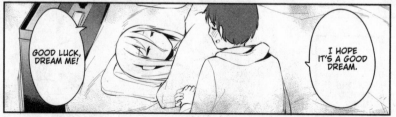

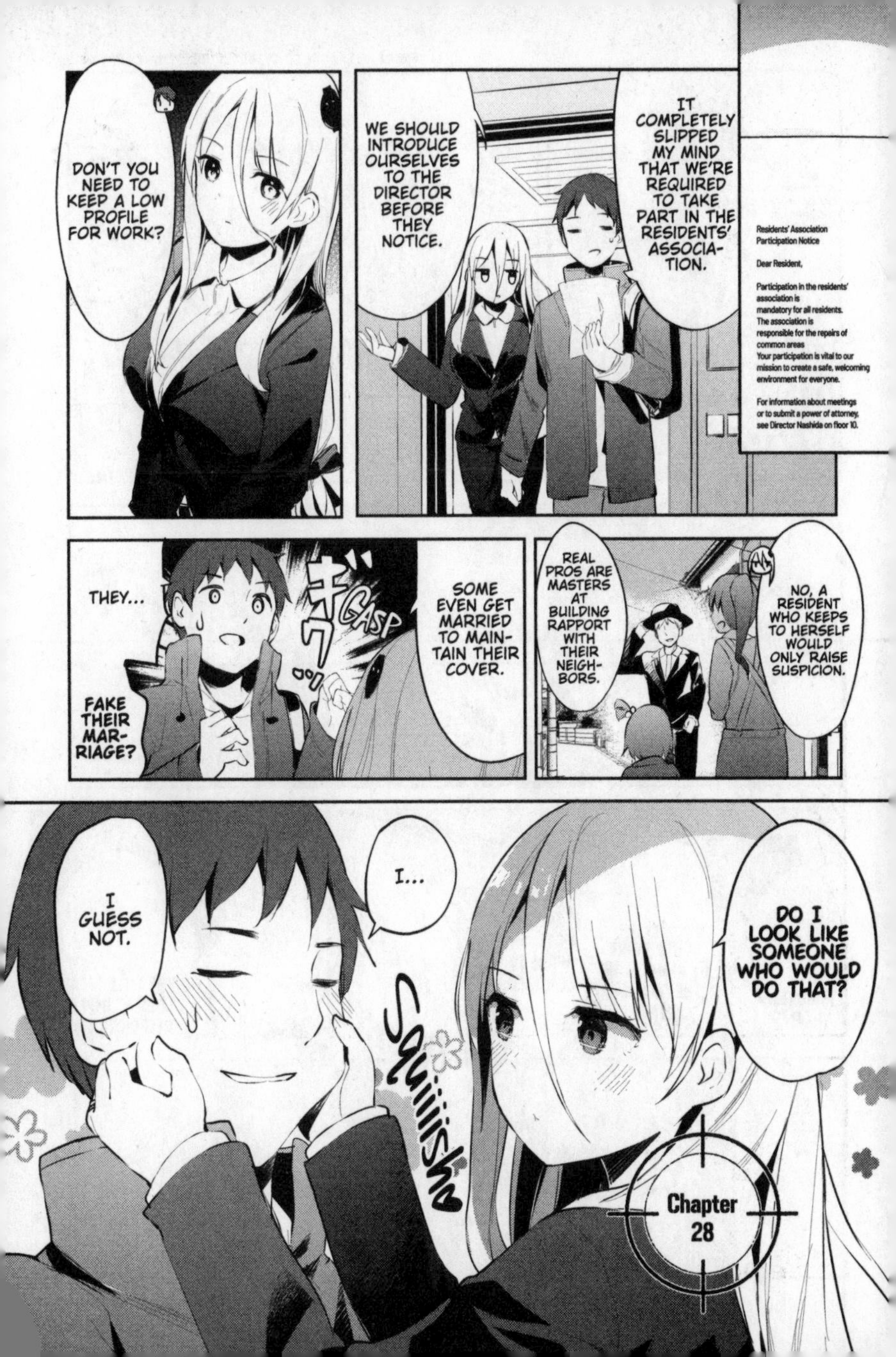
Residents' Association
Participation Notice
Dear Resident,
Participation in the residents' association is mandatory for all residents. The association is responsible for the repairs of common areas
Your participation is vital to our mission to create a safe, welcoming environment for everyone.
For information about meetings or to submit a power of attorney, see Director Nashida on floor 10.
IT COMPLETELY SLIPPED MY MIND THAT WE'RE REQUIRED TO TAKE PART IN THE RESIDENTS' ASSOCIATION.
WE SHOULD INTRODUCE OURSELVES TO THE DIRECTOR BEFORE THEY NOTICE.
DON'T YOU NEED TO KEEP A LOW PROFILE FOR WORK?
NO, A RESIDENT WHO KEEPS TO HERSELF WOULD ONLY RAISE SUSPICION.
REAL PROS ARE MASTERS AT BUILDING RAPPORT WITH THEIR NEIGHBORS.
SOME EVEN GET MARRIED TO MAINTAIN THEIR COVER.
GASP
THEY...
FAKE THEIR MARRIAGE?
DO I LOOK LIKE SOMEONE WHO WOULD DO THAT?
I...
I GUESS NOT.
Squiiiish
Chapter 28

FROM ASSASSIN TO DISASTER RESPONSE LEADER.

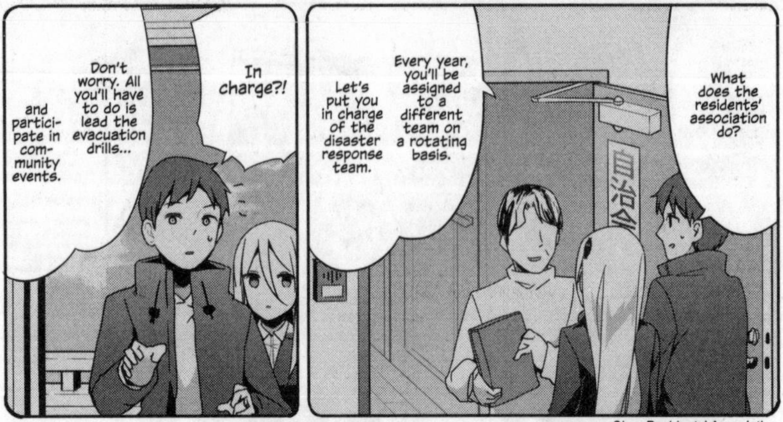
What does the residents' association do?
Every year, you'll be assigned to a different team on a rotating basis.
Let's put you in charge of the disaster response team.
In charge?!
Don't worry. All you'll have to do is lead the evacuation drills...
and partici-pate in com-munity events.

Sign: Residents' Association

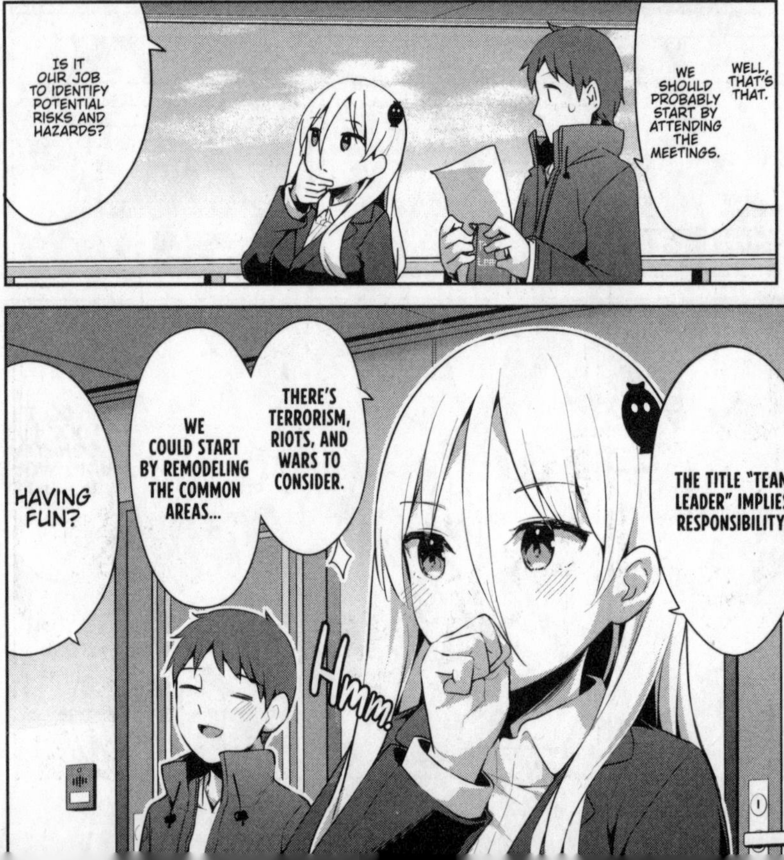
WELL, THAT'S THAT.
WE SHOULD PROBABLY START BY ATTENDING THE MEETINGS.
IS IT OUR JOB TO IDENTIFY POTENTIAL RISKS AND HAZARDS?
THE TITLE "TEAM LEADER" IMPLIES RESPONSIBILITY.
Hmm.
THERE'S TERRORISM, RIOTS, AND WARS TO CONSIDER.
WE COULD START BY REMODELING THE COMMON AREAS...
HAVING FUN?

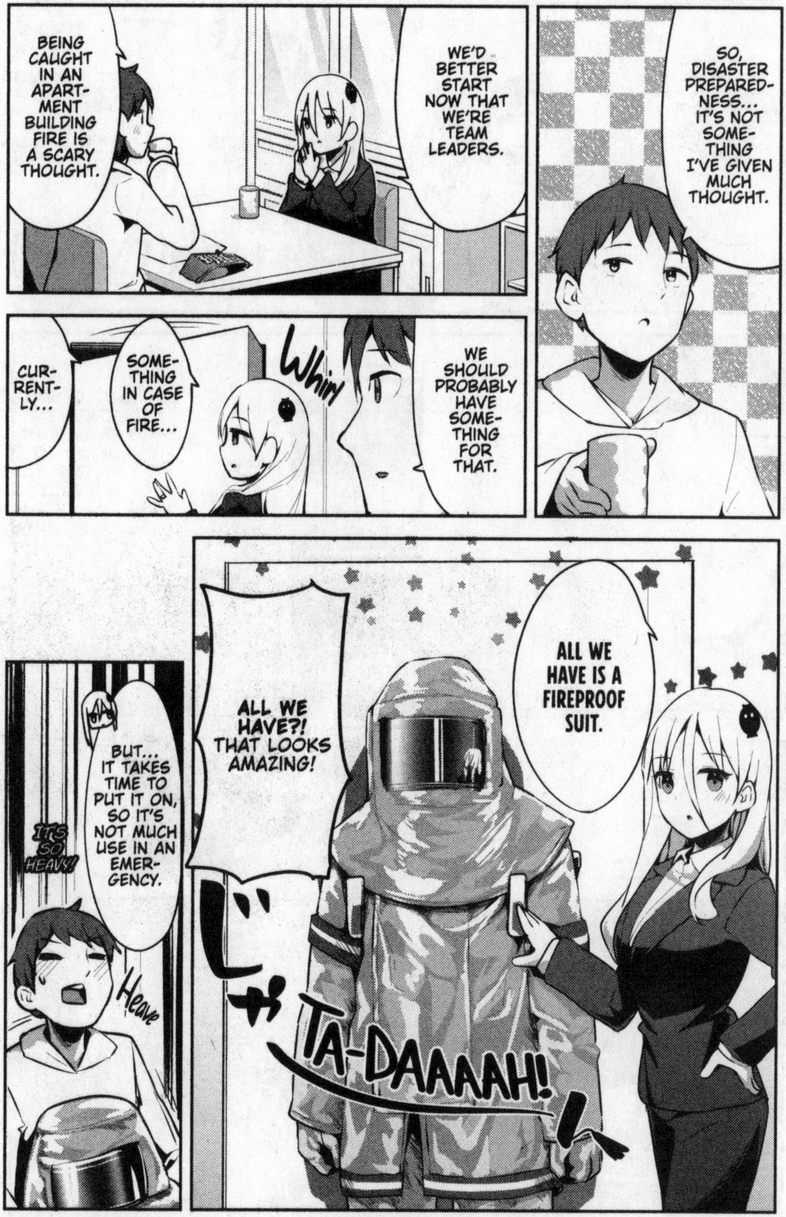
SO, DISASTER PREPAREDNESS... IT'S NOT SOMETHING I'VE GIVEN MUCH THOUGHT.
WE'D BETTER START NOW THAT WE'RE TEAM LEADERS.
BEING CAUGHT IN AN APARTMENT BUILDING FIRE IS A SCARY THOUGHT.
WE SHOULD PROBABLY HAVE SOMETHING FOR THAT.
Whirl
SOMETHING IN CASE OF FIRE...
CURRENTLY...
ALL WE HAVE IS A FIREPROOF SUIT.
TA-DAAAAH!
ALL WE HAVE?! THAT LOOKS AMAZING!
BUT... IT TAKES TIME TO PUT IT ON, SO IT'S NOT MUCH USE IN AN EMERGENCY.
IT'S SO HEAVY!
Heave

FIND A SAFE ROOM.

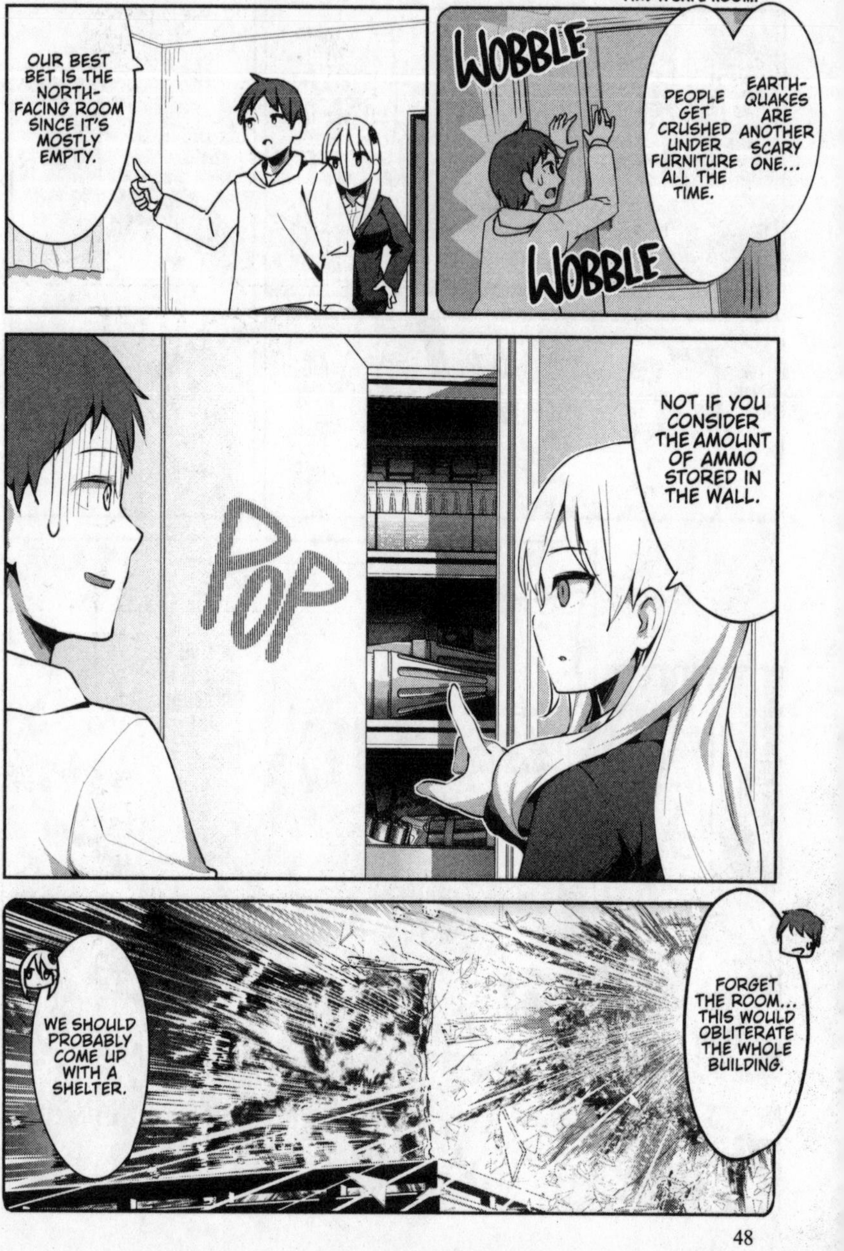

EARTH-QUAKES ARE ANOTHER SCARY ONE...
PEOPLE GET CRUSHED UNDER FURNITURE ALL THE TIME.
WOBBLE
WOBBLE
OUR BEST BET IS THE NORTH-FACING ROOM SINCE IT'S MOSTLY EMPTY.
NOT IF YOU CONSIDER THE AMOUNT OF AMMO STORED IN THE WALL.
POP
FORGET THE ROOM... THIS WOULD OBLITERATE THE WHOLE BUILDING.
WE SHOULD PROBABLY COME UP WITH A SHELTER.

PLAN AN ESCAPE ROUTE.

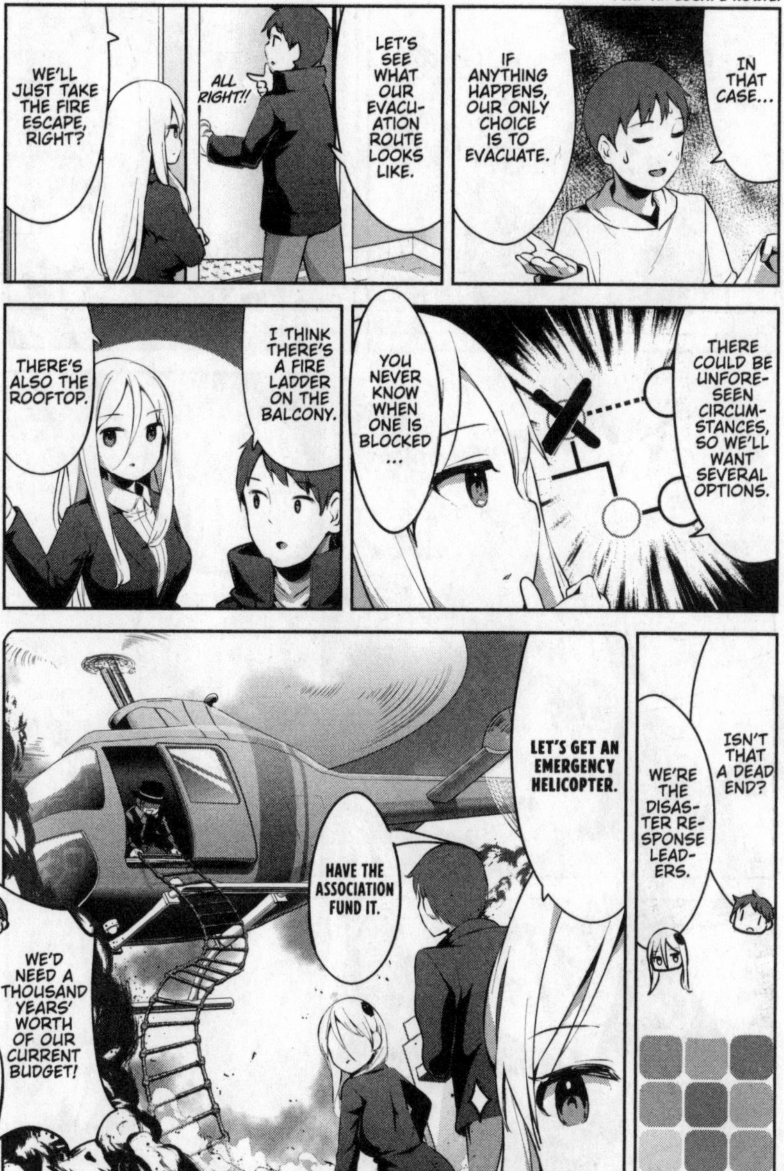
IN THAT CASE...
IF ANYTHING HAPPENS, OUR ONLY CHOICE IS TO EVACUATE.
LET'S SEE WHAT OUR EVACUATION ROUTE LOOKS LIKE.
ALL RIGHT!!
WE'LL JUST TAKE THE FIRE ESCAPE, RIGHT?
THERE COULD BE UNFORESEEN CIRCUMSTANCES, SO WE'LL WANT SEVERAL OPTIONS.
YOU NEVER KNOW WHEN ONE IS BLOCKED...
I THINK THERE'S A FIRE LADDER ON THE BALCONY.
THERE'S ALSO THE ROOFTOP.
ISN'T THAT A DEAD END?
WE'RE THE DISASTER RESPONSE LEADERS.
LET'S GET AN EMERGENCY HELICOPTER.
HAVE THE ASSOCIATION FUND IT.
WE'D NEED A THOUSAND YEARS' WORTH OF OUR CURRENT BUDGET!

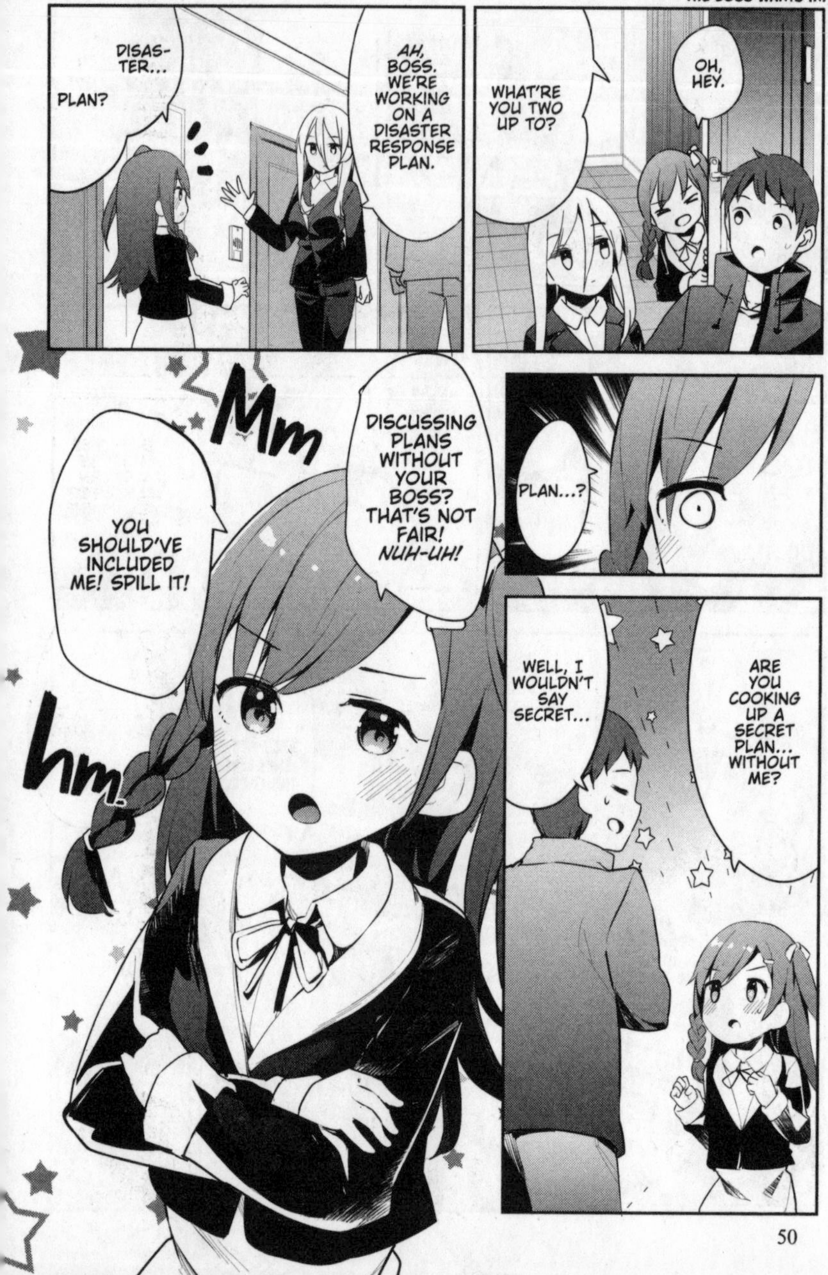
OH, HEY.
WHAT'RE YOU TWO UP TO?
AH, BOSS. WE'RE WORKING ON A DISASTER RESPONSE PLAN.
DISASTER... PLAN?
PLAN...?
ARE YOU COOKING UP A SECRET PLAN... WITHOUT ME?
WELL, I WOULDN'T SAY SECRET...
Mm hm
DISCUSSING PLANS WITHOUT YOUR BOSS? THAT'S NOT FAIR! NUH-UH!
YOU SHOULD'VE INCLUDED ME! SPILL IT!

THE NEW BOSS OF DISASTER RESPONSE.

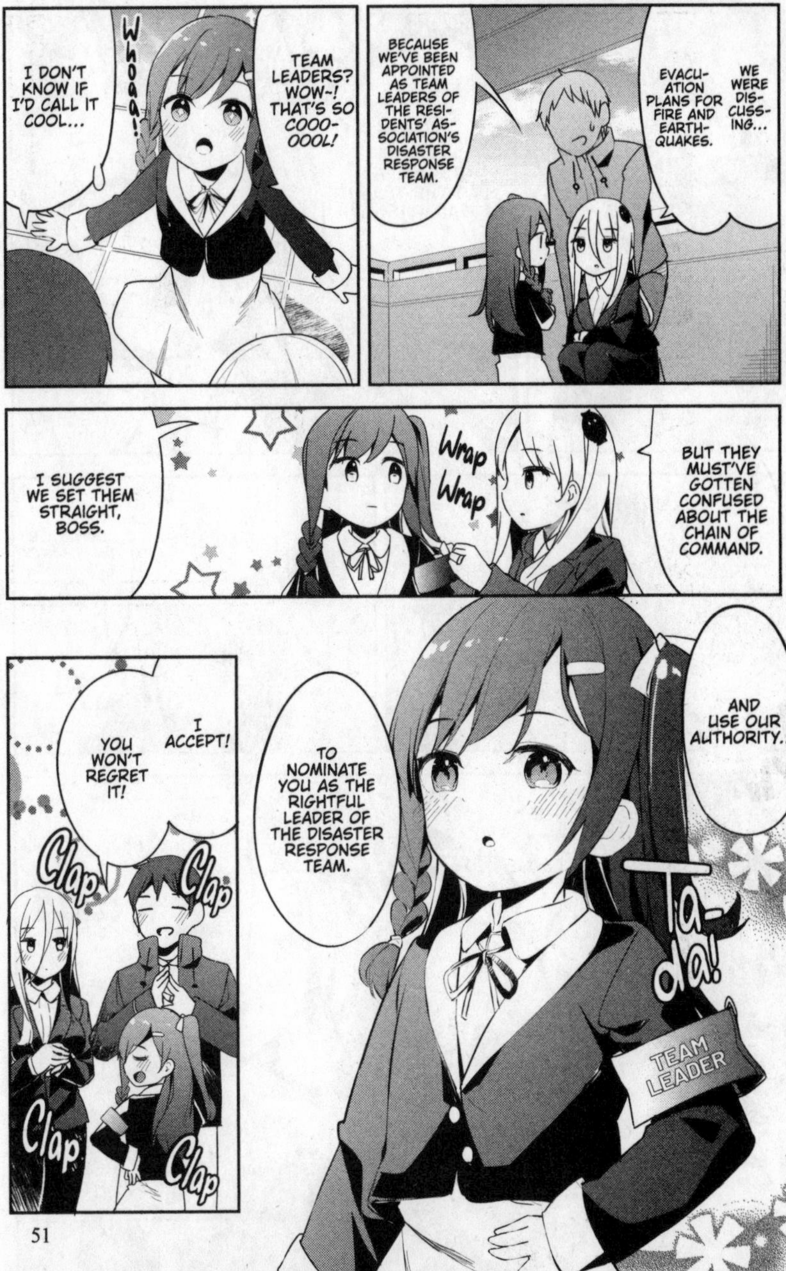

WE WERE DISCUSSING...
EVACUATION PLANS FOR FIRE AND EARTHQUAKES.
BECAUSE WE'VE BEEN APPOINTED AS TEAM LEADERS OF THE RESIDENTS' ASSOCIATION'S DISASTER RESPONSE TEAM.
TEAM LEADERS? WOW~! THAT'S SO COOOOOOL!
Whoaaa!
I DON'T KNOW IF I'D CALL IT COOL...
BUT THEY MUST'VE GOTTEN CONFUSED ABOUT THE CHAIN OF COMMAND.
Wrap Wrap
I SUGGEST WE SET THEM STRAIGHT, BOSS.
AND USE OUR AUTHORITY...
TO NOMINATE YOU AS THE RIGHTFUL LEADER OF THE DISASTER RESPONSE TEAM.
Ta-da!
TEAM LEADER
I ACCEPT!
YOU WON'T REGRET IT!
Clap
Clap
Clap
Clap

BE PREPARED!

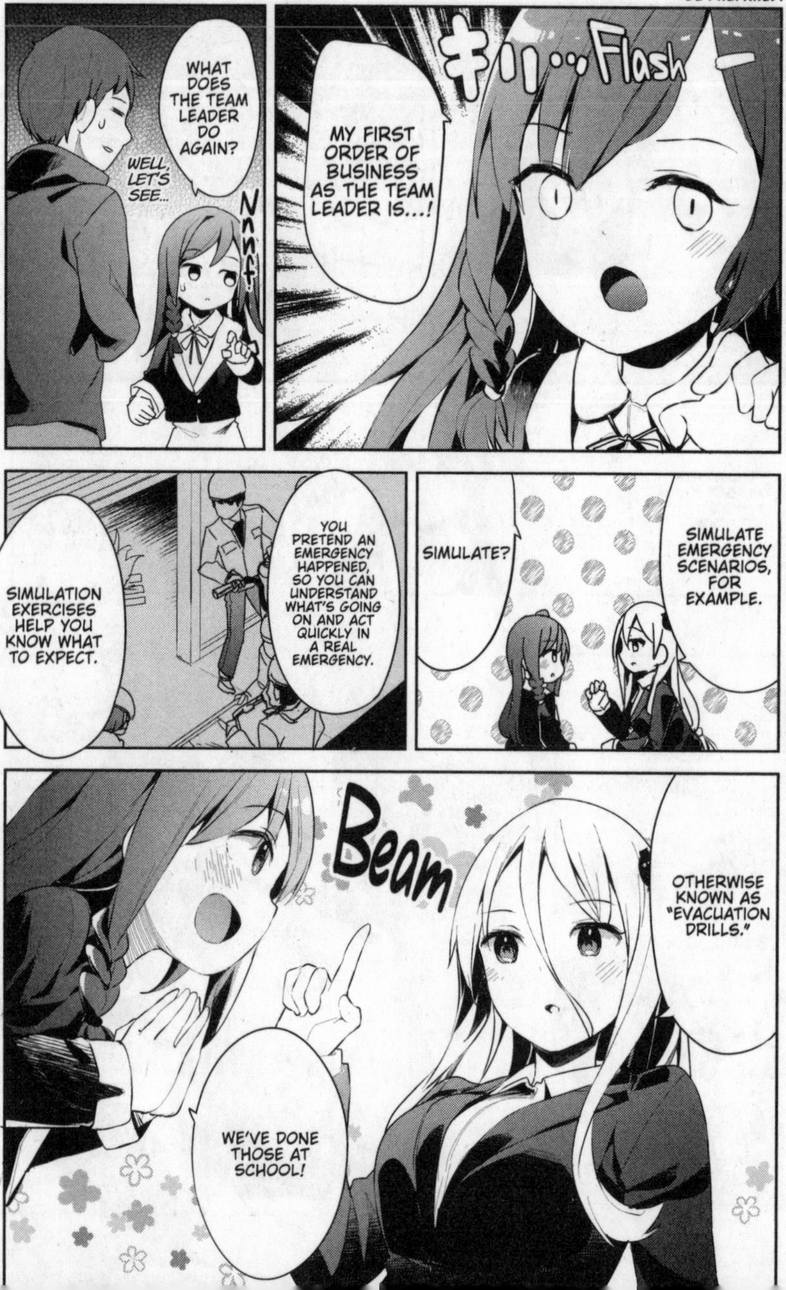

Flash
MY FIRST ORDER OF BUSINESS AS THE TEAM LEADER IS...!
WHAT DOES THE TEAM LEADER DO AGAIN?
WELL, LET'S SEE...
Nnnf!
SIMULATE EMERGENCY SCENARIOS, FOR EXAMPLE.
SIMULATE?
YOU PRETEND AN EMERGENCY HAPPENED, SO YOU CAN UNDERSTAND WHAT'S GOING ON AND ACT QUICKLY IN A REAL EMERGENCY.
SIMULATION EXERCISES HELP YOU KNOW WHAT TO EXPECT.
OTHERWISE KNOWN AS "EVACUATION DRILLS."
Beam
WE'VE DONE THOSE AT SCHOOL!

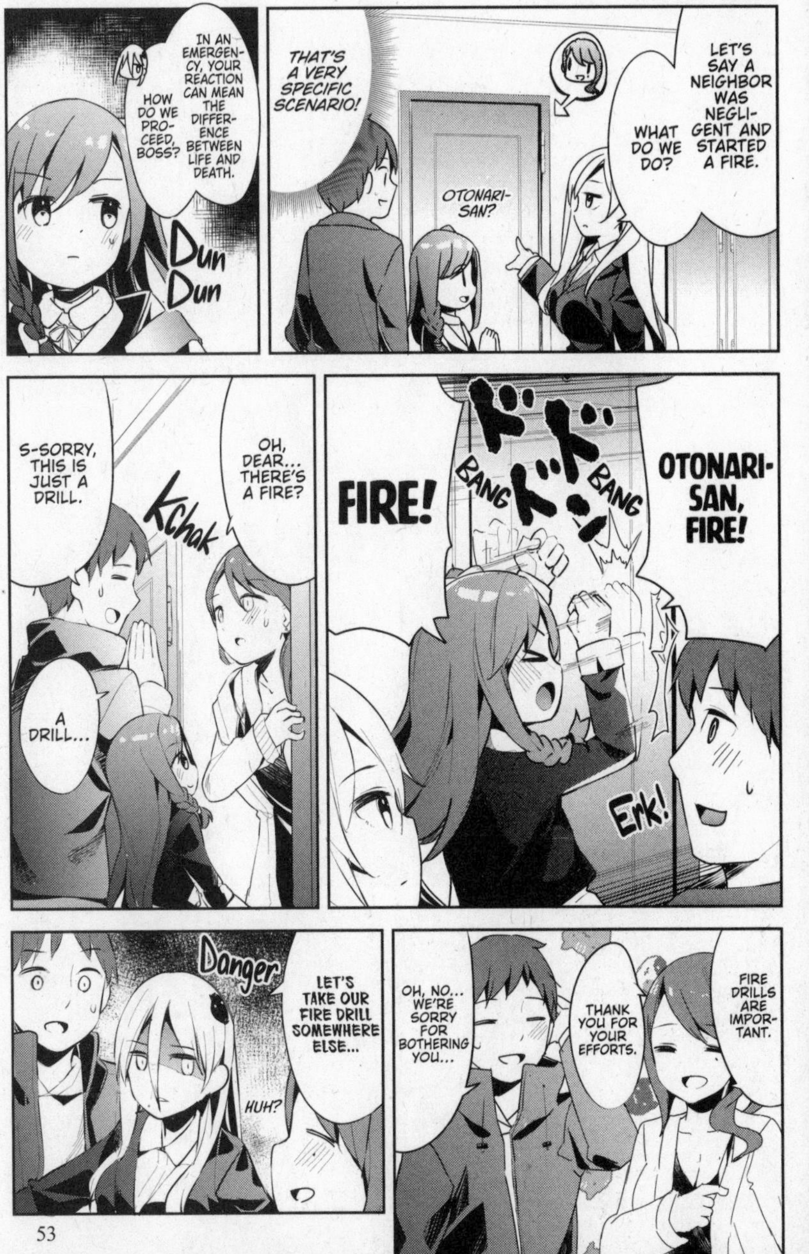
LET'S SAY A NEIGHBOR WAS NEGLIGENT AND STARTED A FIRE.
WHAT DO WE DO?
OTONARI-SAN?
THAT'S A VERY SPECIFIC SCENARIO!
IN AN EMERGENCY, YOUR REACTION CAN MEAN THE DIFFERENCE BETWEEN LIFE AND DEATH.
HOW DO WE PROCEED, BOSS?
Dun Dun
OTONARI-SAN, FIRE!
BANG BANG
FIRE!
Erk!
OH, DEAR... THERE'S A FIRE?
Kchak
S-SORRY, THIS IS JUST A DRILL.
A DRILL...
FIRE DRILLS ARE IMPORTANT.
THANK YOU FOR YOUR EFFORTS.
OH, NO... WE'RE SORRY FOR BOTHERING YOU...
LET'S TAKE OUR FIRE DRILL SOMEWHERE ELSE...
Danger
HUH?

FIRE MEANS SMOKE.

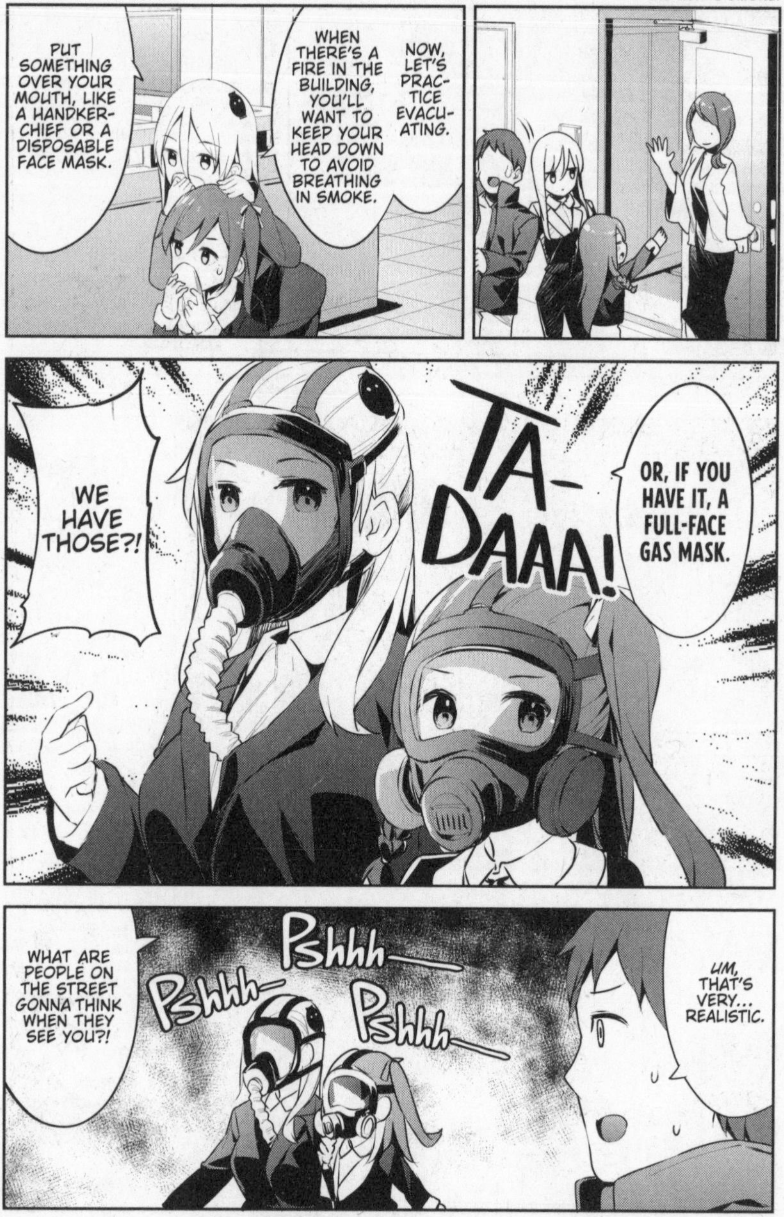
NOW, LET'S PRAC-TICE EVACU-ATING.
WHEN THERE'S A FIRE IN THE BUILDING, YOU'LL WANT TO KEEP YOUR HEAD DOWN TO AVOID BREATHING IN SMOKE.
PUT SOMETHING OVER YOUR MOUTH, LIKE A HANDKER-CHIEF OR A DISPOSABLE FACE MASK.
OR, IF YOU HAVE IT, A FULL-FACE GAS MASK.
TA-DAAA!
WE HAVE THOSE?!
UM, THAT'S VERY... REALISTIC.
Pshhh—
Pshhh—
Pshhh—
WHAT ARE PEOPLE ON THE STREET GONNA THINK WHEN THEY SEE YOU?!

PICTURE A REAL FIRE.

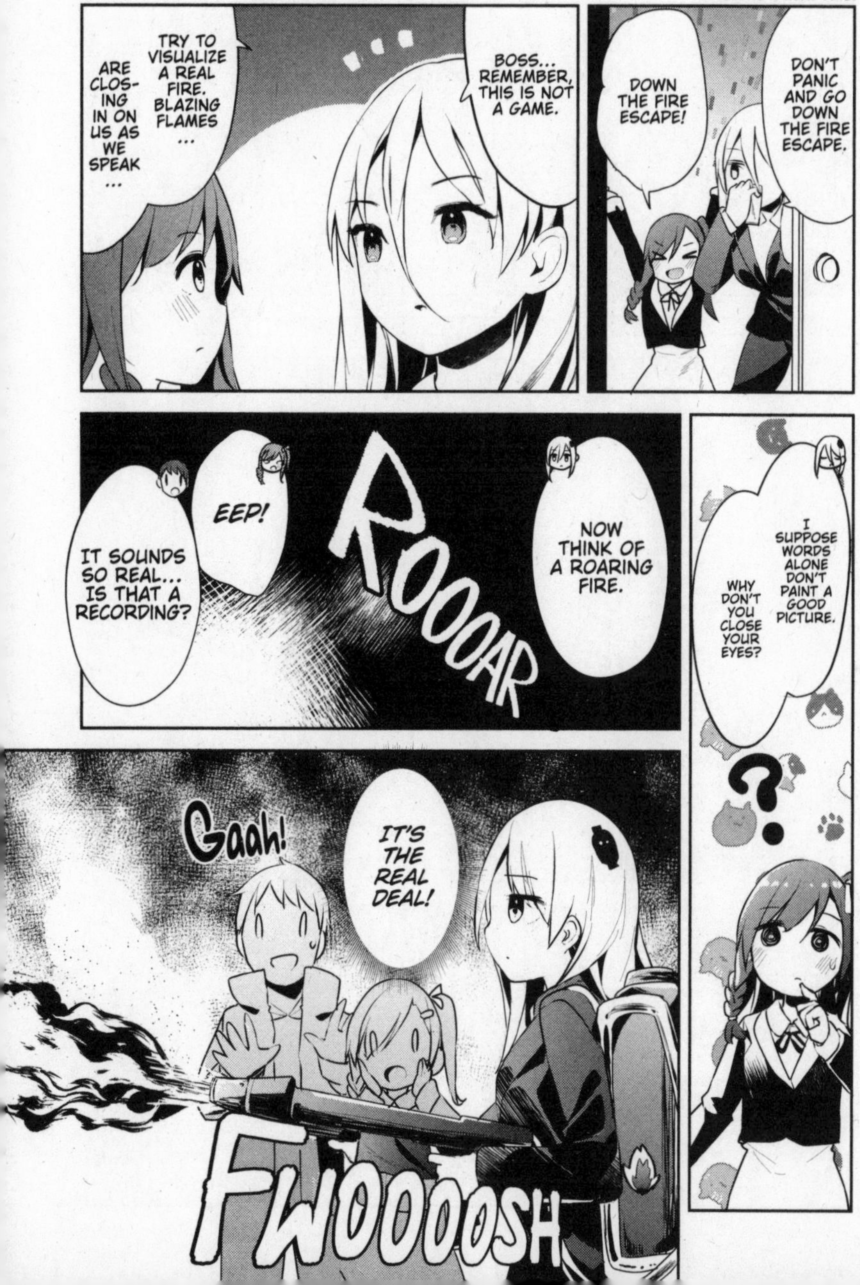

DON'T PANIC AND GO DOWN THE FIRE ESCAPE.
DOWN THE FIRE ESCAPE!
BOSS... REMEMBER, THIS IS NOT A GAME.
TRY TO VISUALIZE A REAL FIRE. BLAZING FLAMES...
ARE CLOSING IN ON US AS WE SPEAK...
I SUPPOSE WORDS ALONE DON'T PAINT A GOOD PICTURE.
WHY DON'T YOU CLOSE YOUR EYES?
?
NOW THINK OF A ROARING FIRE.
ROOOAR
EEP!
IT SOUNDS SO REAL... IS THAT A RECORDING?
IT'S THE REAL DEAL!
Gaah!
FWOOOOSH

A FULL-SCALE SIMULATION.

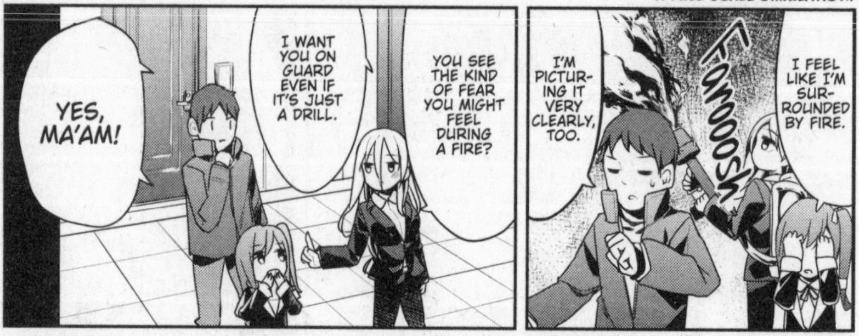
I FEEL LIKE I'M SURROUNDED BY FIRE.
Fwooosh
I'M PICTURING IT VERY CLEARLY, TOO.
YOU SEE THE KIND OF FEAR YOU MIGHT FEEL DURING A FIRE?
I WANT YOU ON GUARD EVEN IF IT'S JUST A DRILL.
YES, MA'AM!

Kids, don't try this at home!

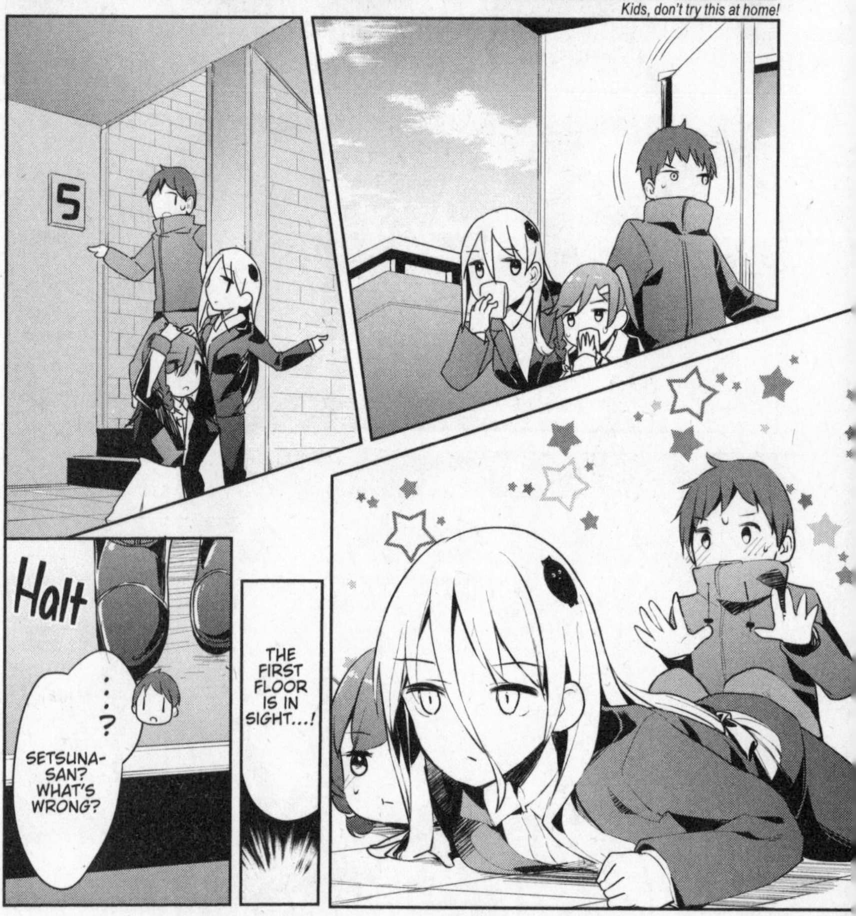
5
THE FIRST FLOOR IS IN SIGHT...!
Halt
...?
SETSUNA-SAN? WHAT'S WRONG?

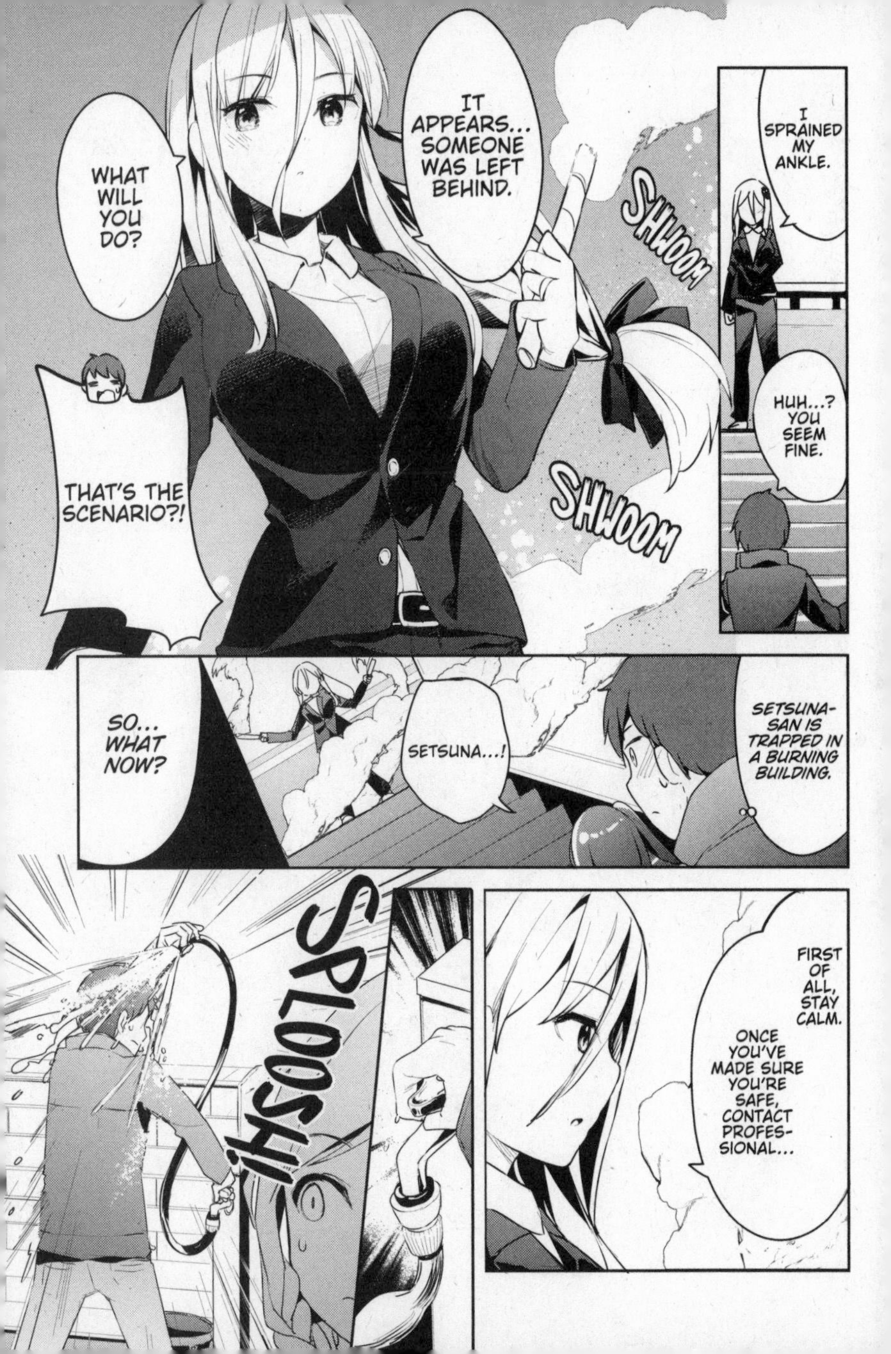
I SPRAINED MY ANKLE.
HUH...? YOU SEEM FINE.
SHWOOM
IT APPEARS... SOMEONE WAS LEFT BEHIND.
SHWOOM
WHAT WILL YOU DO?
THAT'S THE SCENARIO?!
SETSUNA-SAN IS TRAPPED IN A BURNING BUILDING.
SETSUNA...!
SO... WHAT NOW?
FIRST OF ALL, STAY CALM.
ONCE YOU'VE MADE SURE YOU'RE SAFE, CONTACT PROFESSIONAL...
SPLOOSH!

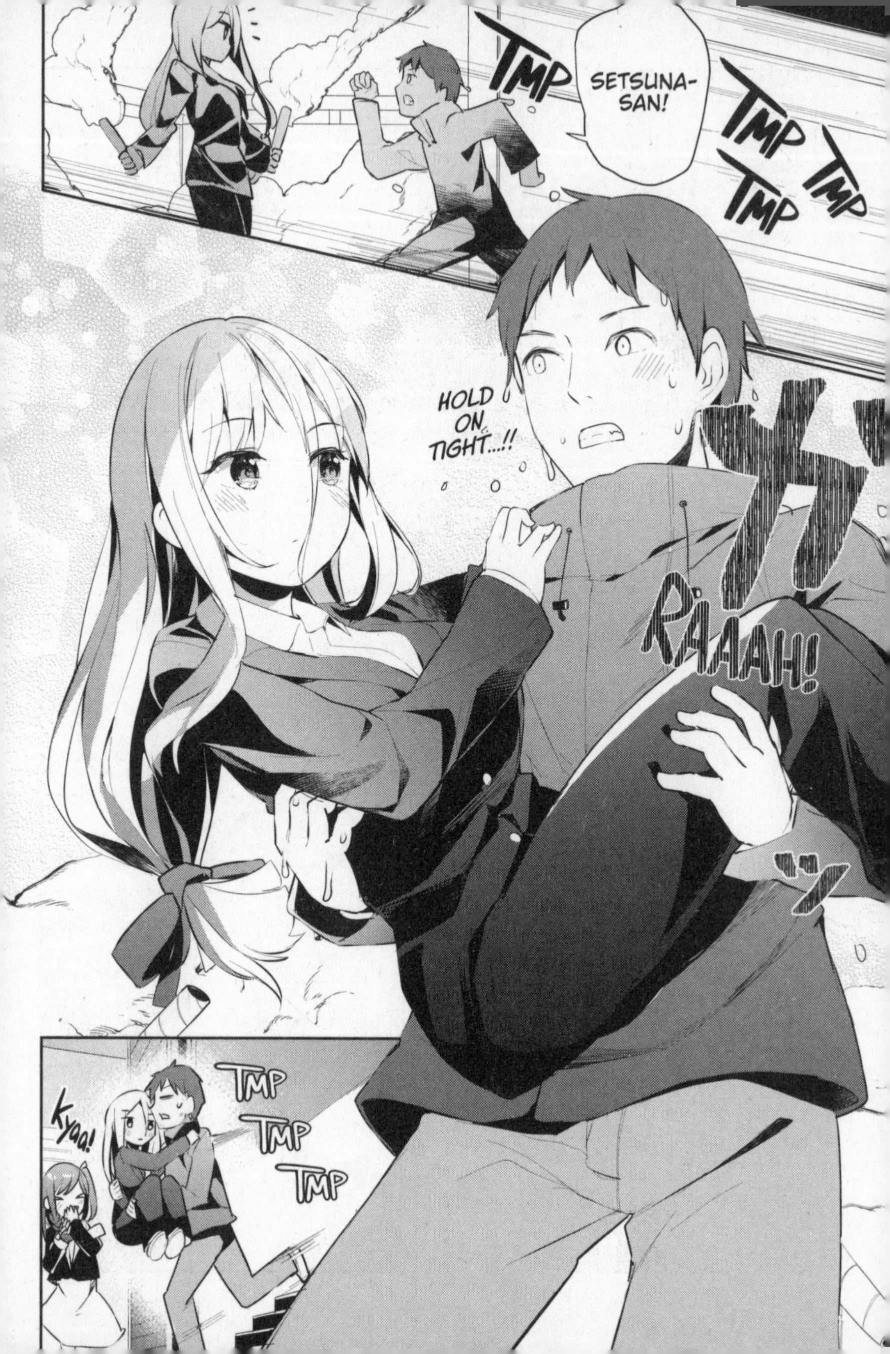

TMP
TMP
TMP
TMP
SETSUNA-SAN!
TMP
RAAAH!
HOLD ON TIGHT...!!
TMP
TMP
TMP
Kyaa!

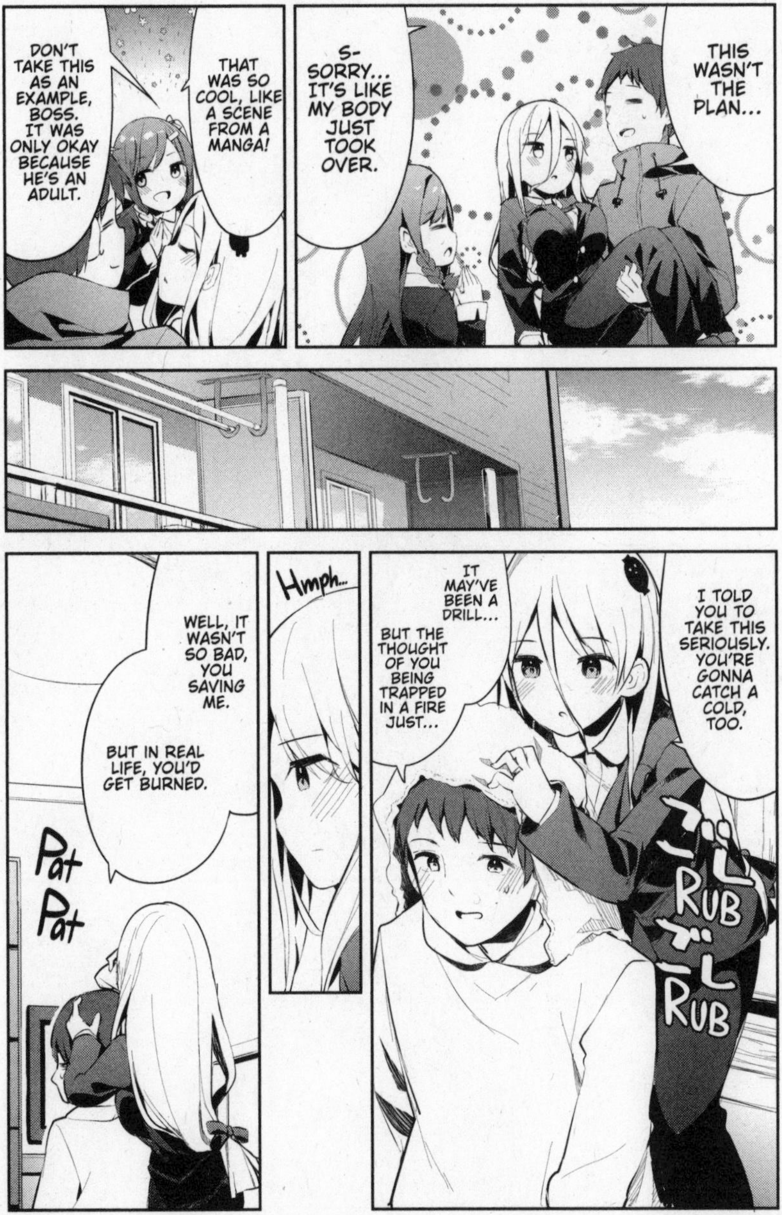
THIS WASN'T THE PLAN...
S-SORRY... IT'S LIKE MY BODY JUST TOOK OVER.
THAT WAS SO COOL, LIKE A SCENE FROM A MANGA!
DON'T TAKE THIS AS AN EXAMPLE, BOSS. IT WAS ONLY OKAY BECAUSE HE'S AN ADULT.
I TOLD YOU TO TAKE THIS SERIOUSLY. YOU'RE GONNA CATCH A COLD, TOO.
RUB RUB
IT MAY'VE BEEN A DRILL...
BUT THE THOUGHT OF YOU BEING TRAPPED IN A FIRE JUST...
Hmph...
WELL, IT WASN'T SO BAD, YOU SAVING ME.
BUT IN REAL LIFE, YOU'D GET BURNED.
Pat Pat

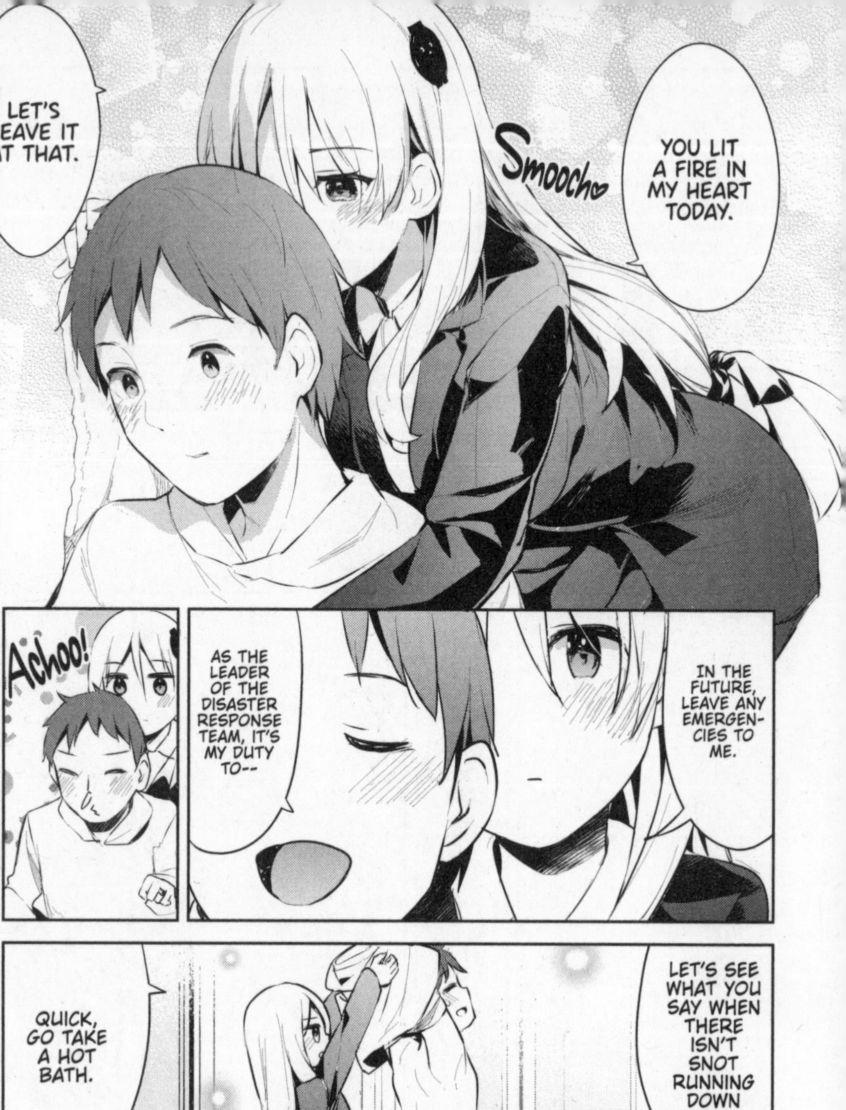
YOU LIT A FIRE IN MY HEART TODAY.
Smooch
LET'S LEAVE IT AT THAT.
IN THE FUTURE, LEAVE ANY EMERGEN-CIES TO ME.
AS THE LEADER OF THE DISASTER RESPONSE TEAM, IT'S MY DUTY TO--
Achoo!
LET'S SEE WHAT YOU SAY WHEN THERE ISN'T SNOT RUNNING DOWN YOUR FACE.
QUICK, GO TAKE A HOT BATH.

HARUKA-CHAN THE ASSASSIN-IN-TRAINING

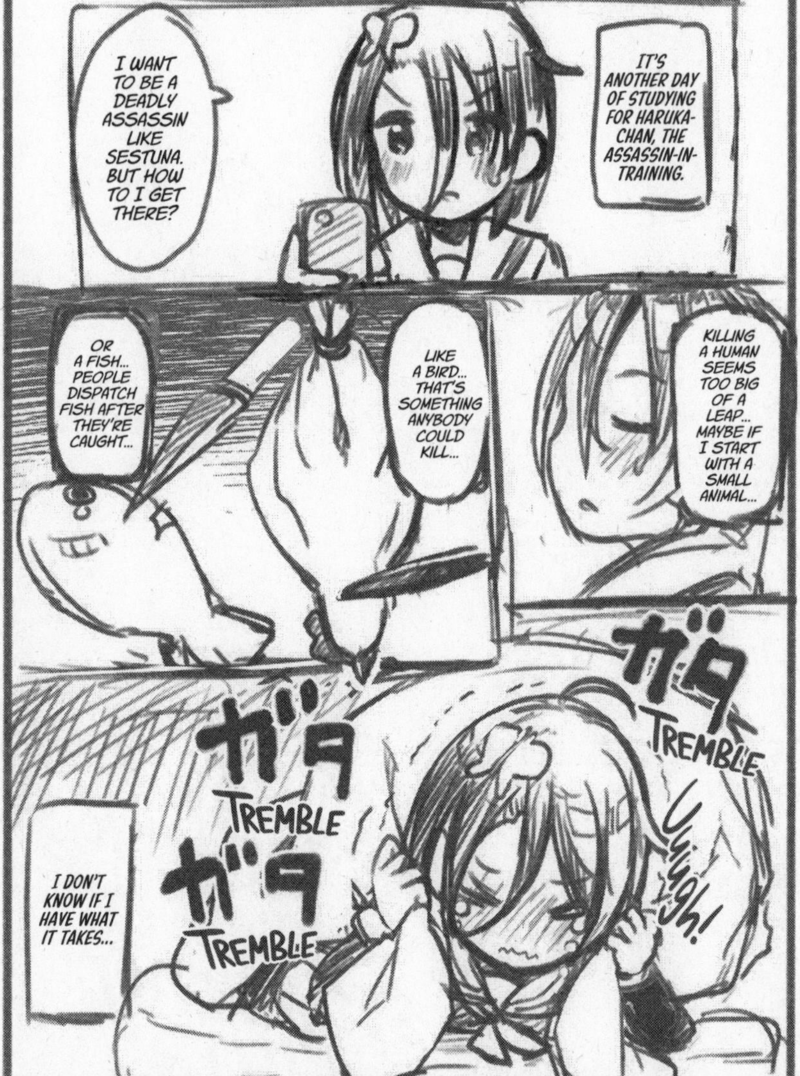
IT'S ANOTHER DAY OF STUDYING FOR HARUKA-CHAN, THE ASSASSIN-IN-TRAINING.
I WANT TO BE A DEADLY ASSASSIN LIKE SESTUNA. BUT HOW TO I GET THERE?
KILLING A HUMAN SEEMS TOO BIG OF A LEAP... MAYBE IF I START WITH A SMALL ANIMAL...
LIKE A BIRD... THAT'S SOMETHING ANYBODY COULD KILL...
OR A FISH... PEOPLE DISPATCH FISH AFTER THEY'RE CAUGHT...
ガタ
TREMBLE
Uuugh!
ガタ
TREMBLE
ガタ
TREMBLE
I DON'T KNOW IF I HAVE WHAT IT TAKES...

MY Lovey-Dovey Wife IS A STONE COLD KILLER

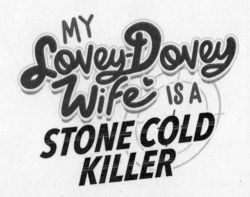

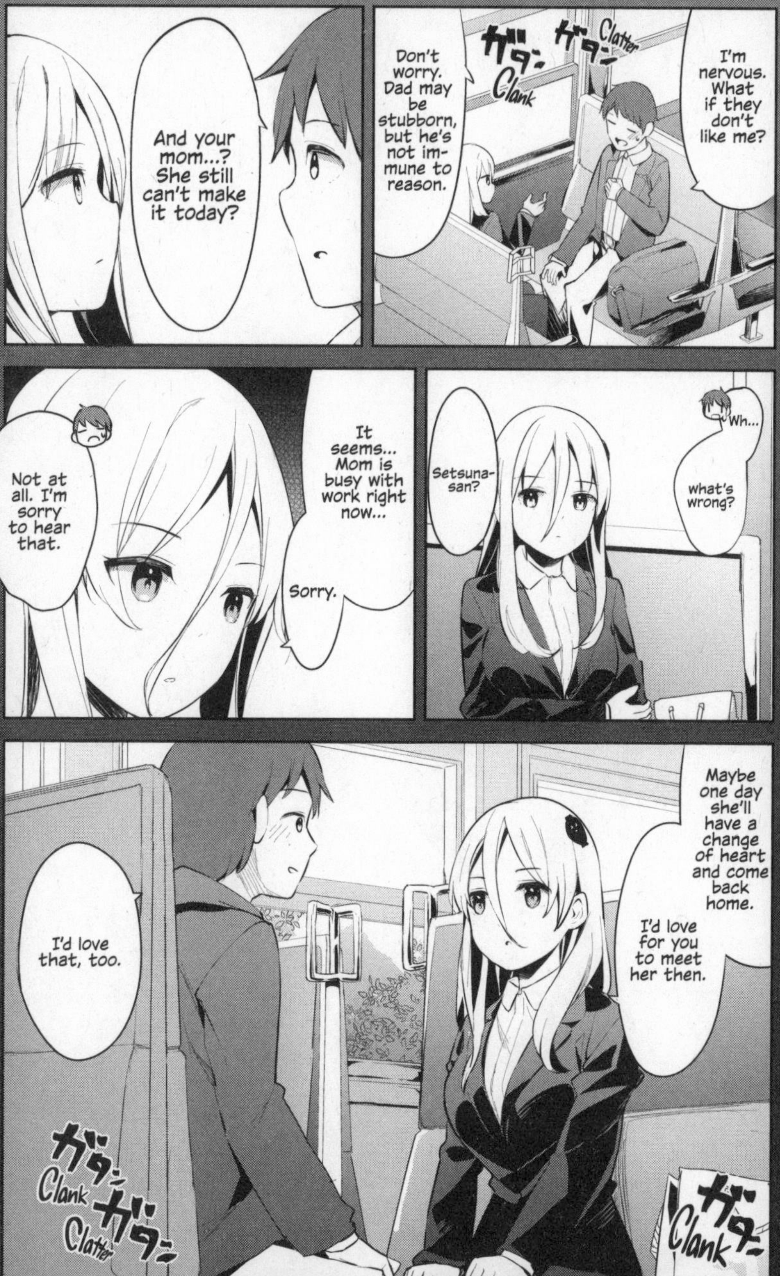
I'm nervous. What if they don't like me?
ガタン Clatter
ガタン Clank
Don't worry. Dad may be stubborn, but he's not immune to reason.
And your mom...? She still can't make it today?
Wh...
what's wrong?
Setsuna-san?
It seems... Mom is busy with work right now...
Sorry.
Not at all. I'm sorry to hear that.
Maybe one day she'll have a change of heart and come back home.
I'd love for you to meet her then.
ガタン Clank
I'd love that, too.
ガタン Clank
ガタン Clatter

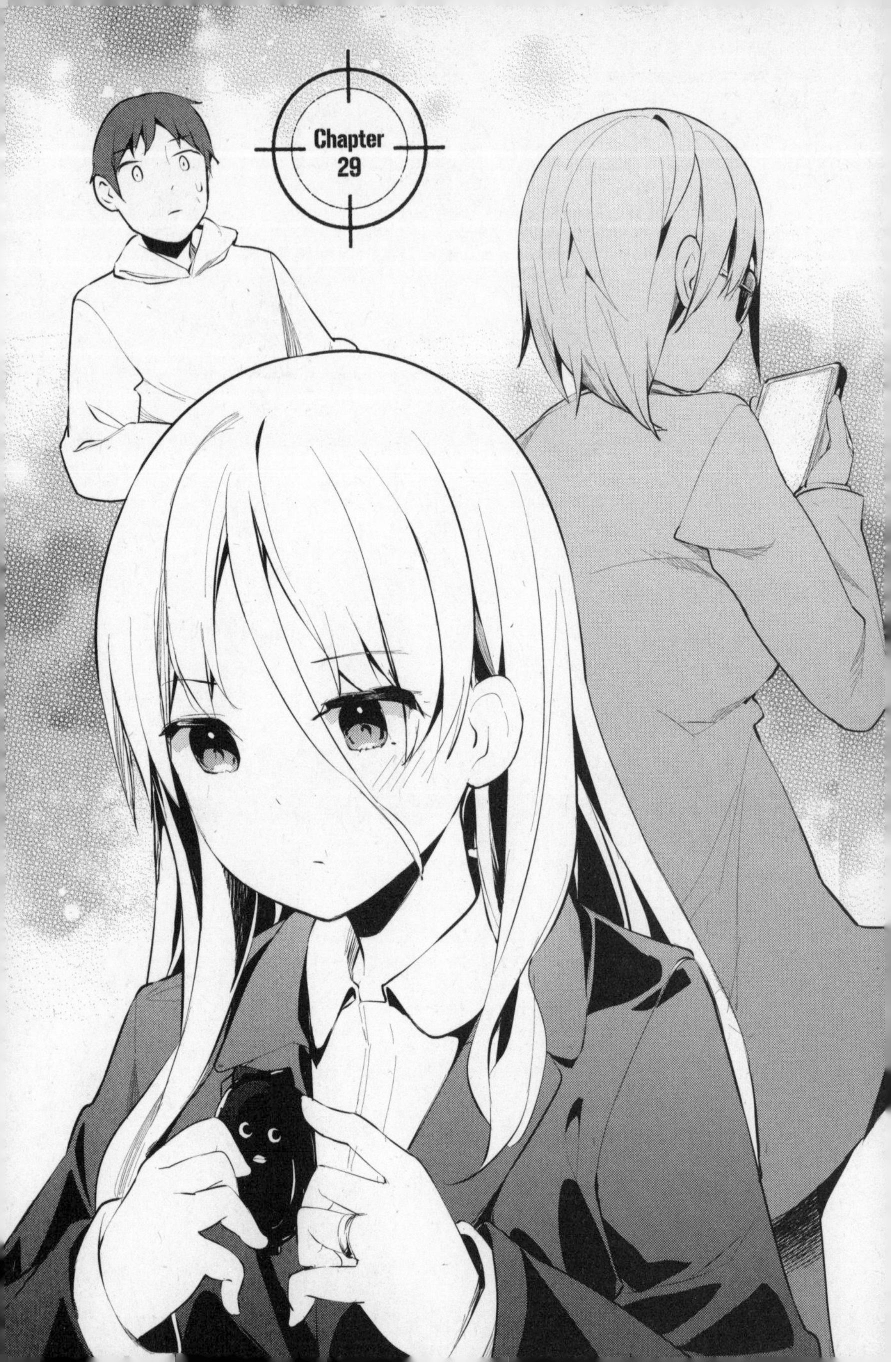
Chapter
29

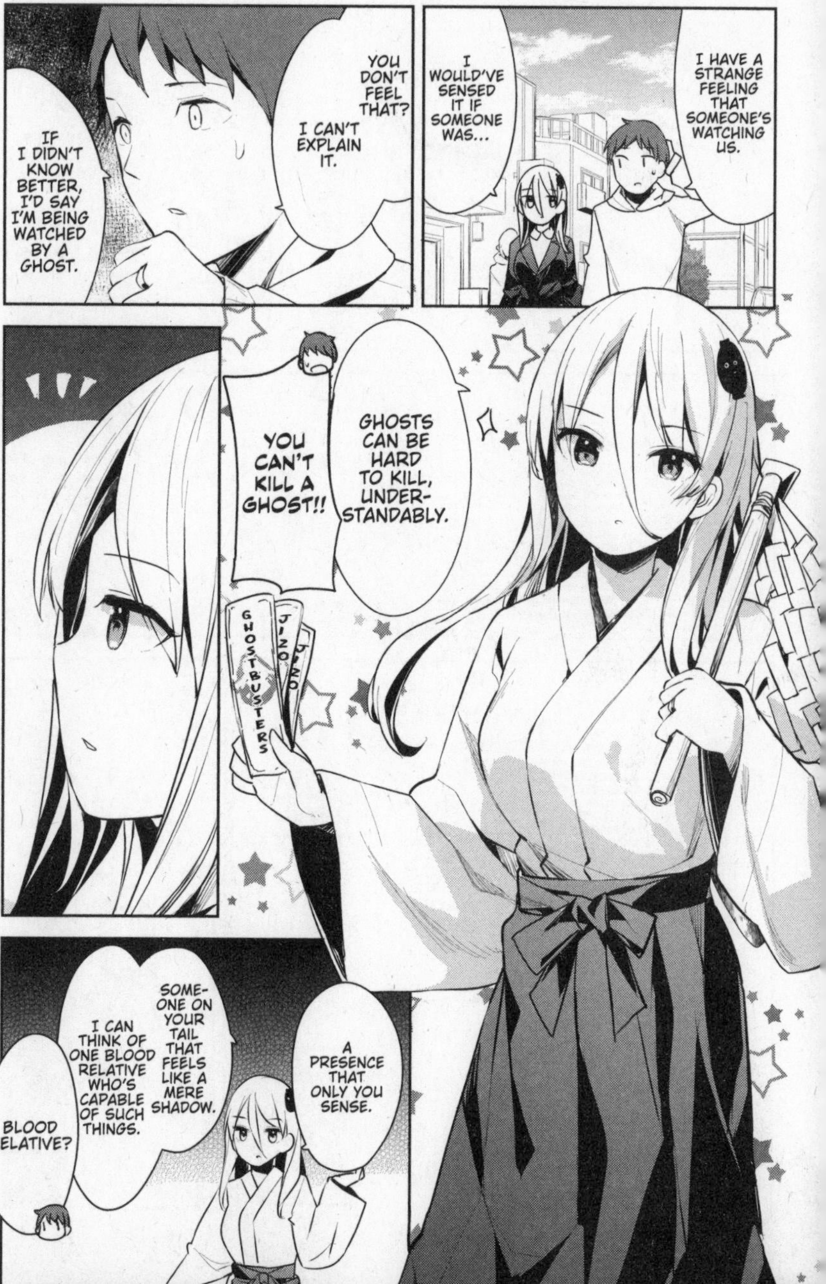
I HAVE A STRANGE FEELING THAT SOMEONE'S WATCHING US.
I WOULD'VE SENSED IT IF SOMEONE WAS...
YOU DON'T FEEL THAT? I CAN'T EXPLAIN IT.
IF I DIDN'T KNOW BETTER, I'D SAY I'M BEING WATCHED BY A GHOST.
GHOSTS CAN BE HARD TO KILL, UNDER-STANDABLY.
YOU CAN'T KILL A GHOST!!
GHOSTBUSTERS
JIZO
JIZO
A PRESENCE THAT ONLY YOU SENSE.
SOME-ONE ON YOUR TAIL THAT FEELS LIKE A MERE SHADOW.
I CAN THINK OF ONE BLOOD RELATIVE WHO'S CAPABLE OF SUCH THINGS.
BLOOD RELATIVE?

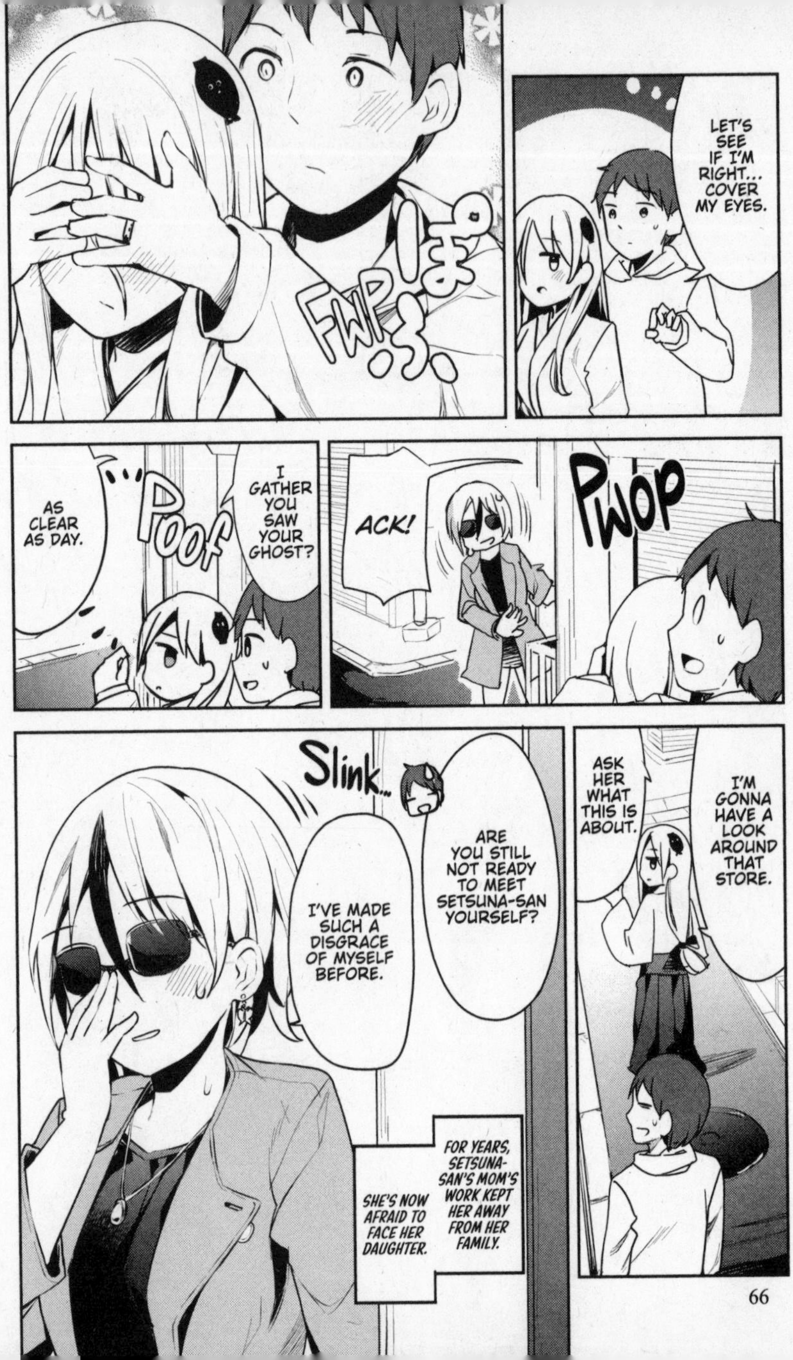
LET'S SEE IF I'M RIGHT... COVER MY EYES.
FWP
ぽふ
PWOP
ACK!
I GATHER YOU SAW YOUR GHOST?
Poof
...AS CLEAR AS DAY.
I'M GONNA HAVE A LOOK AROUND THAT STORE.
ASK HER WHAT THIS IS ABOUT.
Slink...
ARE YOU STILL NOT READY TO MEET SETSUNA-SAN YOURSELF?
I'VE MADE SUCH A DISGRACE OF MYSELF BEFORE.
FOR YEARS, SETSUNA-SAN'S MOM'S WORK KEPT HER AWAY FROM HER FAMILY.
SHE'S NOW AFRAID TO FACE HER DAUGHTER.

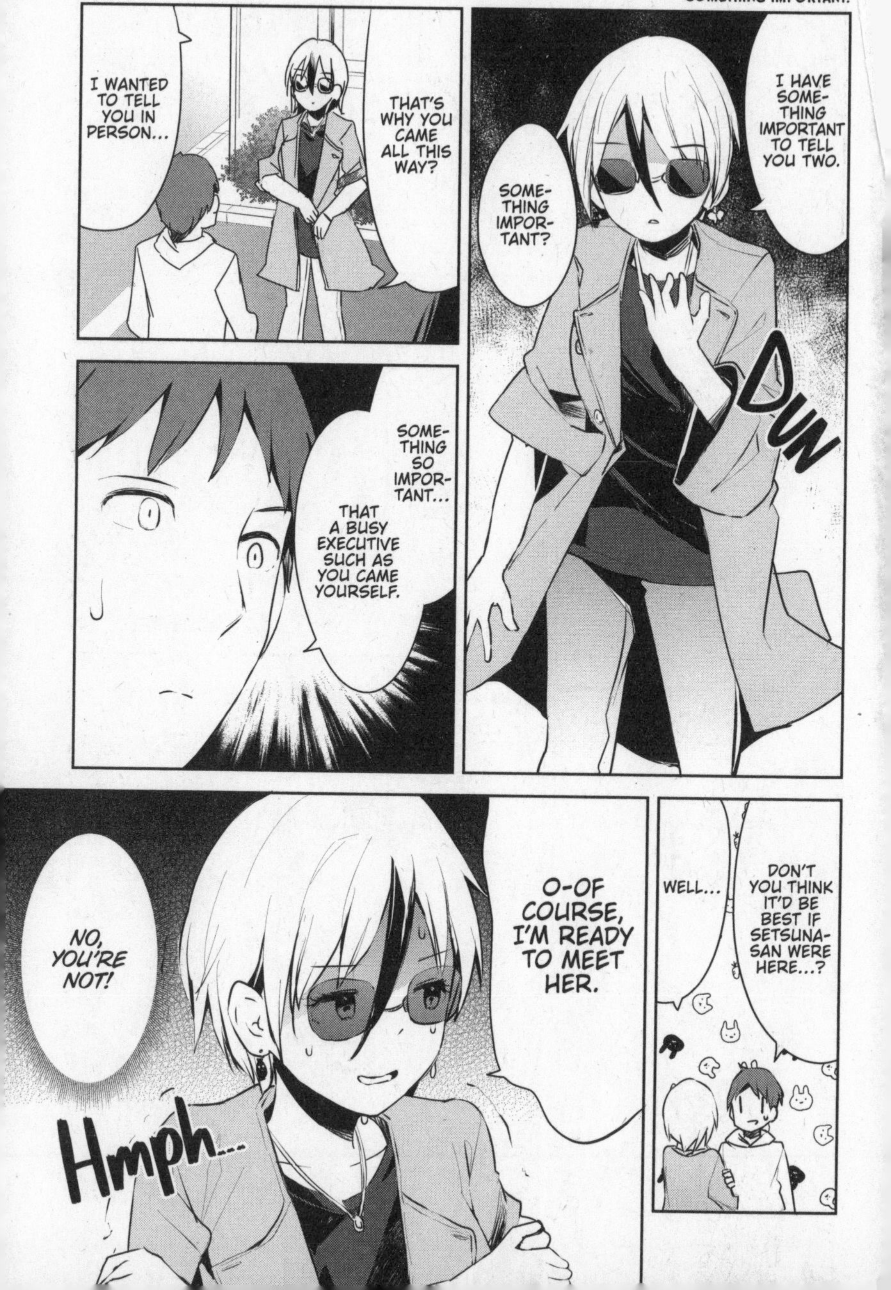
I HAVE SOMETHING IMPORTANT TO TELL YOU TWO.
SOME-THING IMPOR-TANT?
DUN
THAT'S WHY YOU CAME ALL THIS WAY?
I WANTED TO TELL YOU IN PERSON...
SOME-THING SO IMPOR-TANT... THAT A BUSY EXECUTIVE SUCH AS YOU CAME YOURSELF.
DON'T YOU THINK IT'D BE BEST IF SETSUNA-SAN WERE HERE...?
WELL...
O-OF COURSE, I'M READY TO MEET HER.
NO, YOU'RE NOT!
Hmph...

COME WHAT MAY.

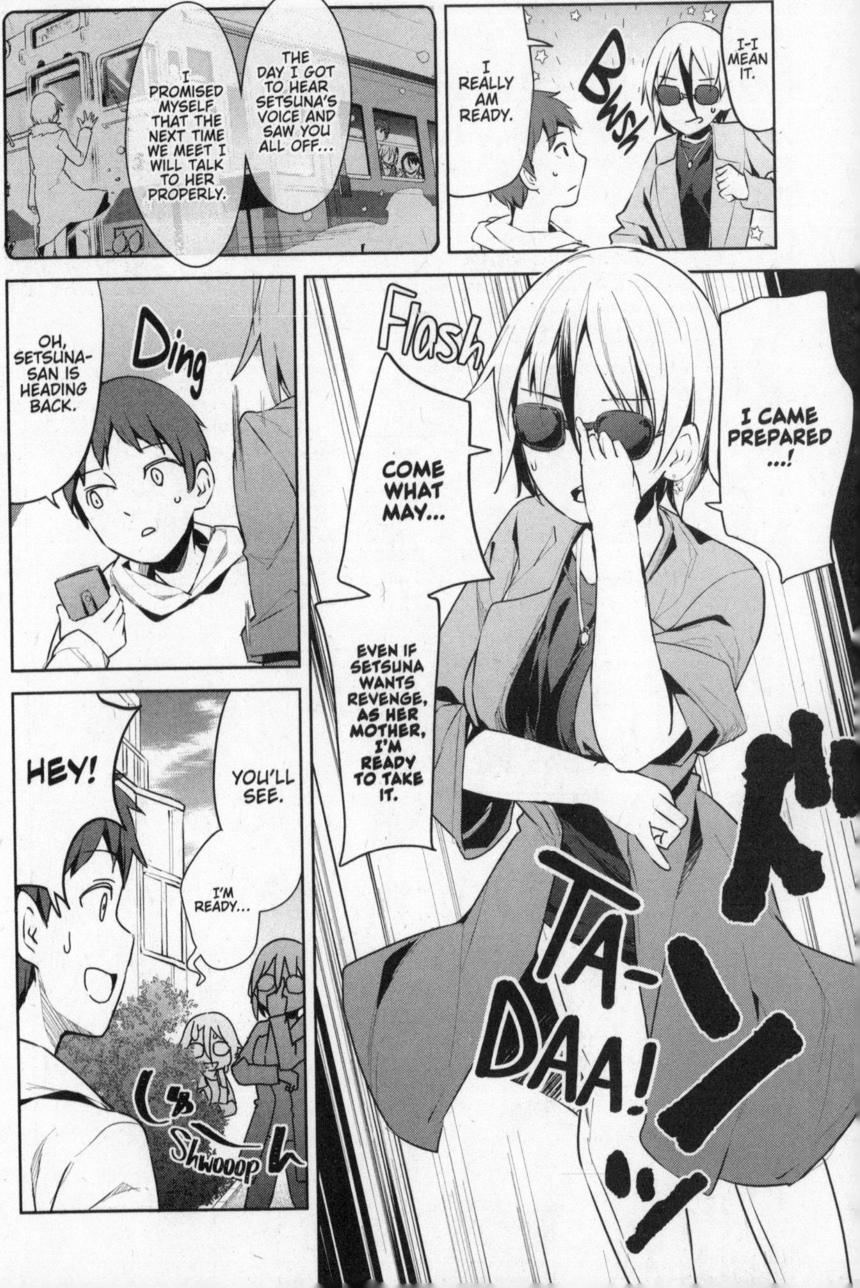

I-I MEAN IT.
Bwsh
I REALLY AM READY.
THE DAY I GOT TO HEAR SETSUNA'S VOICE AND SAW YOU ALL OFF...
I PROMISED MYSELF THAT THE NEXT TIME WE MEET I WILL TALK TO HER PROPERLY.
I CAME PREPARED ...!
Flash
COME WHAT MAY...
EVEN IF SETSUNA WANTS REVENGE, AS HER MOTHER, I'M READY TO TAKE IT.
TA-DAA!
Ding
OH, SETSUNA-SAN IS HEADING BACK.
YOU'LL SEE.
HEY!
I'M READY...
Shwooop

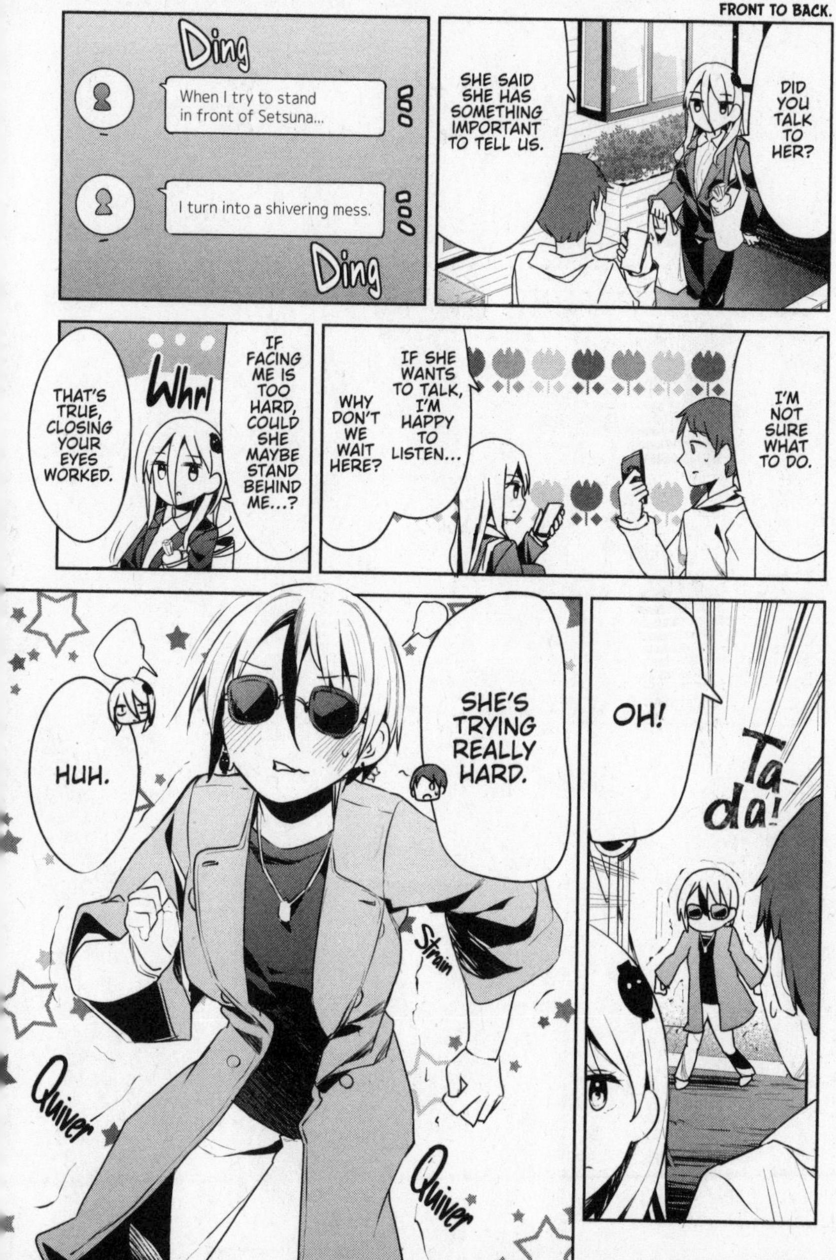
DID YOU TALK TO HER?
SHE SAID SHE HAS SOMETHING IMPORTANT TO TELL US.
Ding
When I try to stand in front of Setsuna...
I turn into a shivering mess.
Ding
I'M NOT SURE WHAT TO DO.
IF SHE WANTS TO TALK, I'M HAPPY TO LISTEN...
WHY DON'T WE WAIT HERE?
IF FACING ME IS TOO HARD, COULD SHE MAYBE STAND BEHIND ME...?
Whrl
THAT'S TRUE, CLOSING YOUR EYES WORKED.
OH!
Ta-da!
SHE'S TRYING REALLY HARD.
HUH.
Strain
Quiver
Quiver

THREE STEPS FORWARD, TWO STEPS BACK.

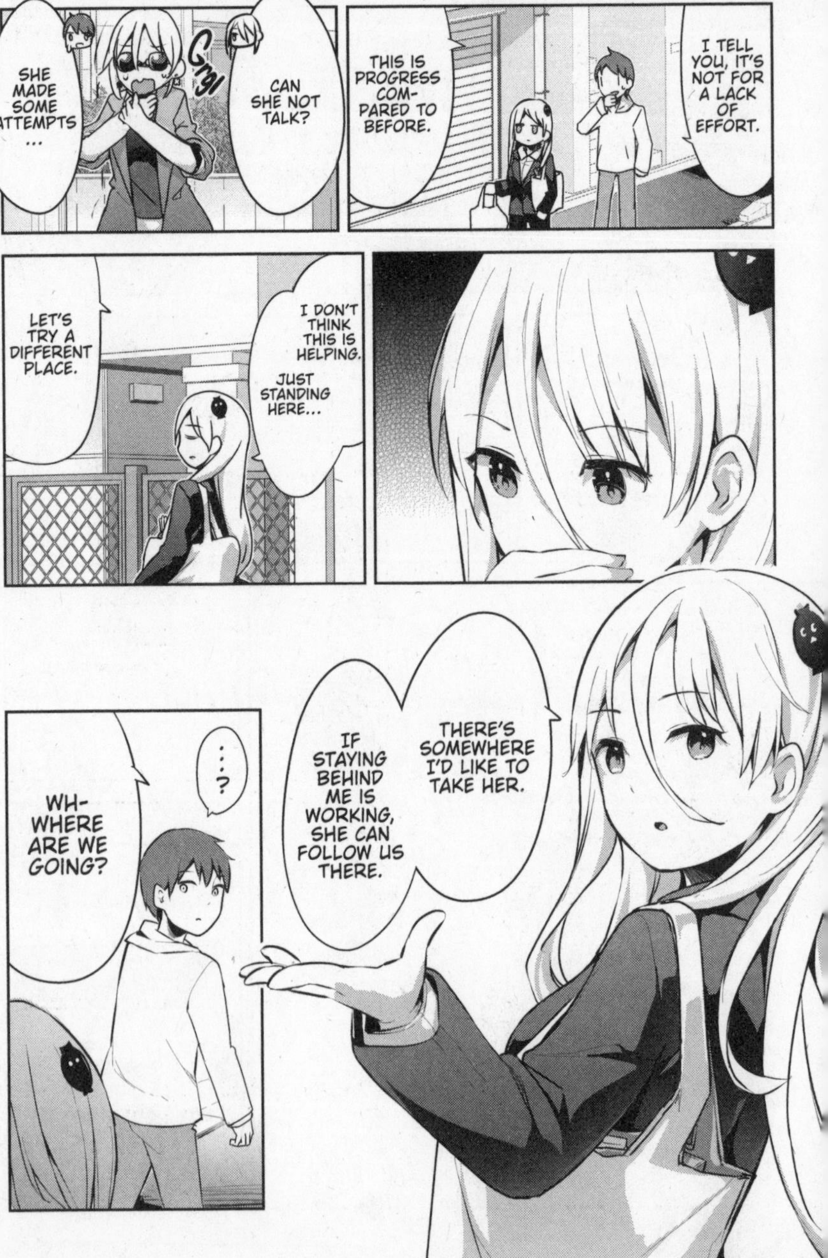
I TELL YOU, IT'S NOT FOR A LACK OF EFFORT.
THIS IS PROGRESS COMPARED TO BEFORE.
CAN SHE NOT TALK?
Grgl
SHE MADE SOME ATTEMPTS...
I DON'T THINK THIS IS HELPING.
JUST STANDING HERE...
LET'S TRY A DIFFERENT PLACE.
THERE'S SOMEWHERE I'D LIKE TO TAKE HER.
IF STAYING BEHIND ME IS WORKING, SHE CAN FOLLOW US THERE.
...?
WH-WHERE ARE WE GOING?

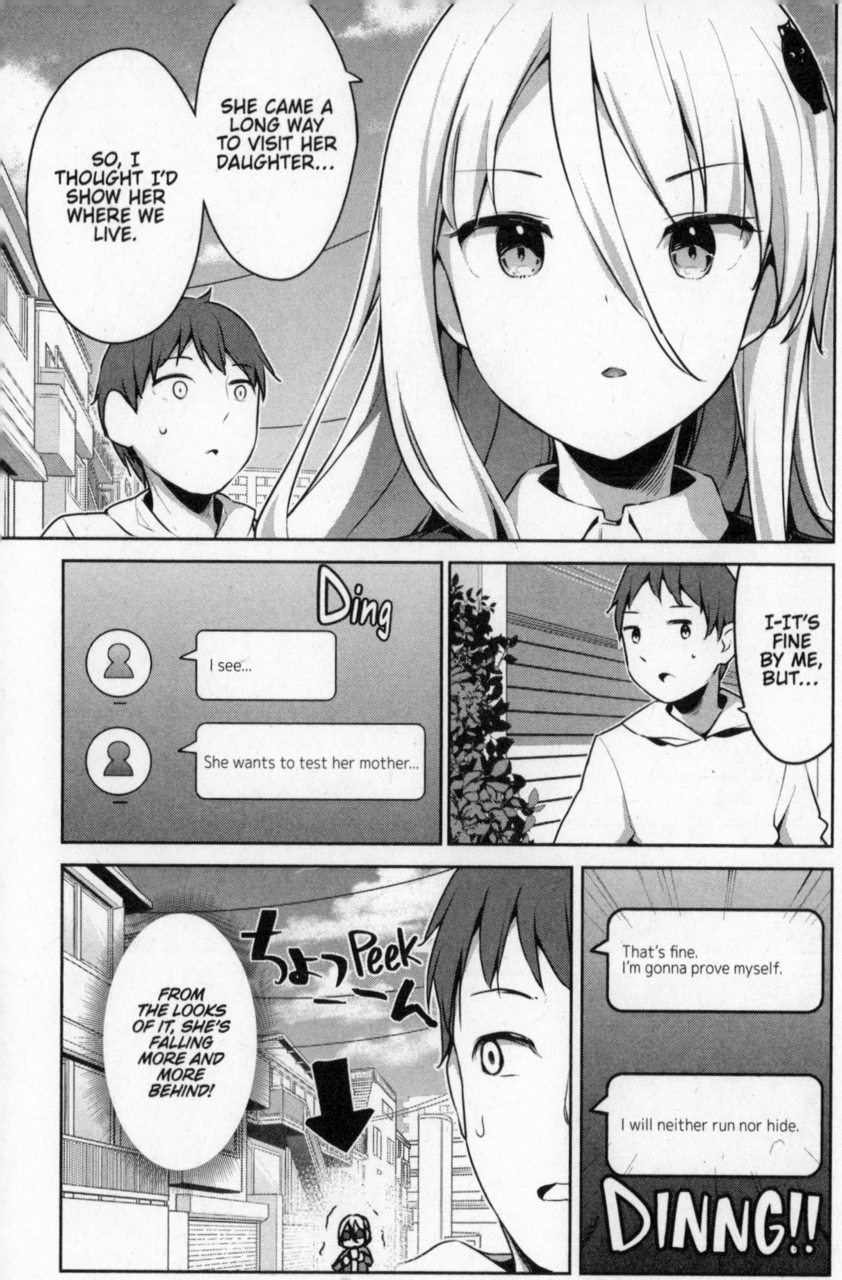
SHE CAME A LONG WAY TO VISIT HER DAUGHTER...
SO, I THOUGHT I'D SHOW HER WHERE WE LIVE.
I-IT'S FINE BY ME, BUT...
Ding
I see...
She wants to test her mother...
That's fine. I'm gonna prove myself.
I will neither run nor hide.
DINNG!!
ちょこーん
Peek
FROM THE LOOKS OF IT, SHE'S FALLING MORE AND MORE BEHIND!

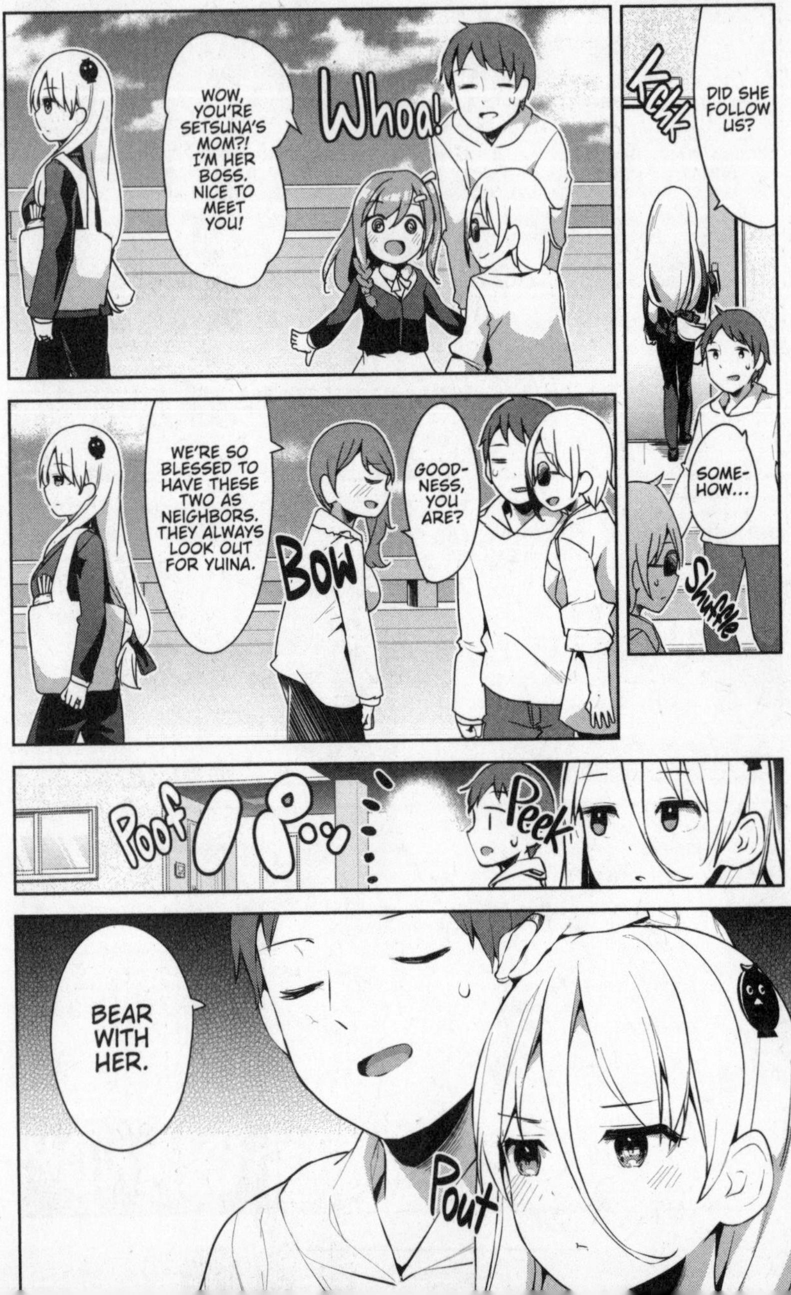
Kchk
DID SHE FOLLOW US?
SOME-HOW...
Shuffle
Whoa!
WOW, YOU'RE SETSUNA'S MOM?! I'M HER BOSS. NICE TO MEET YOU!
GOOD-NESS, YOU ARE?
Bow
WE'RE SO BLESSED TO HAVE THESE TWO AS NEIGHBORS. THEY ALWAYS LOOK OUT FOR YUINA.
Peek
Poof
BEAR WITH HER.
Pout

THE SUMMONING.

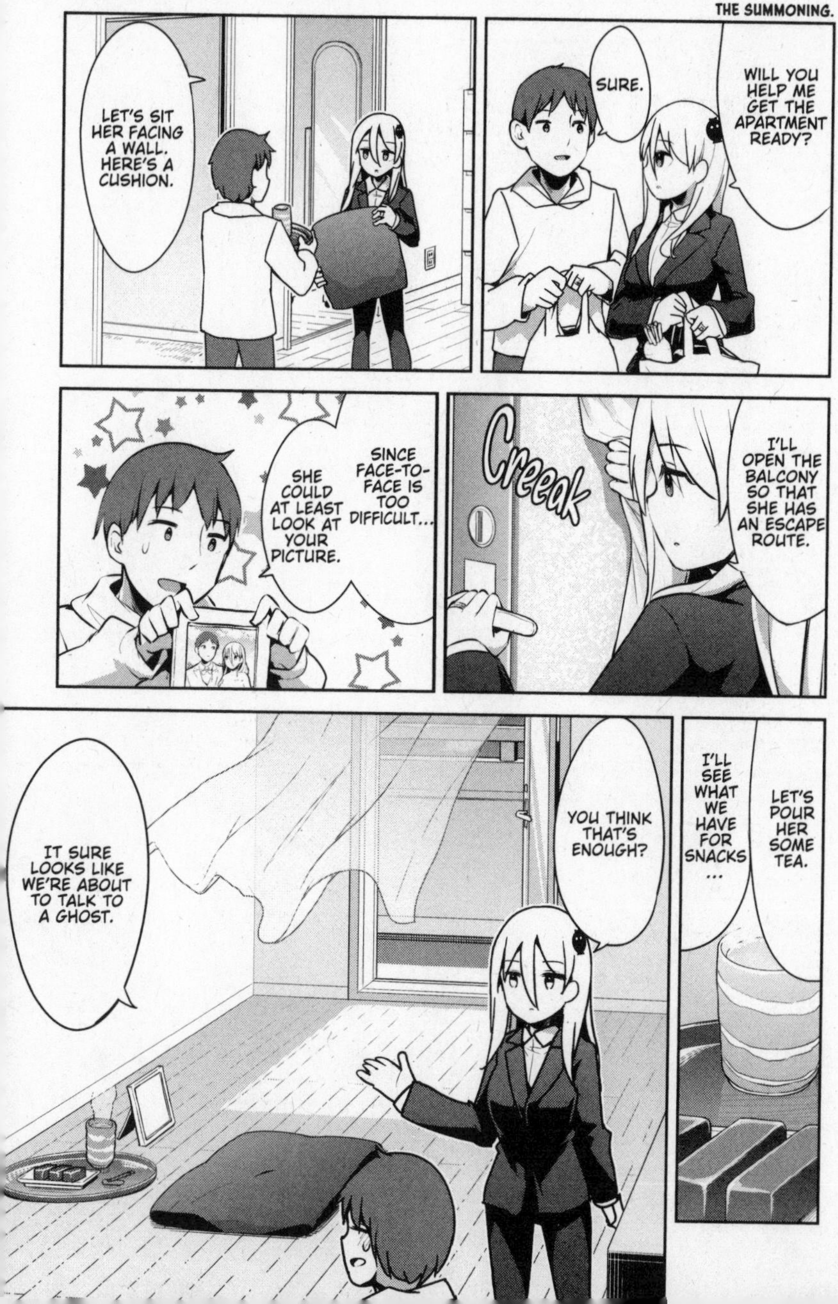

WILL YOU HELP ME GET THE APARTMENT READY?
SURE.
LET'S SIT HER FACING A WALL. HERE'S A CUSHION.
I'LL OPEN THE BALCONY SO THAT SHE HAS AN ESCAPE ROUTE.
Creeak
SINCE FACE-TO-FACE IS TOO DIFFICULT...
SHE COULD AT LEAST LOOK AT YOUR PICTURE.
LET'S POUR HER SOME TEA.
I'LL SEE WHAT WE HAVE FOR SNACKS...
YOU THINK THAT'S ENOUGH?
IT SURE LOOKS LIKE WE'RE ABOUT TO TALK TO A GHOST.

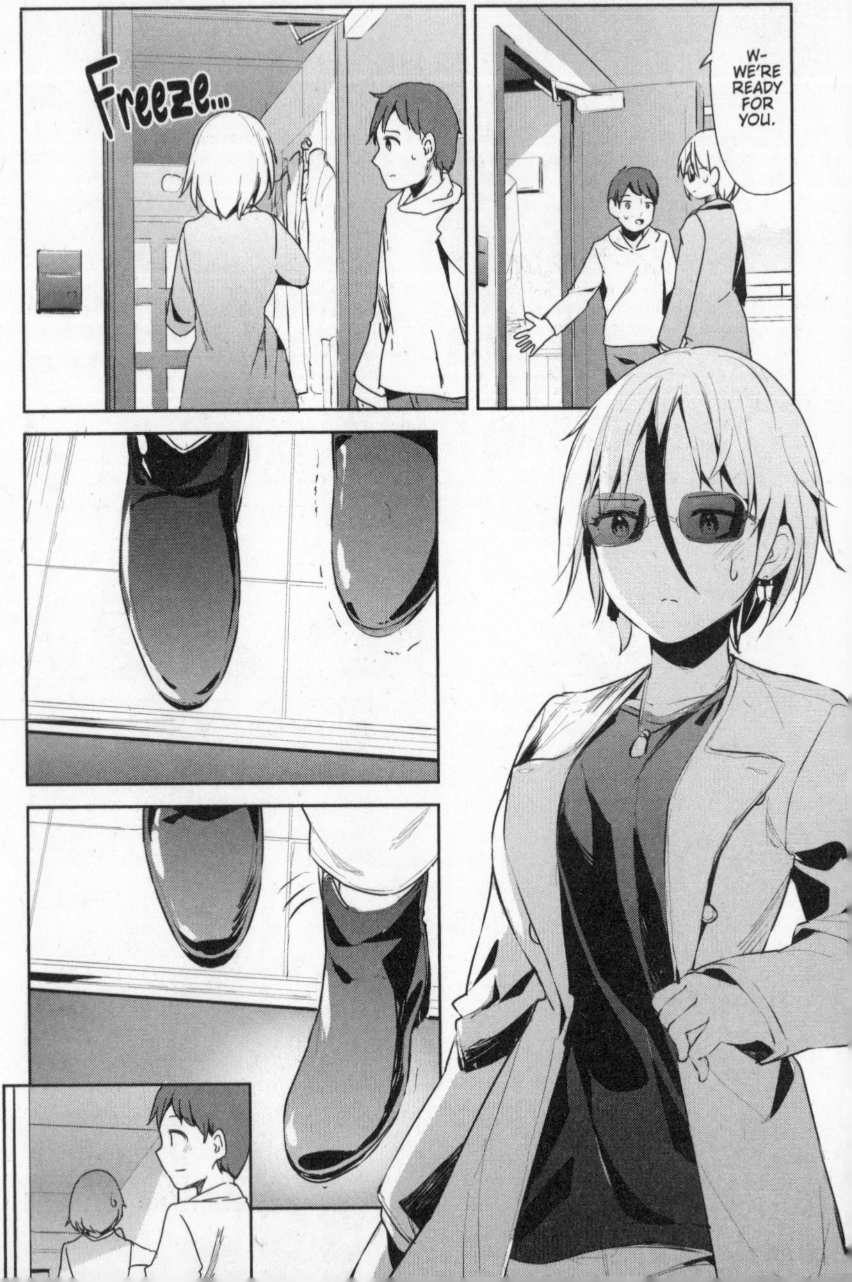
W- WE'RE READY FOR YOU.
Freeze...

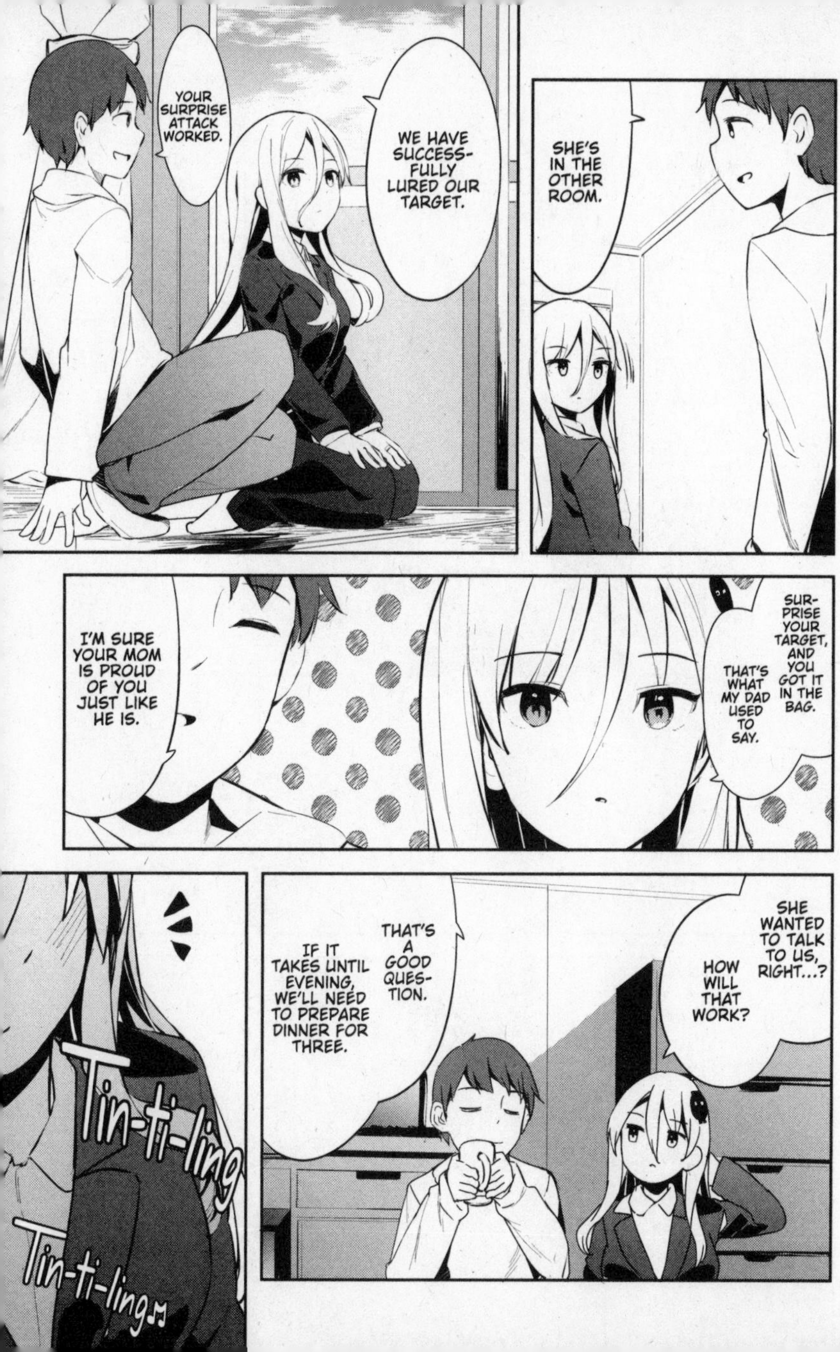
SHE'S IN THE OTHER ROOM.
WE HAVE SUCCESS-FULLY LURED OUR TARGET.
YOUR SURPRISE ATTACK WORKED.
SUR-PRISE YOUR TARGET, AND YOU GOT IT IN THE BAG.
THAT'S WHAT MY DAD USED TO SAY.
I'M SURE YOUR MOM IS PROUD OF YOU JUST LIKE HE IS.
SHE WANTED TO TALK TO US, RIGHT...?
HOW WILL THAT WORK?
THAT'S A GOOD QUES-TION.
IF IT TAKES UNTIL EVENING, WE'LL NEED TO PREPARE DINNER FOR THREE.
Tin-ti-ling
Tin-ti-ling♫

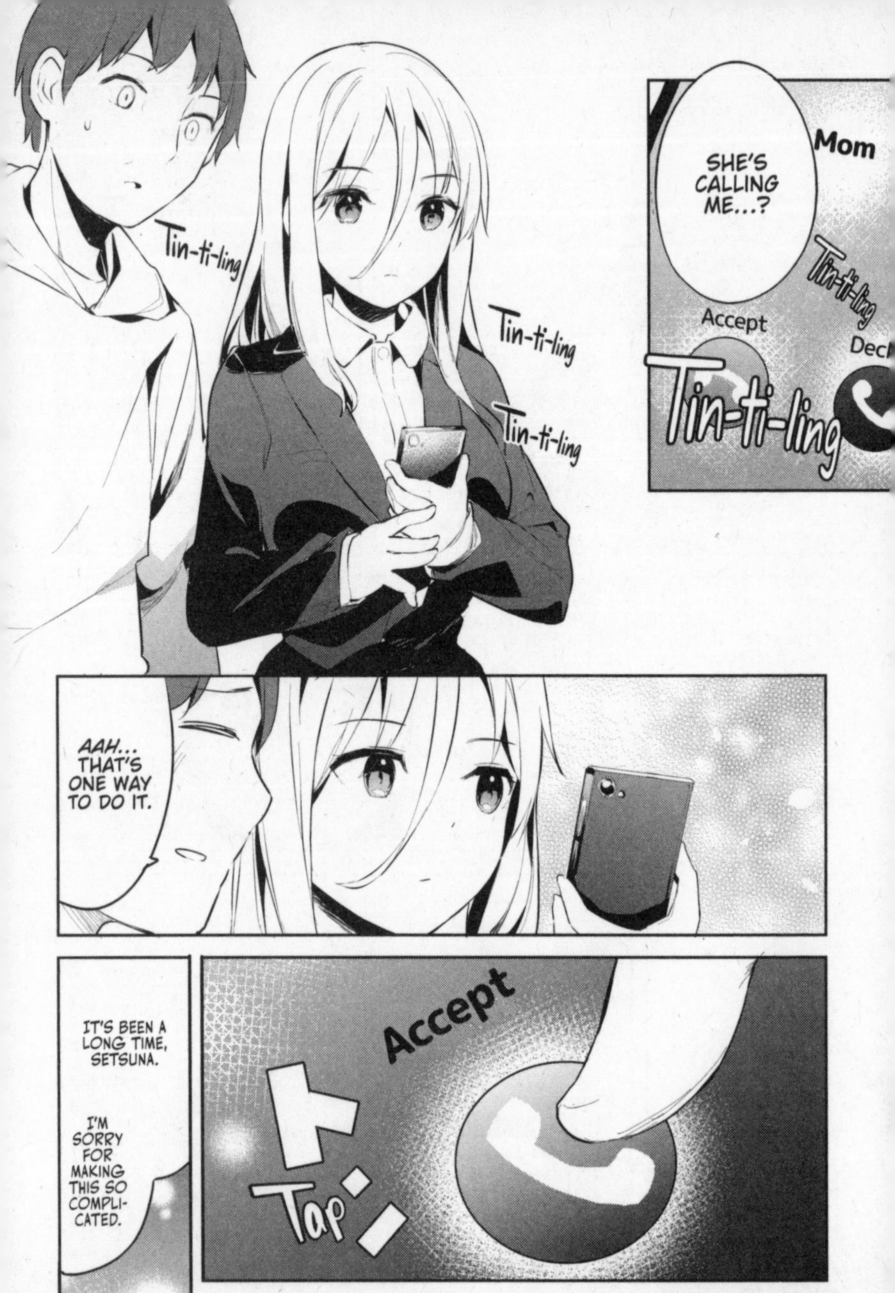
SHE'S CALLING ME...?
Mom
Tin-ti-ling
Accept
Tin-ti-ling
Tin-ti-ling
Tin-ti-ling
Tin-ti-ling
AAH... THAT'S ONE WAY TO DO IT.
Accept
Tap
IT'S BEEN A LONG TIME, SETSUNA.
I'M SORRY FOR MAKING THIS SO COMPLICATED.

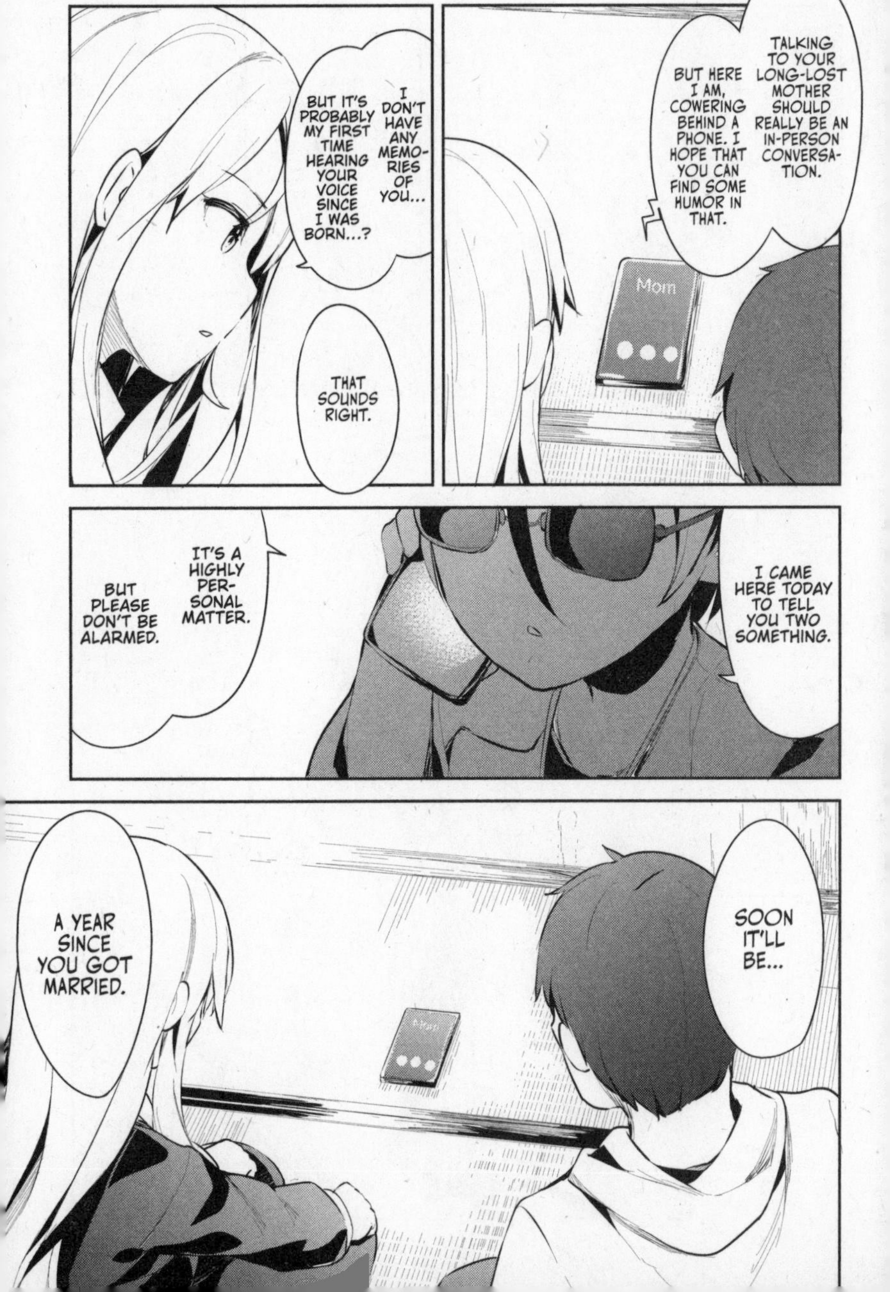
TALKING TO YOUR LONG-LOST MOTHER SHOULD REALLY BE AN IN-PERSON CONVERSATION.
BUT HERE I AM, COWERING BEHIND A PHONE. I HOPE THAT YOU CAN FIND SOME HUMOR IN THAT.
Mom
I DON'T HAVE ANY MEMORIES OF YOU...
BUT IT'S PROBABLY MY FIRST TIME HEARING YOUR VOICE SINCE I WAS BORN...?
THAT SOUNDS RIGHT.
I CAME HERE TODAY TO TELL YOU TWO SOMETHING.
IT'S A HIGHLY PERSONAL MATTER.
BUT PLEASE DON'T BE ALARMED.
SOON IT'LL BE...
A YEAR SINCE YOU GOT MARRIED.

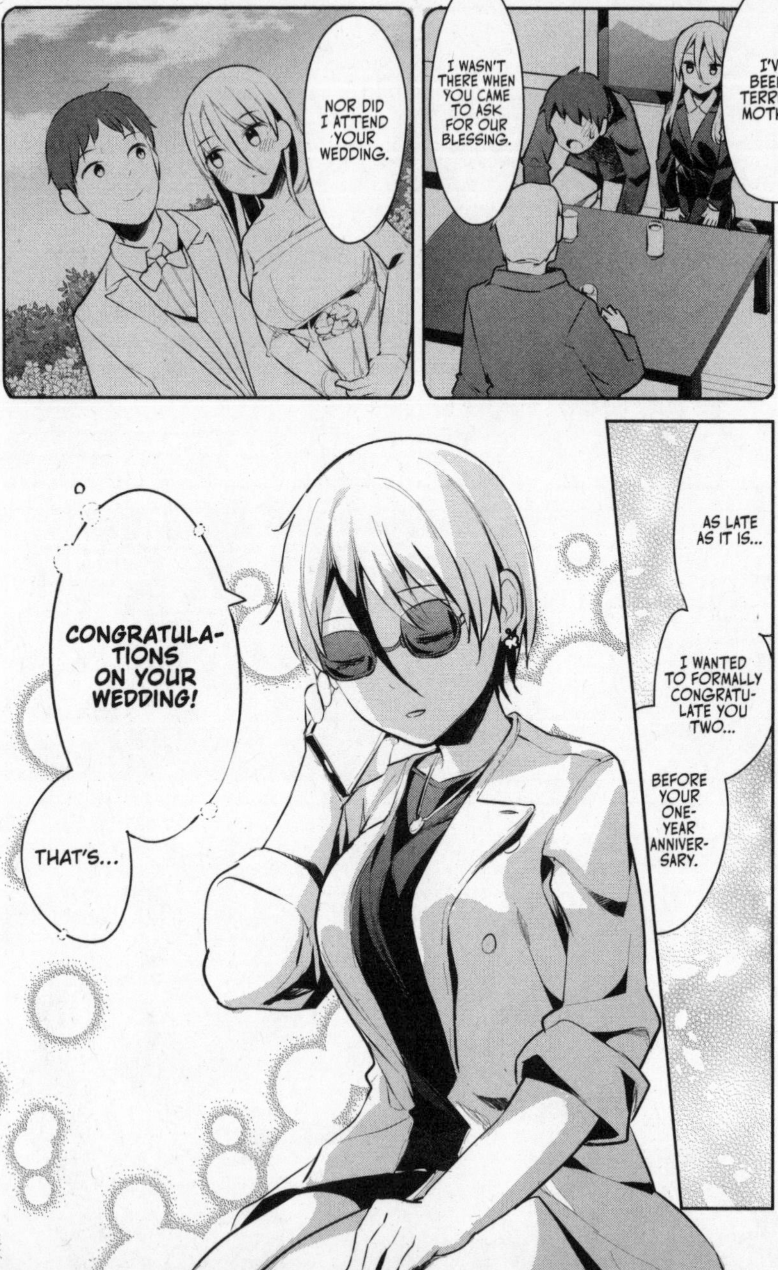
I'VE BEEN A TERRIBLE MOTHER.
I WASN'T THERE WHEN YOU CAME TO ASK FOR OUR BLESSING.
NOR DID I ATTEND YOUR WEDDING.
AS LATE AS IT IS...
I WANTED TO FORMALLY CONGRATU-LATE YOU TWO...
BEFORE YOUR ONE-YEAR ANNIVER-SARY.
CONGRATULA-TIONS ON YOUR WEDDING!
THAT'S...

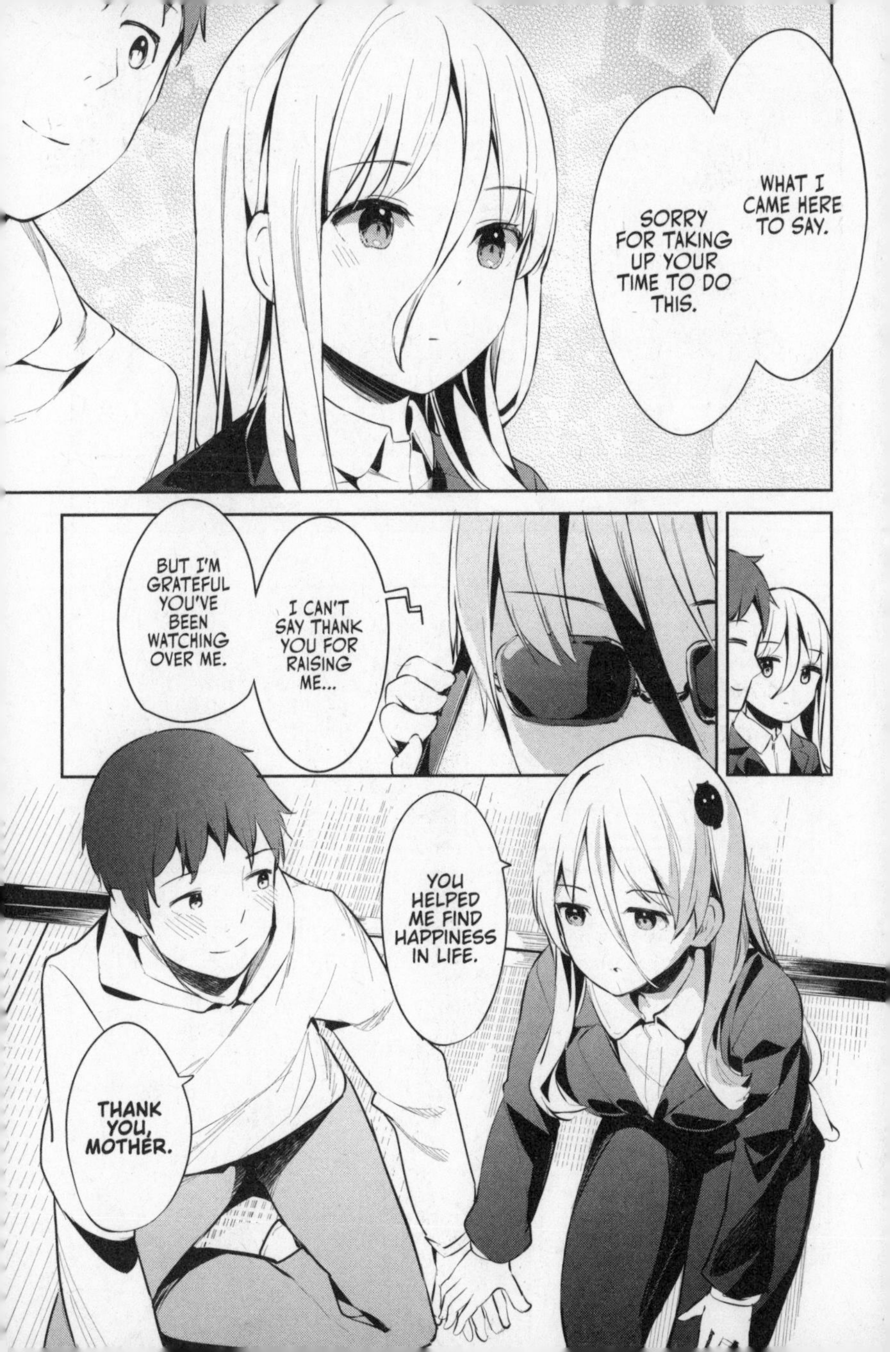
WHAT I CAME HERE TO SAY.
SORRY FOR TAKING UP YOUR TIME TO DO THIS.
I CAN'T SAY THANK YOU FOR RAISING ME...
BUT I'M GRATEFUL YOU'VE BEEN WATCHING OVER ME.
YOU HELPED ME FIND HAPPINESS IN LIFE.
THANK YOU, MOTHER.

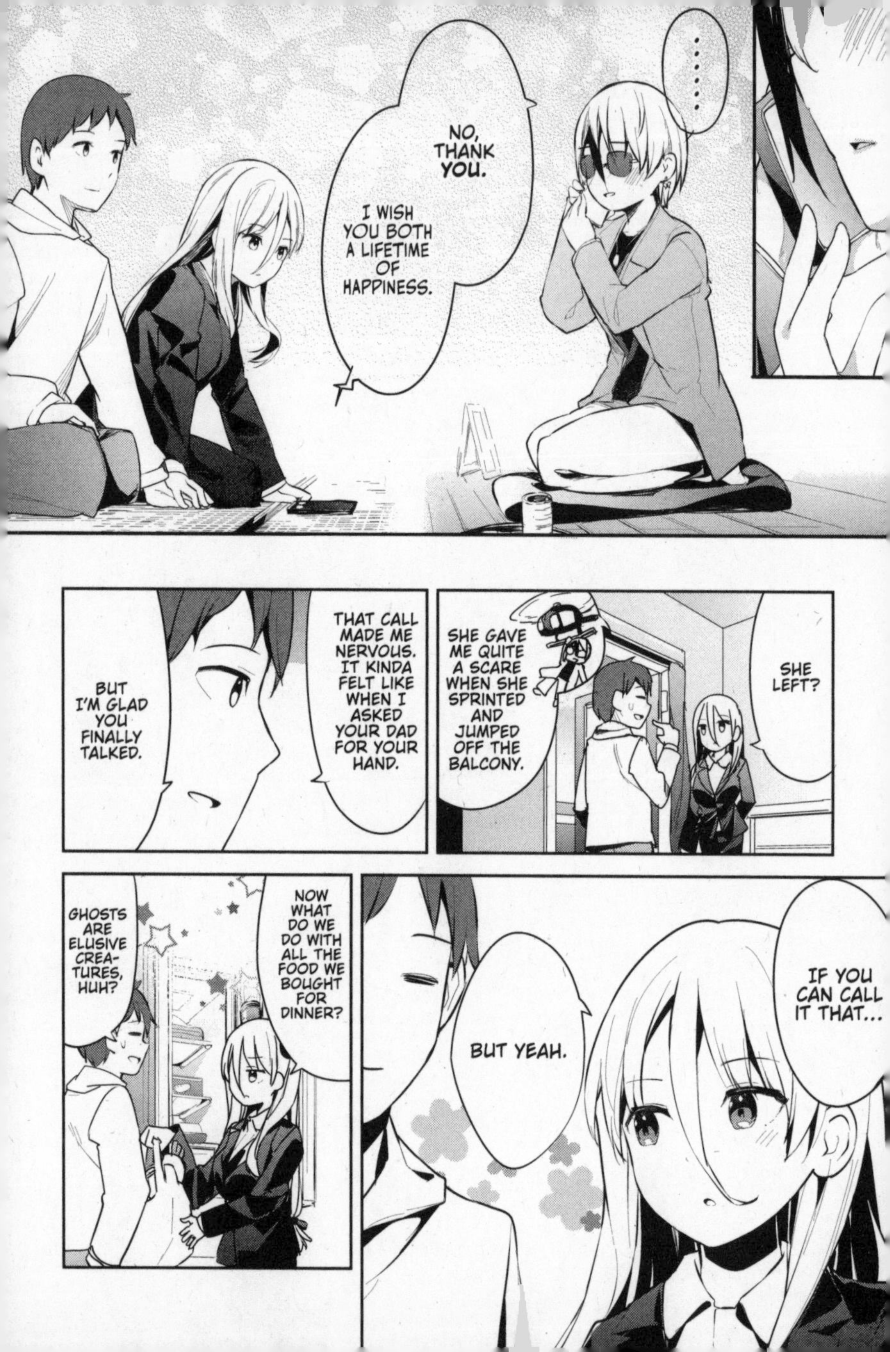
......
NO, THANK YOU. I WISH YOU BOTH A LIFETIME OF HAPPINESS.
SHE LEFT?
SHE GAVE ME QUITE A SCARE WHEN SHE SPRINTED AND JUMPED OFF THE BALCONY.
THAT CALL MADE ME NERVOUS. IT KINDA FELT LIKE WHEN I ASKED YOUR DAD FOR YOUR HAND.
BUT I'M GLAD YOU FINALLY TALKED.
IF YOU CAN CALL IT THAT...
BUT YEAH.
NOW WHAT DO WE DO WITH ALL THE FOOD WE BOUGHT FOR DINNER?
GHOSTS ARE ELUSIVE CREA-TURES, HUH?

MOTHER AND HARUKA-CHAN

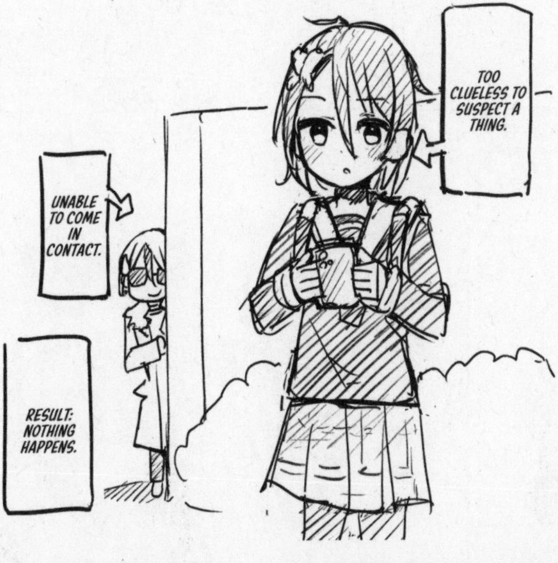
TOO CLUELESS TO SUSPECT A THING.
UNABLE TO COME IN CONTACT.
RESULT: NOTHING HAPPENS.

MY LOVEY-DOVEY WIFE IS A STONE COLD KILLER

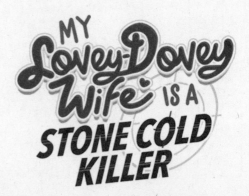

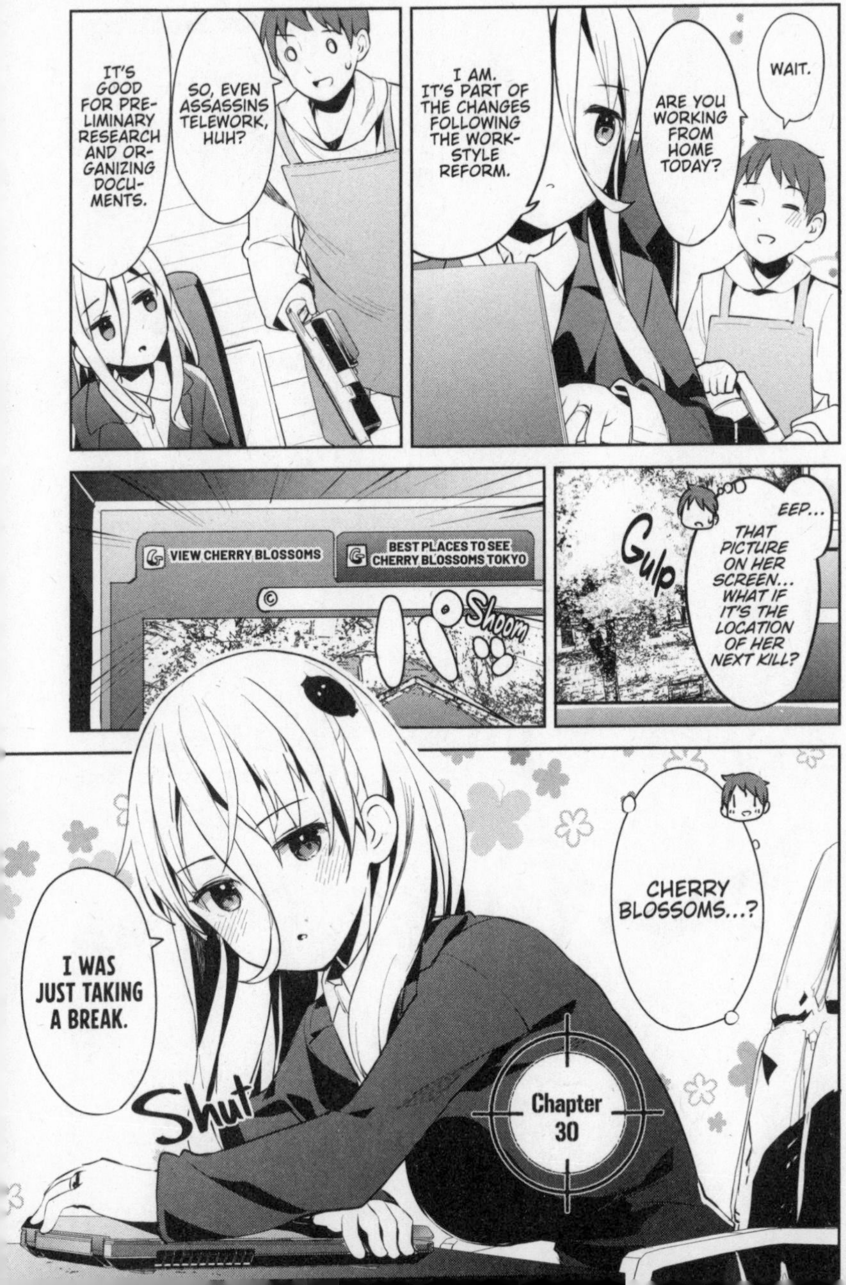
WAIT.
ARE YOU WORKING FROM HOME TODAY?
I AM. IT'S PART OF THE CHANGES FOLLOWING THE WORK-STYLE REFORM.
SO, EVEN ASSASSINS TELEWORK, HUH?
IT'S GOOD FOR PRE-LIMINARY RESEARCH AND OR-GANIZING DOCU-MENTS.
EEP... THAT PICTURE ON HER SCREEN... WHAT IF IT'S THE LOCATION OF HER NEXT KILL?
Gulp
BEST PLACES TO SEE CHERRY BLOSSOMS TOKYO
VIEW CHERRY BLOSSOMS
Shoom
CHERRY BLOSSOMS...?
I WAS JUST TAKING A BREAK.
Shut
Chapter 30

PLANS TO SEE CHERRY BLOSSOMS.

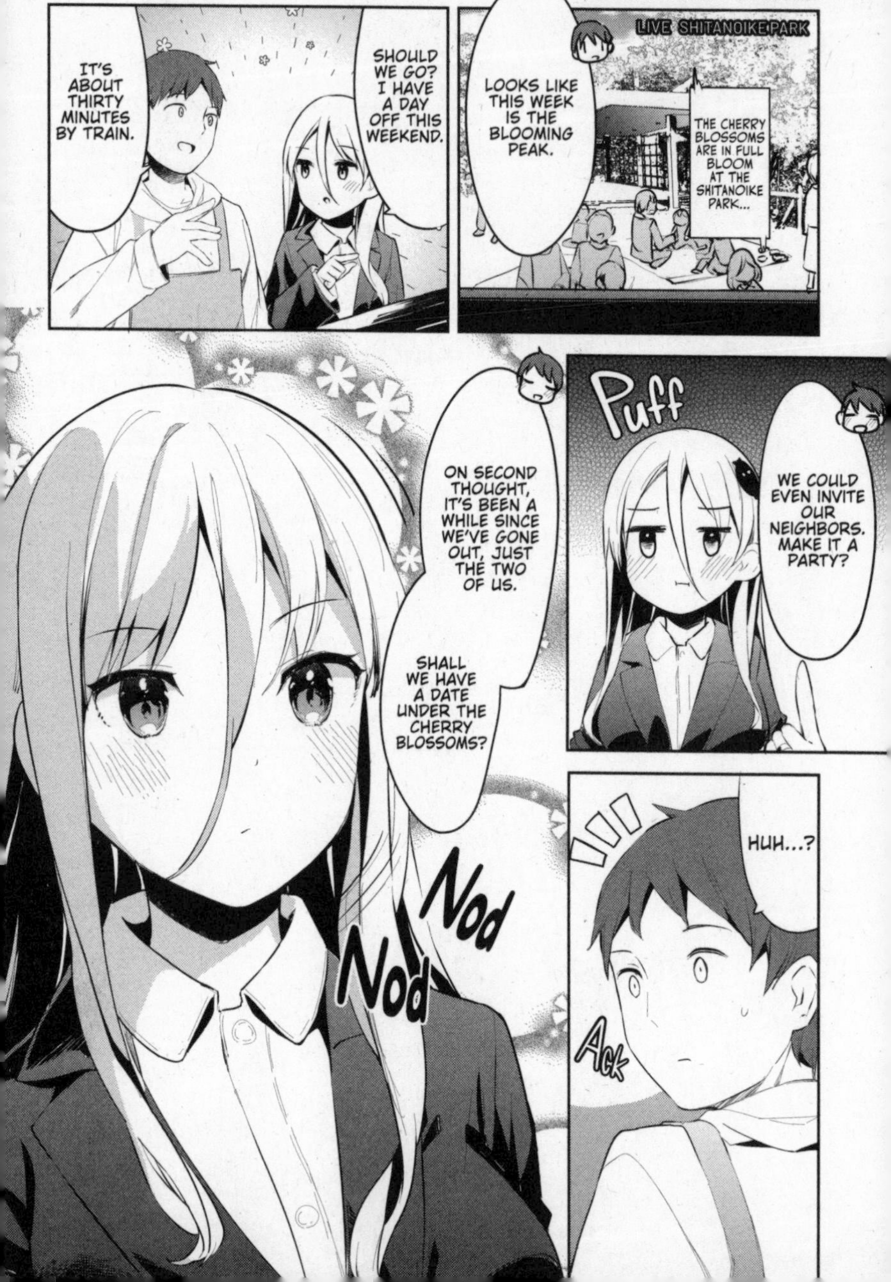
LIVE SHITANOIKE PARK
THE CHERRY BLOSSOMS ARE IN FULL BLOOM AT THE SHITANOIKE PARK...
LOOKS LIKE THIS WEEK IS THE BLOOMING PEAK.
SHOULD WE GO? I HAVE A DAY OFF THIS WEEKEND.
IT'S ABOUT THIRTY MINUTES BY TRAIN.
Puff
WE COULD EVEN INVITE OUR NEIGHBORS. MAKE IT A PARTY?
HUH...?
Ack
ON SECOND THOUGHT, IT'S BEEN A WHILE SINCE WE'VE GONE OUT, JUST THE TWO OF US.
SHALL WE HAVE A DATE UNDER THE CHERRY BLOSSOMS?
Nod
Nod

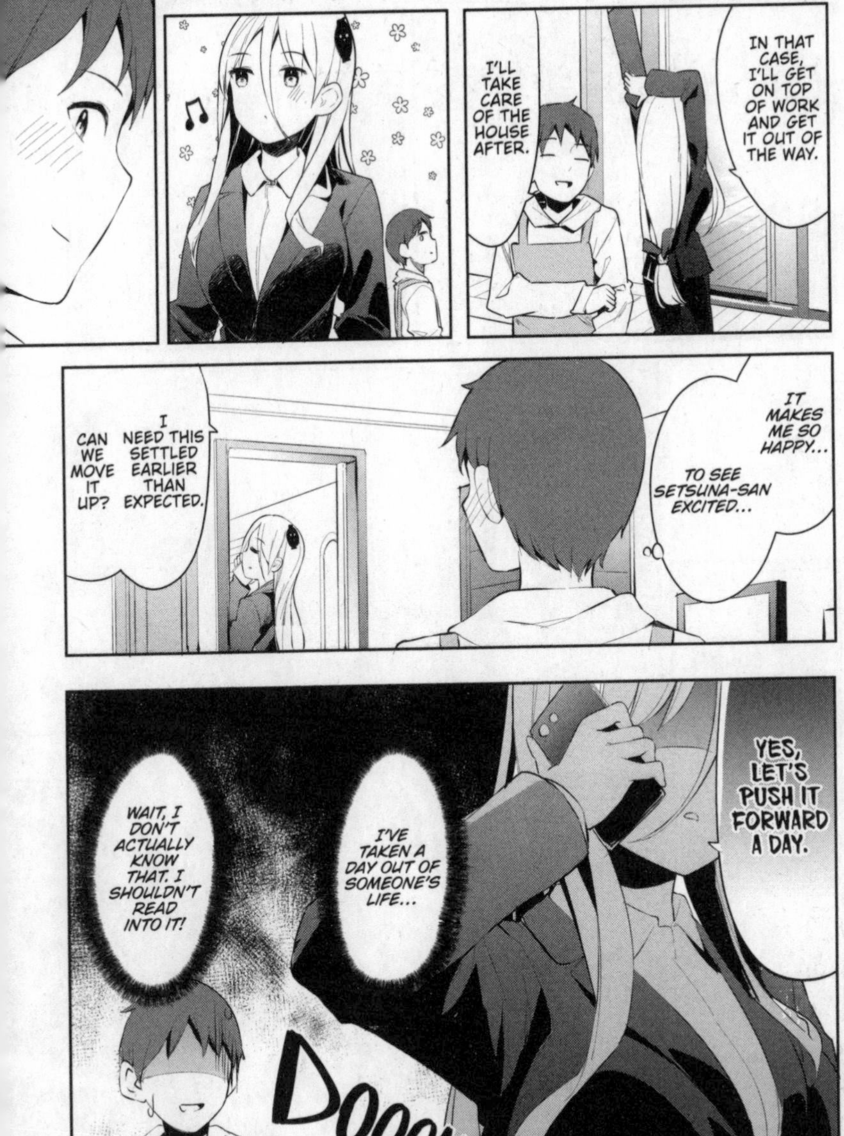
IN THAT CASE, I'LL GET ON TOP OF WORK AND GET IT OUT OF THE WAY.
I'LL TAKE CARE OF THE HOUSE AFTER.
IT MAKES ME SO HAPPY...
TO SEE SETSUNA-SAN EXCITED...
I NEED THIS SETTLED EARLIER THAN EXPECTED.
CAN WE MOVE IT UP?
YES, LET'S PUSH IT FORWARD A DAY.
I'VE TAKEN A DAY OUT OF SOMEONE'S LIFE...
WAIT, I DON'T ACTUALLY KNOW THAT. I SHOULDN'T READ INTO IT!
DOOOM

SETSUNA-SAN'S AUSTERE TASTE.

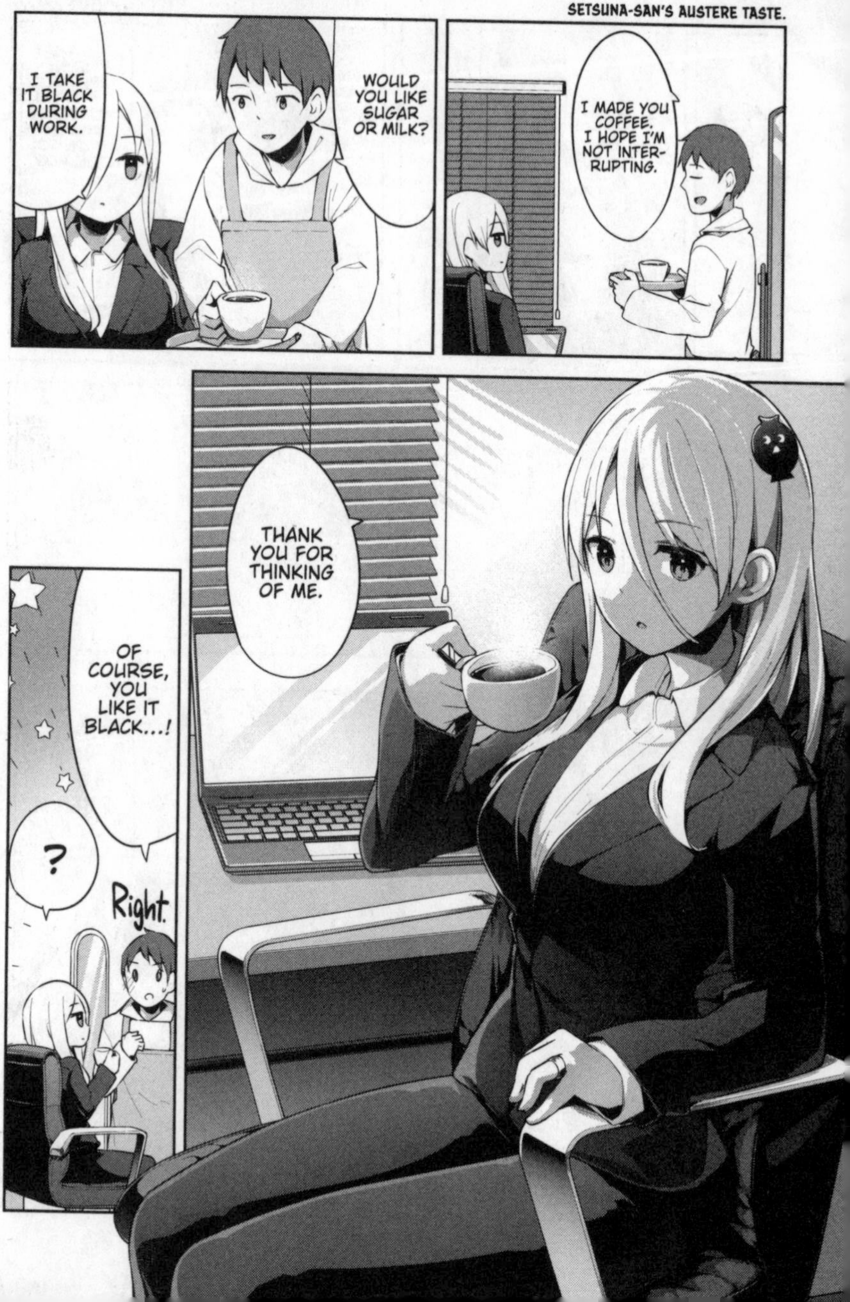
I MADE YOU COFFEE. I HOPE I'M NOT INTER-RUPTING.
WOULD YOU LIKE SUGAR OR MILK?
I TAKE IT BLACK DURING WORK.
THANK YOU FOR THINKING OF ME.
OF COURSE, YOU LIKE IT BLACK...!
?
Right.

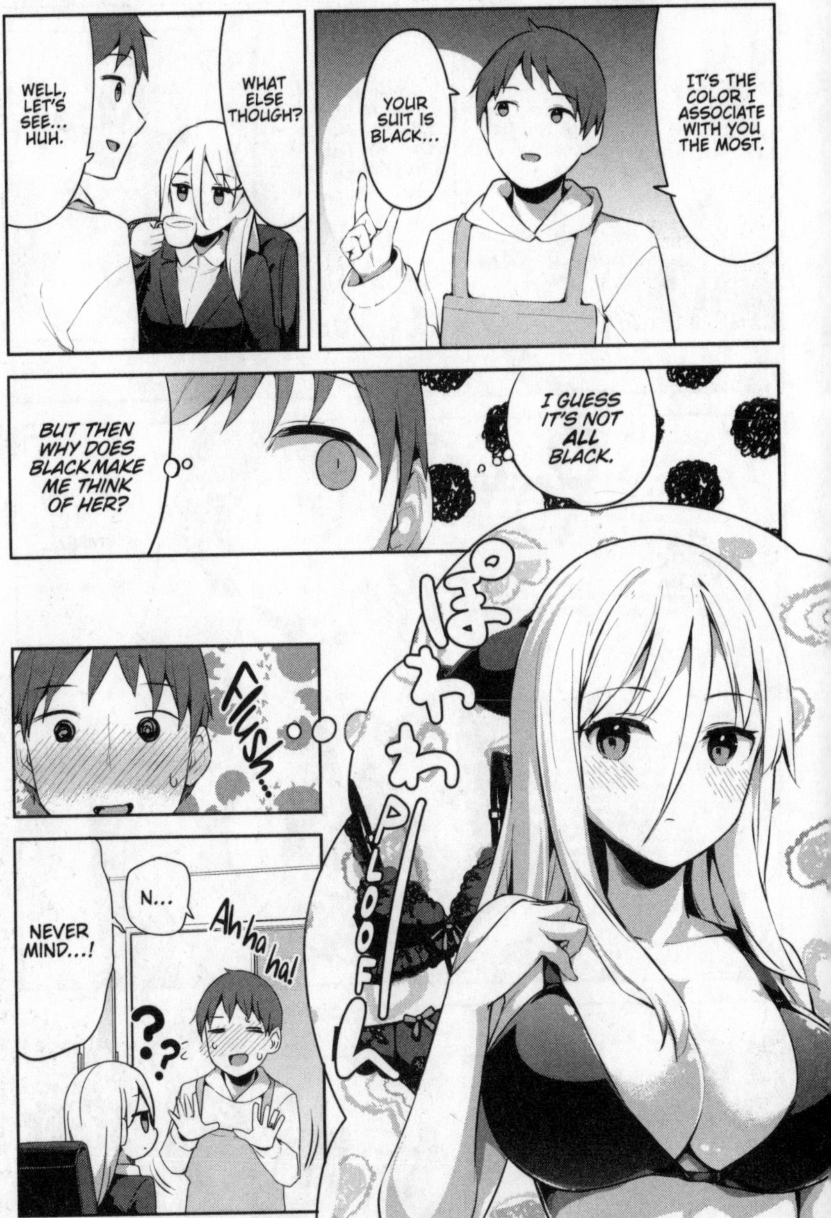
IT'S THE COLOR I ASSOCIATE WITH YOU THE MOST.
YOUR SUIT IS BLACK...
WHAT ELSE THOUGH?
WELL, LET'S SEE... HUH.
I GUESS IT'S NOT ALL BLACK.
BUT THEN WHY DOES BLACK MAKE ME THINK OF HER?
ぽわわん
PLOOF
Flush...
N...
Ah-ha ha!
NEVER MIND...!
??

MAKING HEADWAY.

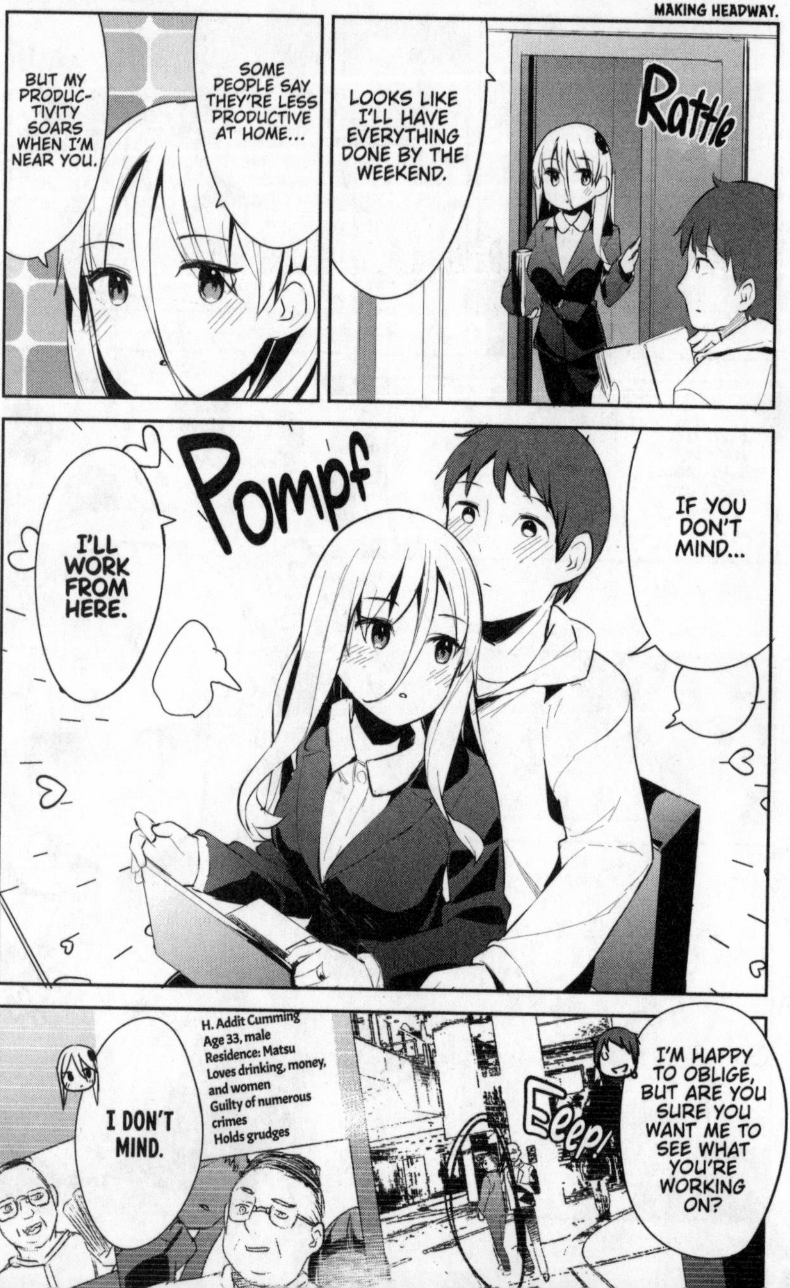
Rattle
LOOKS LIKE I'LL HAVE EVERYTHING DONE BY THE WEEKEND.
SOME PEOPLE SAY THEY'RE LESS PRODUCTIVE AT HOME...
BUT MY PRODUC-TIVITY SOARS WHEN I'M NEAR YOU.
IF YOU DON'T MIND...
Pompf
I'LL WORK FROM HERE.
I'M HAPPY TO OBLIGE, BUT ARE YOU SURE YOU WANT ME TO SEE WHAT YOU'RE WORKING ON?
Eeep!
H. Addit Cumming
Age 33, male
Residence: Matsu
Loves drinking, money, and women
Guilty of numerous crimes
Holds grudges
I DON'T MIND.

SLIM, SOFT: I LIKE IT ALL.

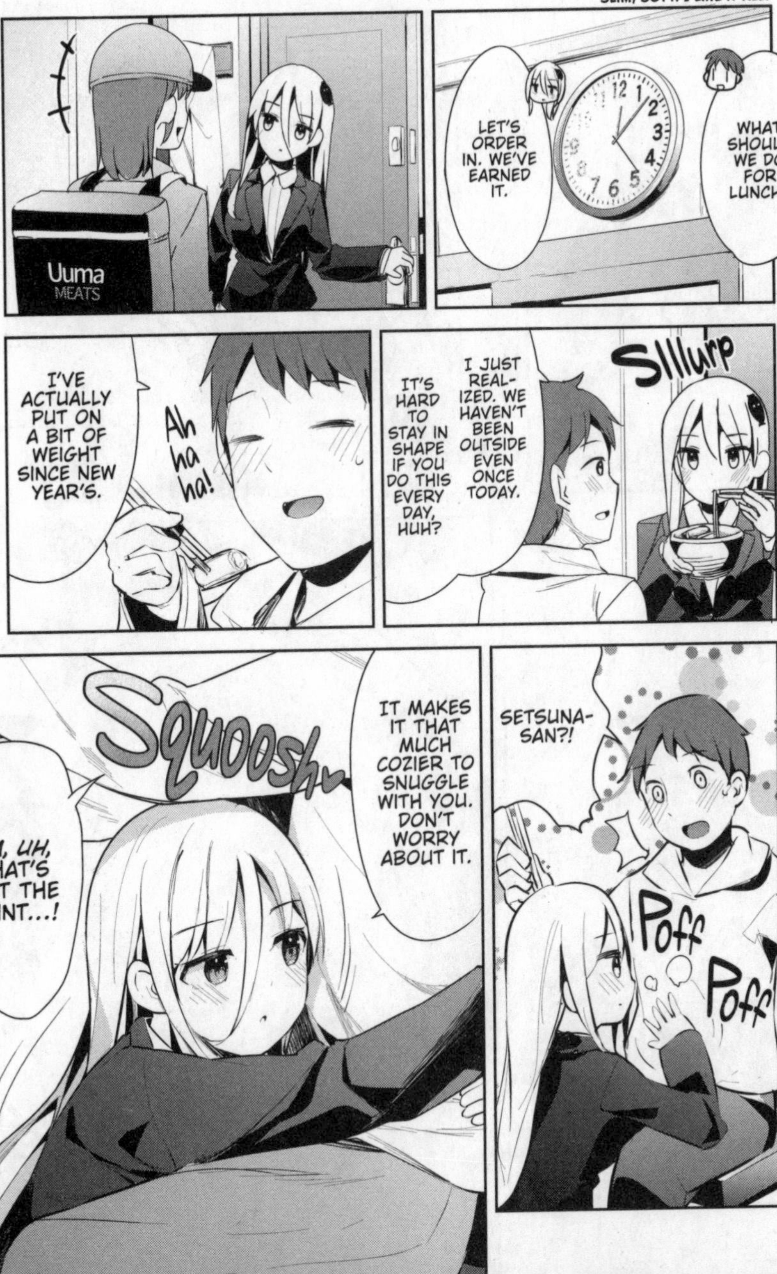
WHAT SHOULD WE DO FOR LUNCH?
LET'S ORDER IN. WE'VE EARNED IT.
Uuma MEATS
Slllurp
I JUST REALIZED. WE HAVEN'T BEEN OUTSIDE EVEN ONCE TODAY.
IT'S HARD TO STAY IN SHAPE IF YOU DO THIS EVERY DAY, HUH?
Ah ha ha!
I'VE ACTUALLY PUT ON A BIT OF WEIGHT SINCE NEW YEAR'S.
SETSUNA-SAN?!
Poff
Poff
Squoosh
IT MAKES IT THAT MUCH COZIER TO SNUGGLE WITH YOU. DON'T WORRY ABOUT IT.
UM, UH, THAT'S NOT THE POINT...!

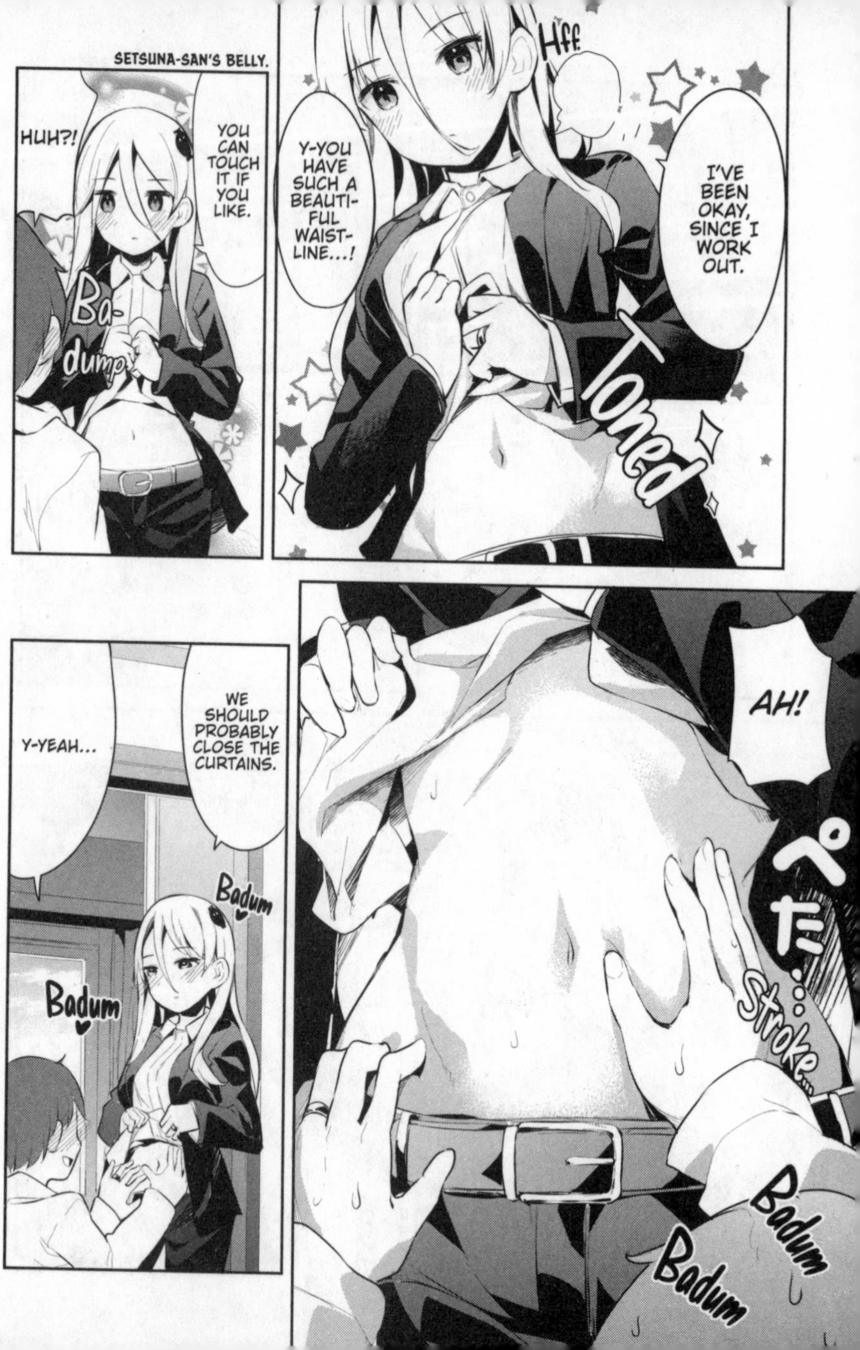
Hff
I'VE BEEN OKAY, SINCE I WORK OUT.
Y-YOU HAVE SUCH A BEAUTI-FUL WAIST-LINE...!
Toned
SETSUNA-SAN'S BELLY.
YOU CAN TOUCH IT IF YOU LIKE.
HUH?!
Ba-dump
AH!
ペた…
Stroke...
Badum
Badum
WE SHOULD PROBABLY CLOSE THE CURTAINS.
Y-YEAH...
Badum
Badum

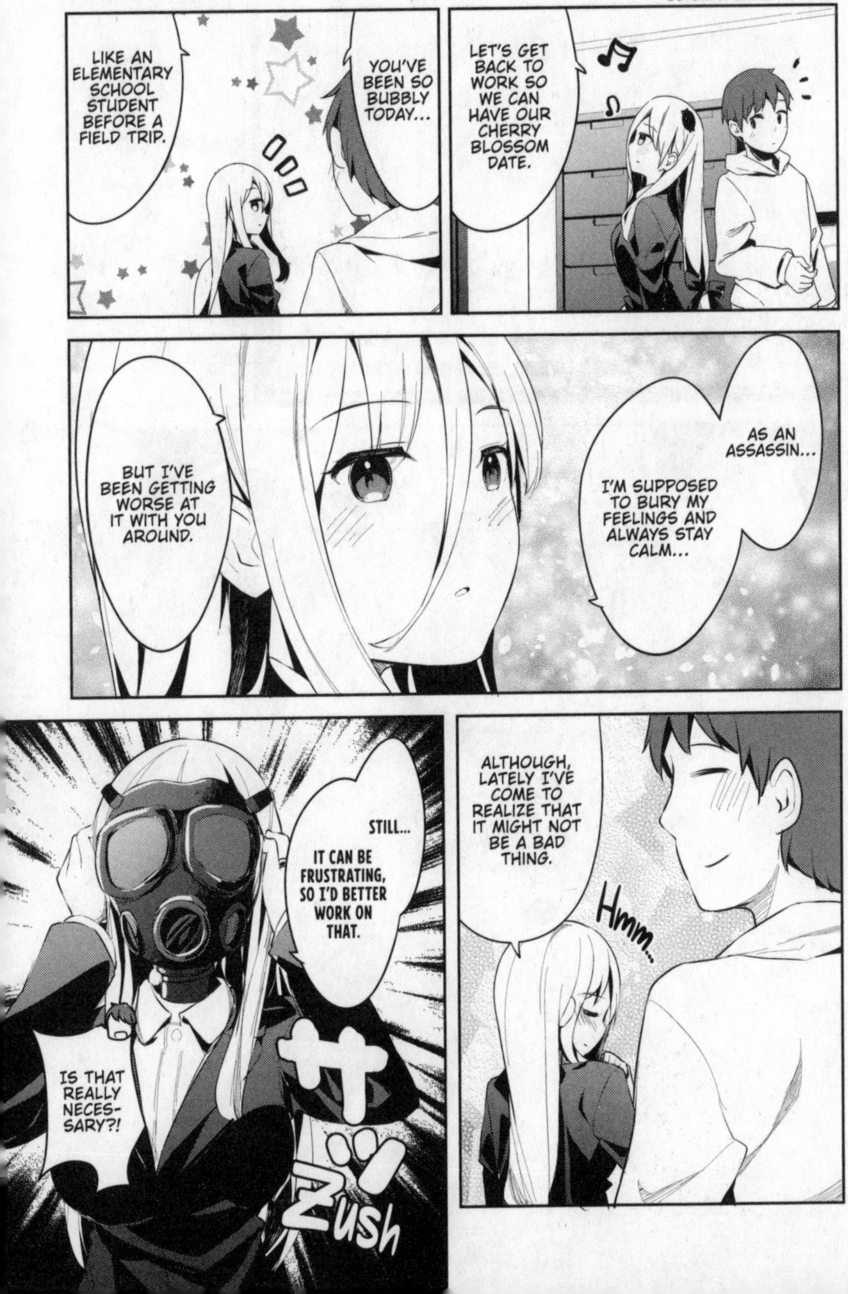
LET'S GET BACK TO WORK SO WE CAN HAVE OUR CHERRY BLOSSOM DATE.
YOU'VE BEEN SO BUBBLY TODAY...
LIKE AN ELEMENTARY SCHOOL STUDENT BEFORE A FIELD TRIP.
AS AN ASSASSIN...
I'M SUPPOSED TO BURY MY FEELINGS AND ALWAYS STAY CALM...
BUT I'VE BEEN GETTING WORSE AT IT WITH YOU AROUND.
ALTHOUGH, LATELY I'VE COME TO REALIZE THAT IT MIGHT NOT BE A BAD THING.
Hmm...
STILL...
IT CAN BE FRUSTRATING, SO I'D BETTER WORK ON THAT.
IS THAT REALLY NECES-SARY?!
Zush

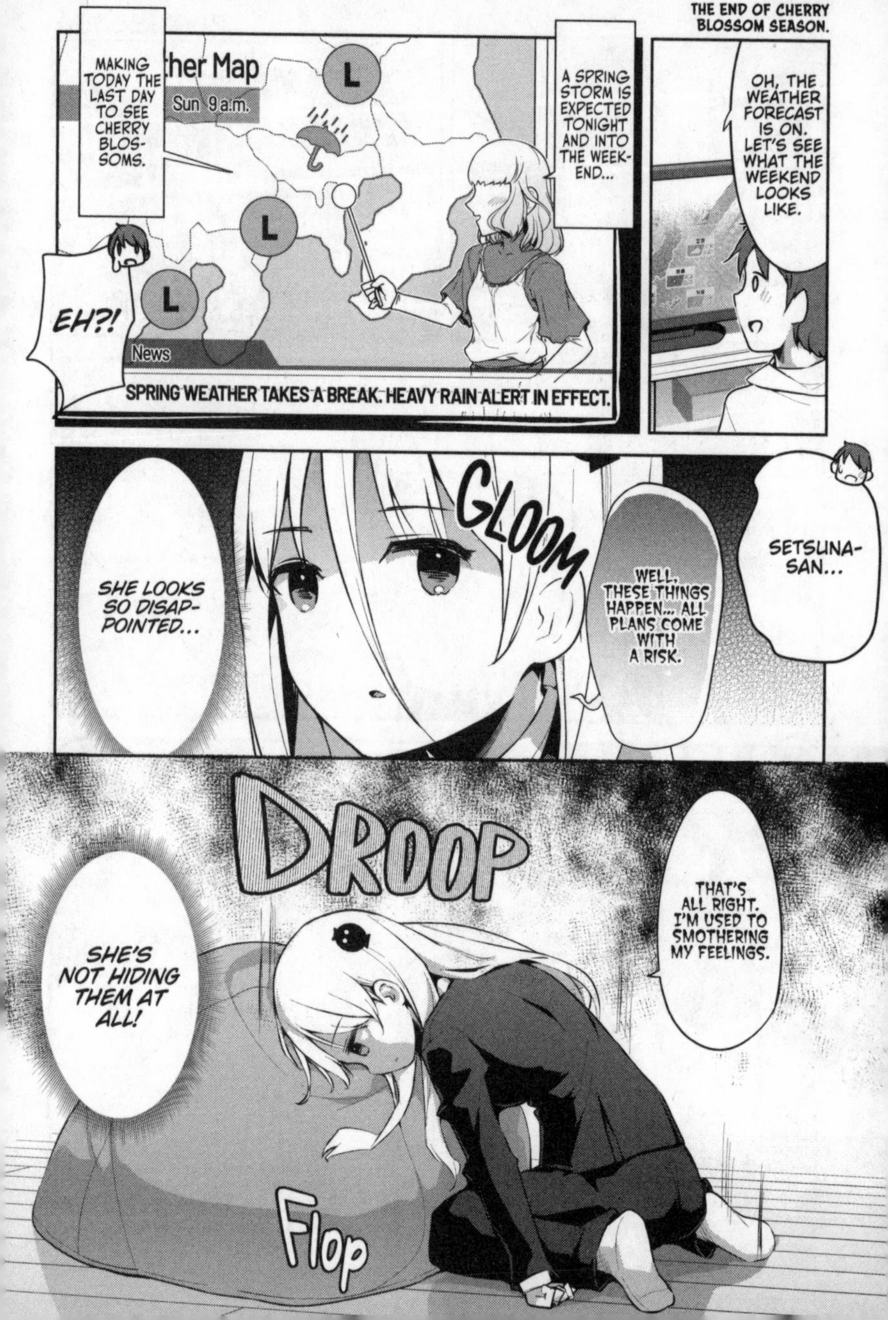
THE END OF CHERRY BLOSSOM SEASON.
OH, THE WEATHER FORECAST IS ON. LET'S SEE WHAT THE WEEKEND LOOKS LIKE.
A SPRING STORM IS EXPECTED TONIGHT AND INTO THE WEEK-END...
MAKING TODAY THE LAST DAY TO SEE CHERRY BLOS-SOMS.
ther Map
Sun 9 a.m.
News
SPRING WEATHER TAKES A BREAK. HEAVY RAIN ALERT IN EFFECT.
EH?!
SETSUNA-SAN...
GLOOM
WELL, THESE THINGS HAPPEN... ALL PLANS COME WITH A RISK.
SHE LOOKS SO DISAP-POINTED...
DROOP
THAT'S ALL RIGHT. I'M USED TO SMOTHERING MY FEELINGS.
SHE'S NOT HIDING THEM AT ALL!
Flop

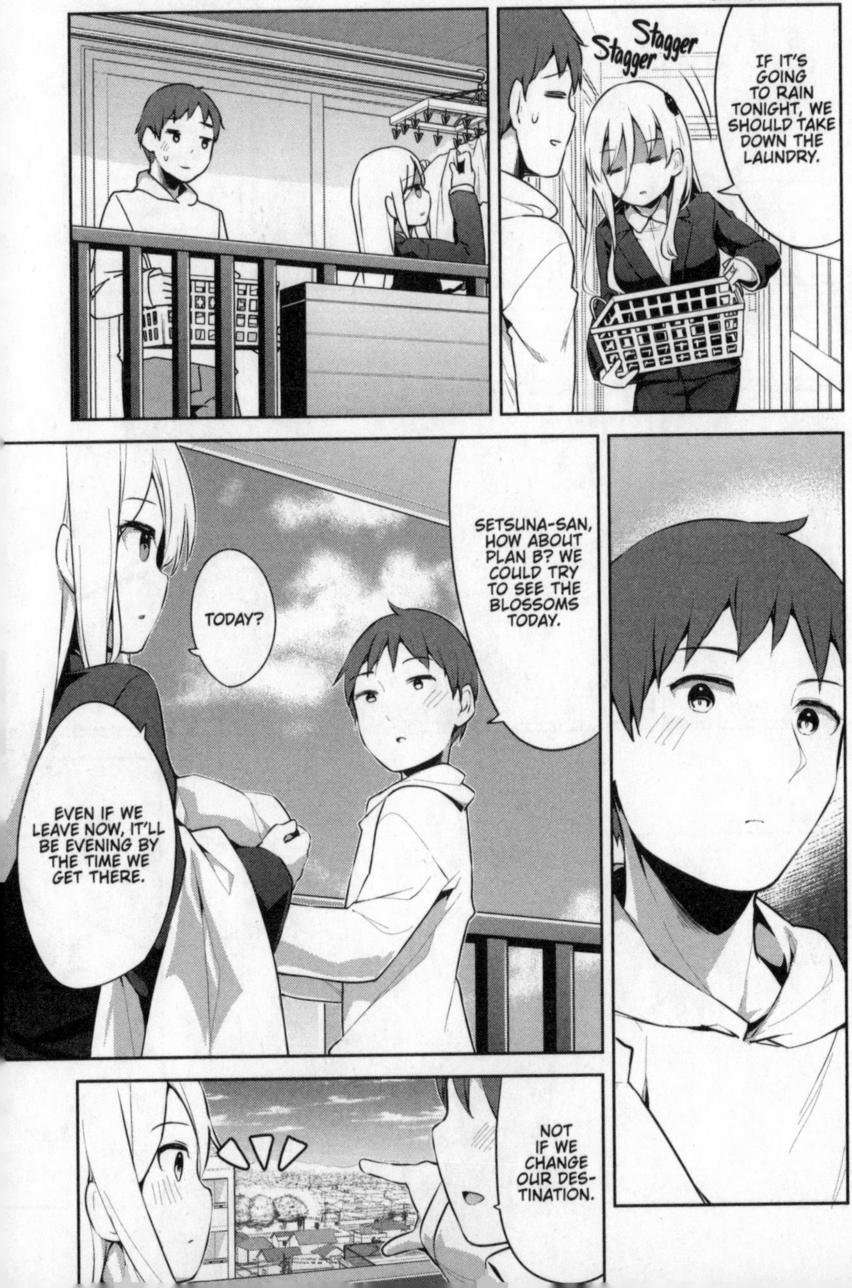
Stagger
Stagger
IF IT'S GOING TO RAIN TONIGHT, WE SHOULD TAKE DOWN THE LAUNDRY.
SETSUNA-SAN, HOW ABOUT PLAN B? WE COULD TRY TO SEE THE BLOSSOMS TODAY.
TODAY?
EVEN IF WE LEAVE NOW, IT'LL BE EVENING BY THE TIME WE GET THERE.
NOT IF WE CHANGE OUR DES-TINATION.

CHERRY BLOSSOM VIEWING: PLAN B.

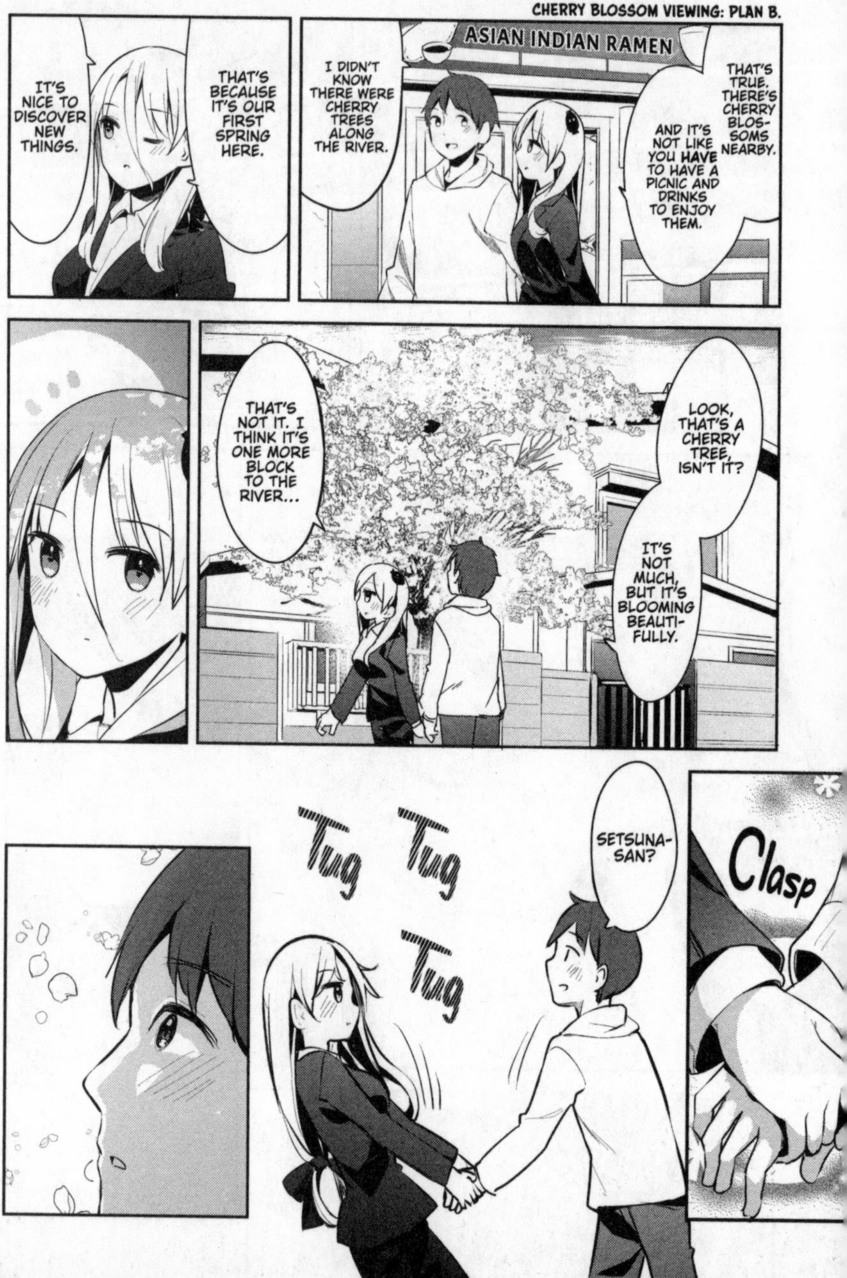
ASIAN INDIAN RAMEN
THAT'S TRUE. THERE'S CHERRY BLOSSOMS NEARBY.
AND IT'S NOT LIKE YOU **HAVE** TO HAVE A PICNIC AND DRINKS TO ENJOY THEM.
I DIDN'T KNOW THERE WERE CHERRY TREES ALONG THE RIVER.
THAT'S BECAUSE IT'S OUR FIRST SPRING HERE.
IT'S NICE TO DISCOVER NEW THINGS.
LOOK, THAT'S A CHERRY TREE, ISN'T IT?
IT'S NOT MUCH, BUT IT'S BLOOMING BEAUTIFULLY.
THAT'S NOT IT. I THINK IT'S ONE MORE BLOCK TO THE RIVER...
Clasp
SETSUNA-SAN?
Tug
Tug
Tug

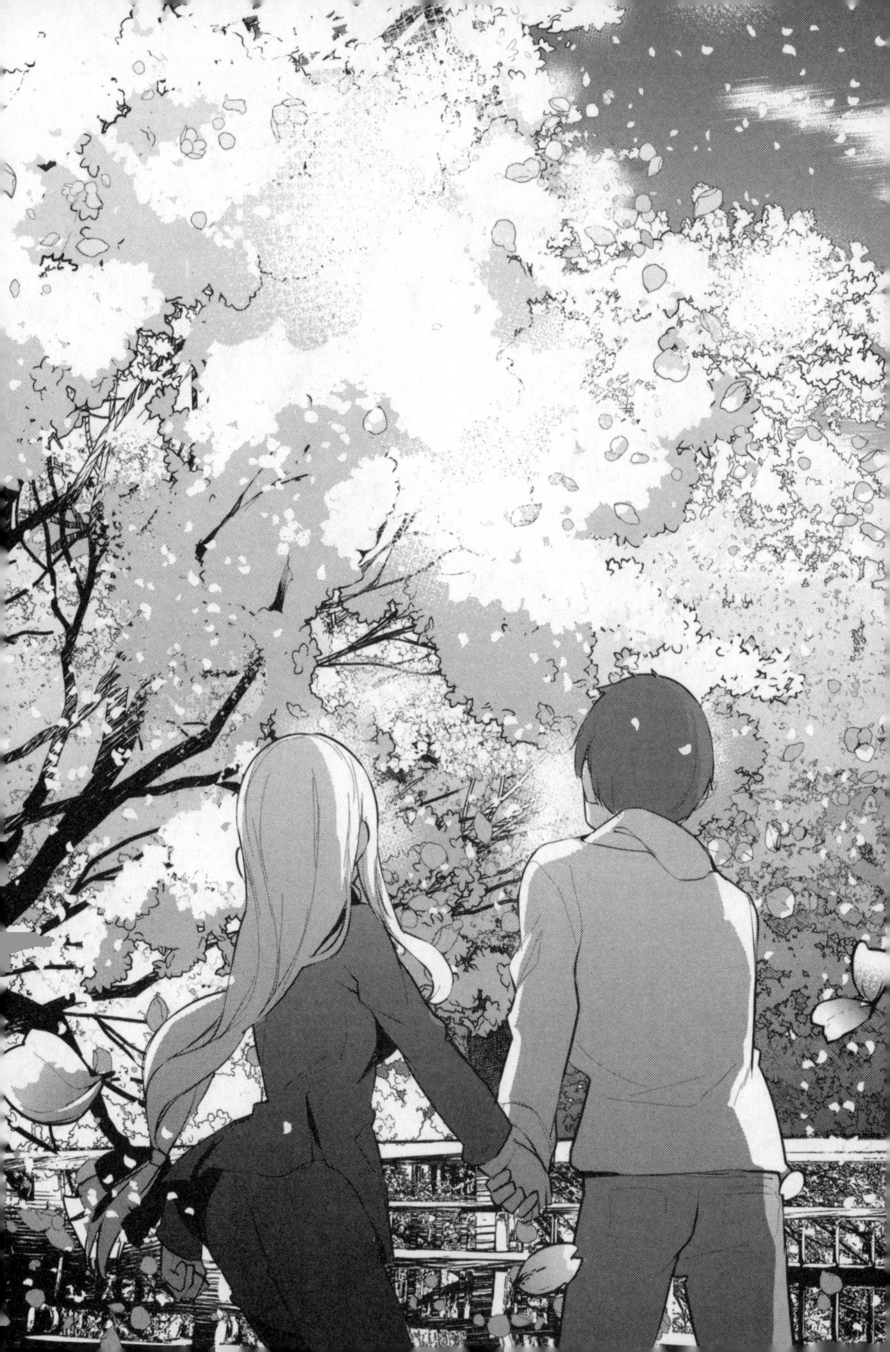

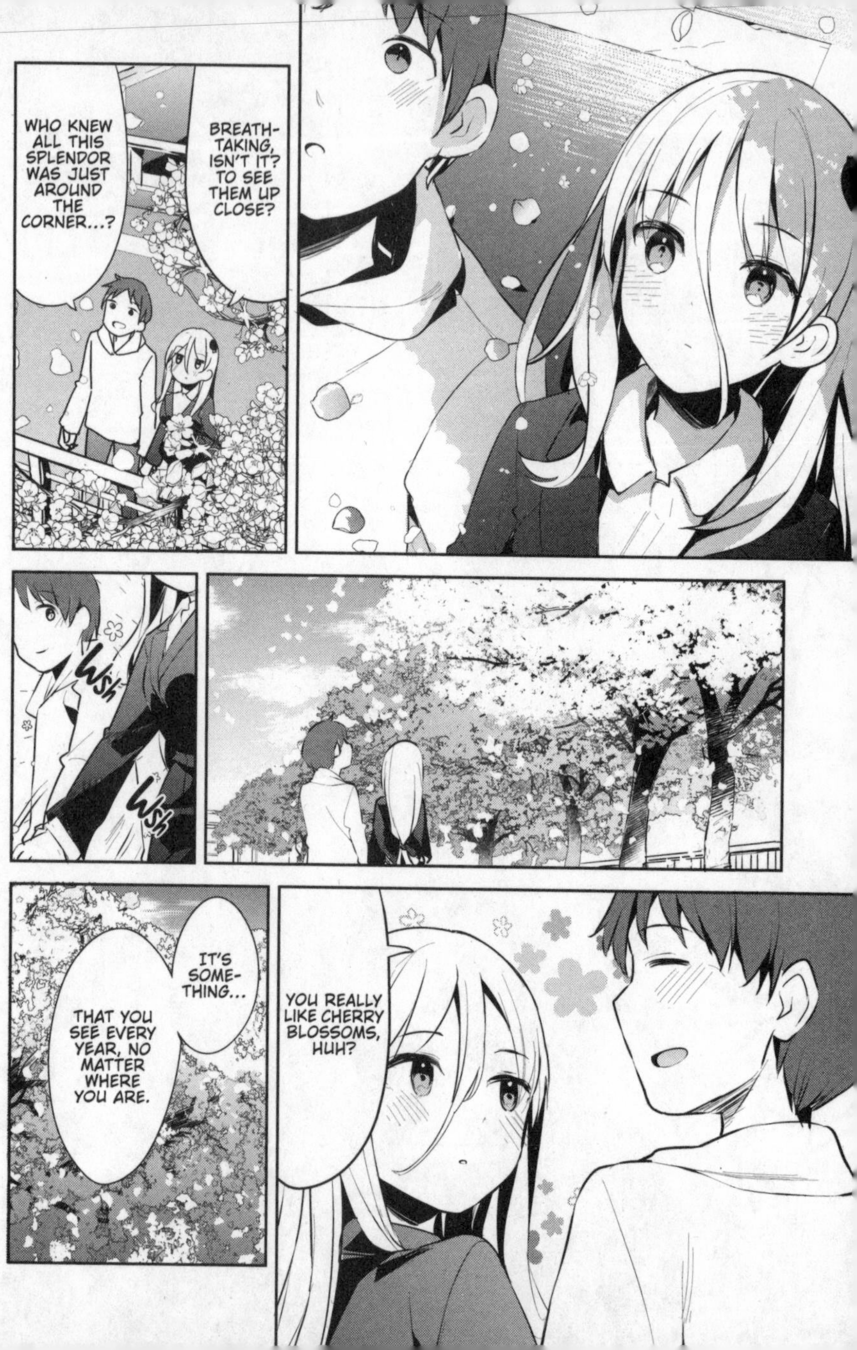
BREATH-TAKING, ISN'T IT? TO SEE THEM UP CLOSE?
WHO KNEW ALL THIS SPLENDOR WAS JUST AROUND THE CORNER...?
Wsh
Wsh
YOU REALLY LIKE CHERRY BLOSSOMS, HUH?
IT'S SOME-THING...
THAT YOU SEE EVERY YEAR, NO MATTER WHERE YOU ARE.

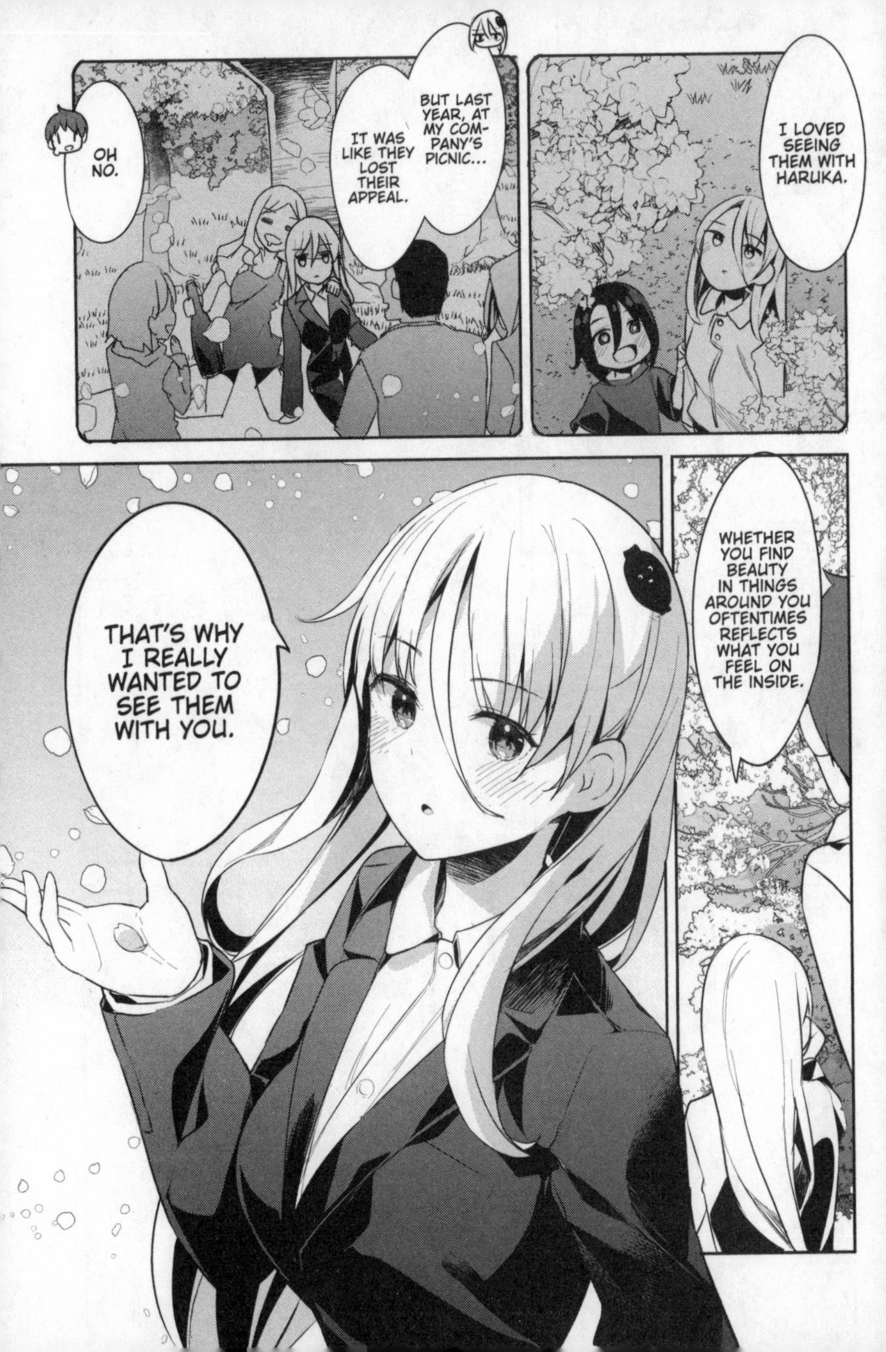
I LOVED SEEING THEM WITH HARUKA.
BUT LAST YEAR, AT MY COMPANY'S PICNIC...
IT WAS LIKE THEY LOST THEIR APPEAL.
OH NO.
WHETHER YOU FIND BEAUTY IN THINGS AROUND YOU OFTENTIMES REFLECTS WHAT YOU FEEL ON THE INSIDE.
THAT'S WHY I REALLY WANTED TO SEE THEM WITH YOU.

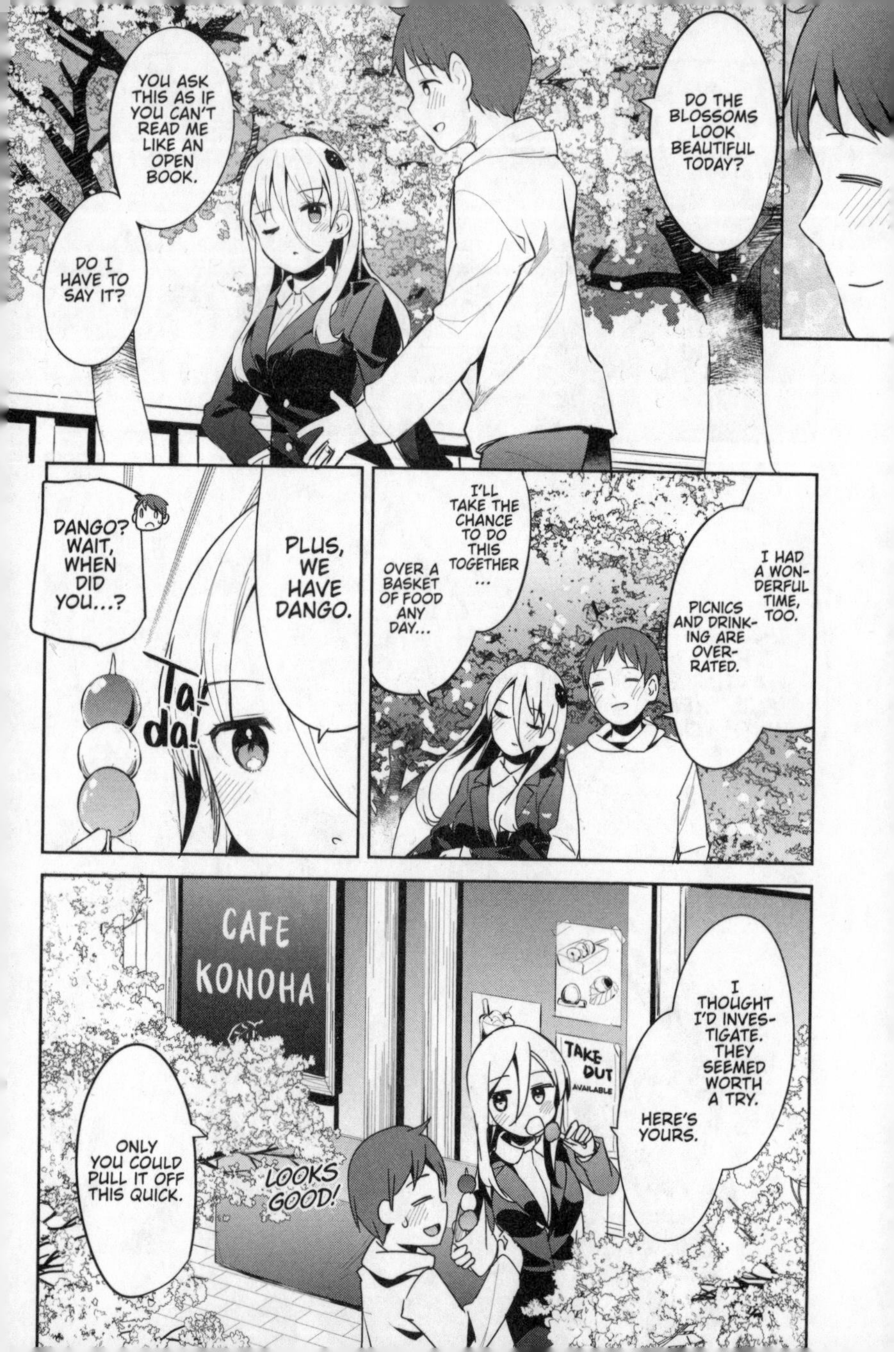
DO THE BLOSSOMS LOOK BEAUTIFUL TODAY?
YOU ASK THIS AS IF YOU CAN'T READ ME LIKE AN OPEN BOOK.
DO I HAVE TO SAY IT?
I HAD A WONDERFUL TIME, TOO.
PICNICS AND DRINKING ARE OVERRATED.
I'LL TAKE THE CHANCE TO DO THIS TOGETHER...
OVER A BASKET OF FOOD ANY DAY...
PLUS, WE HAVE DANGO.
Ta-da!
DANGO? WAIT, WHEN DID YOU...?
CAFE KONOHA
TAKE OUT AVAILABLE
I THOUGHT I'D INVESTIGATE. THEY SEEMED WORTH A TRY.
HERE'S YOURS.
LOOKS GOOD!
ONLY YOU COULD PULL IT OFF THIS QUICK.

HARUKA-CHAN IS TRAINING HARD
TO BECOME AN ACE ASSASSIN.

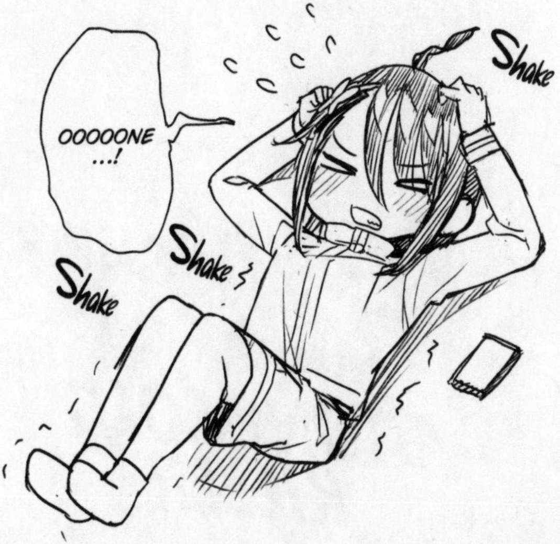
Shake
OOOOONE ...!
Shake
Shake

MY Lovey-Dovey Wife IS A STONE COLD KILLER

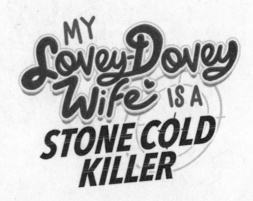

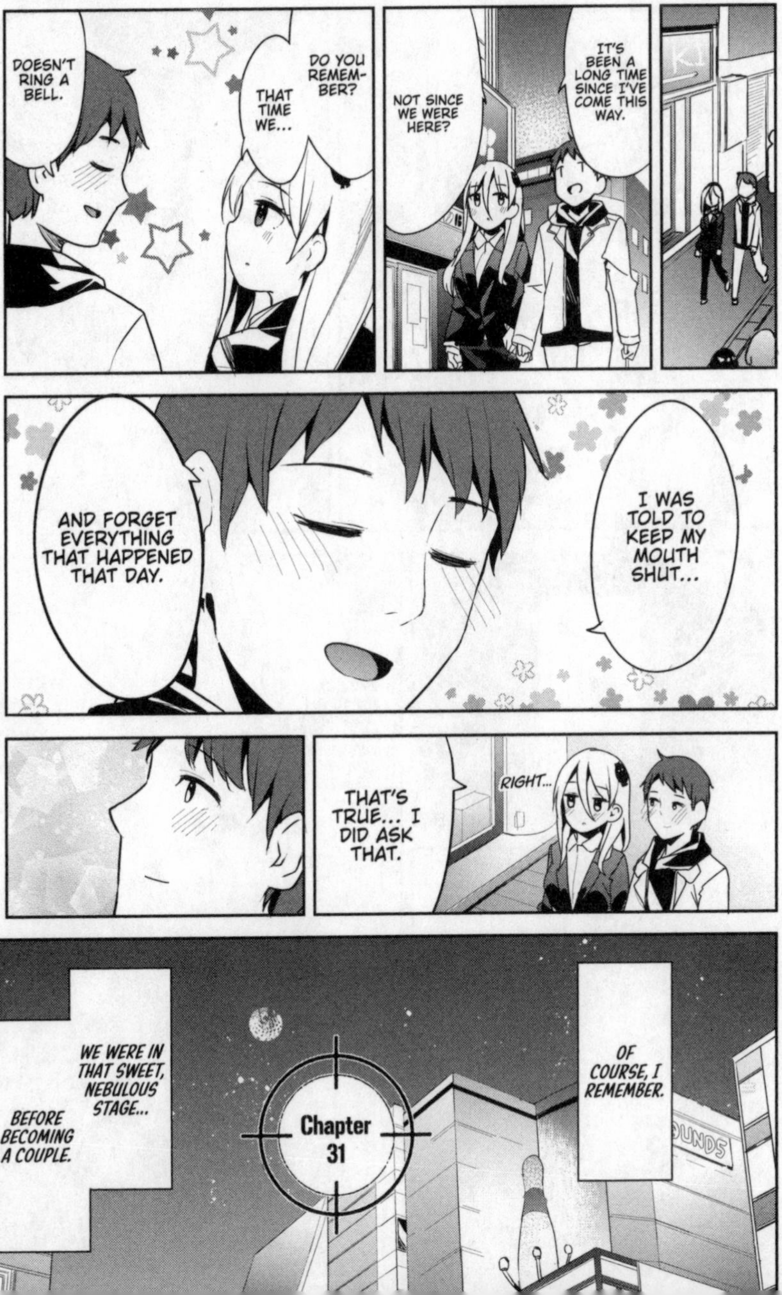
IT'S BEEN A LONG TIME SINCE I'VE COME THIS WAY.
NOT SINCE WE WERE HERE?
DO YOU REMEMBER?
THAT TIME WE...
DOESN'T RING A BELL.
I WAS TOLD TO KEEP MY MOUTH SHUT...
AND FORGET EVERYTHING THAT HAPPENED THAT DAY.
RIGHT...
THAT'S TRUE... I DID ASK THAT.
OF COURSE, I REMEMBER.
Chapter 31
WE WERE IN THAT SWEET, NEBULOUS STAGE...
BEFORE BECOMING A COUPLE.

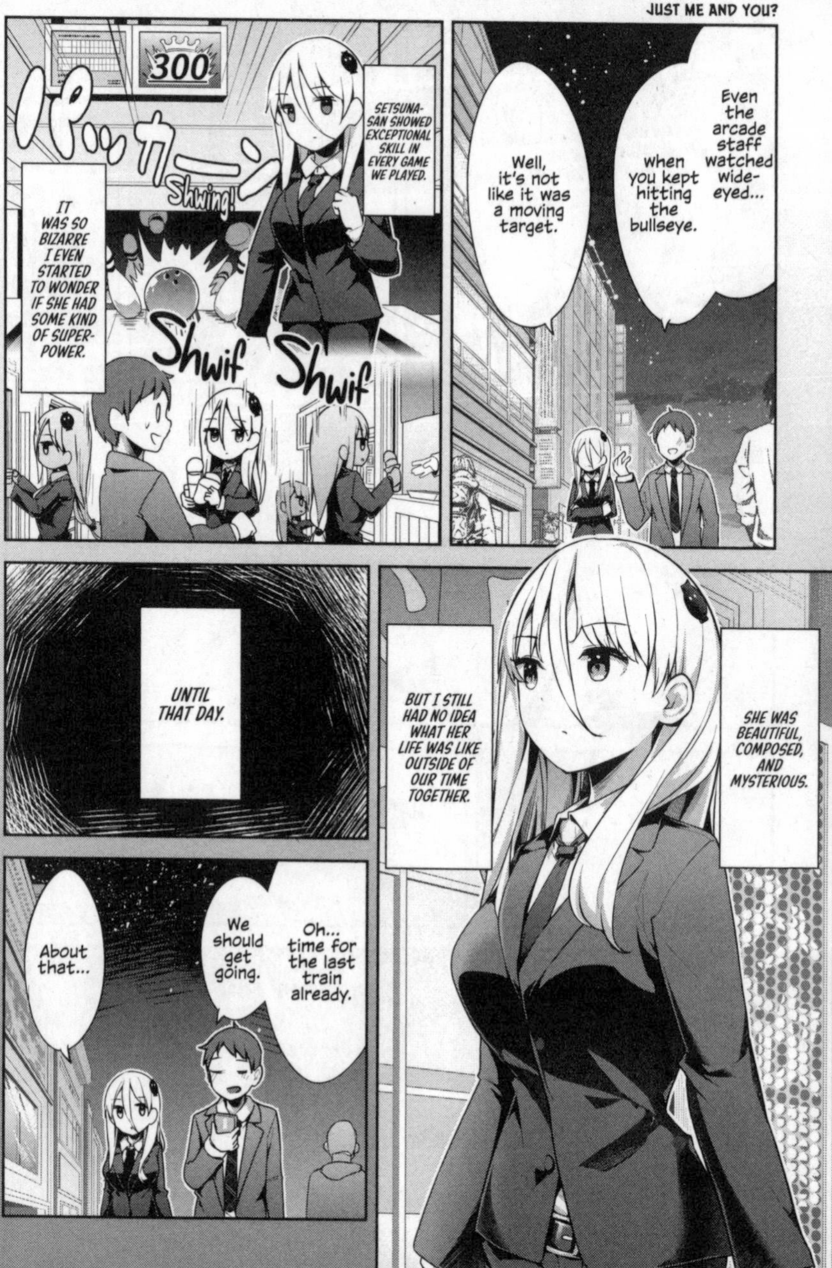
Even the arcade staff watched wide-eyed...
when you kept hitting the bullseye.
Well, it's not like it was a moving target.
SETSUNA-SAN SHOWED EXCEPTIONAL SKILL IN EVERY GAME WE PLAYED.
300
パッカーン
Shwing!
IT WAS SO BIZARRE I EVEN STARTED TO WONDER IF SHE HAD SOME KIND OF SUPER-POWER.
Shwif Shwif
SHE WAS BEAUTIFUL, COMPOSED, AND MYSTERIOUS.
BUT I STILL HAD NO IDEA WHAT HER LIFE WAS LIKE OUTSIDE OF OUR TIME TOGETHER.
UNTIL THAT DAY.
Oh... time for the last train already.
We should get going.
About that...

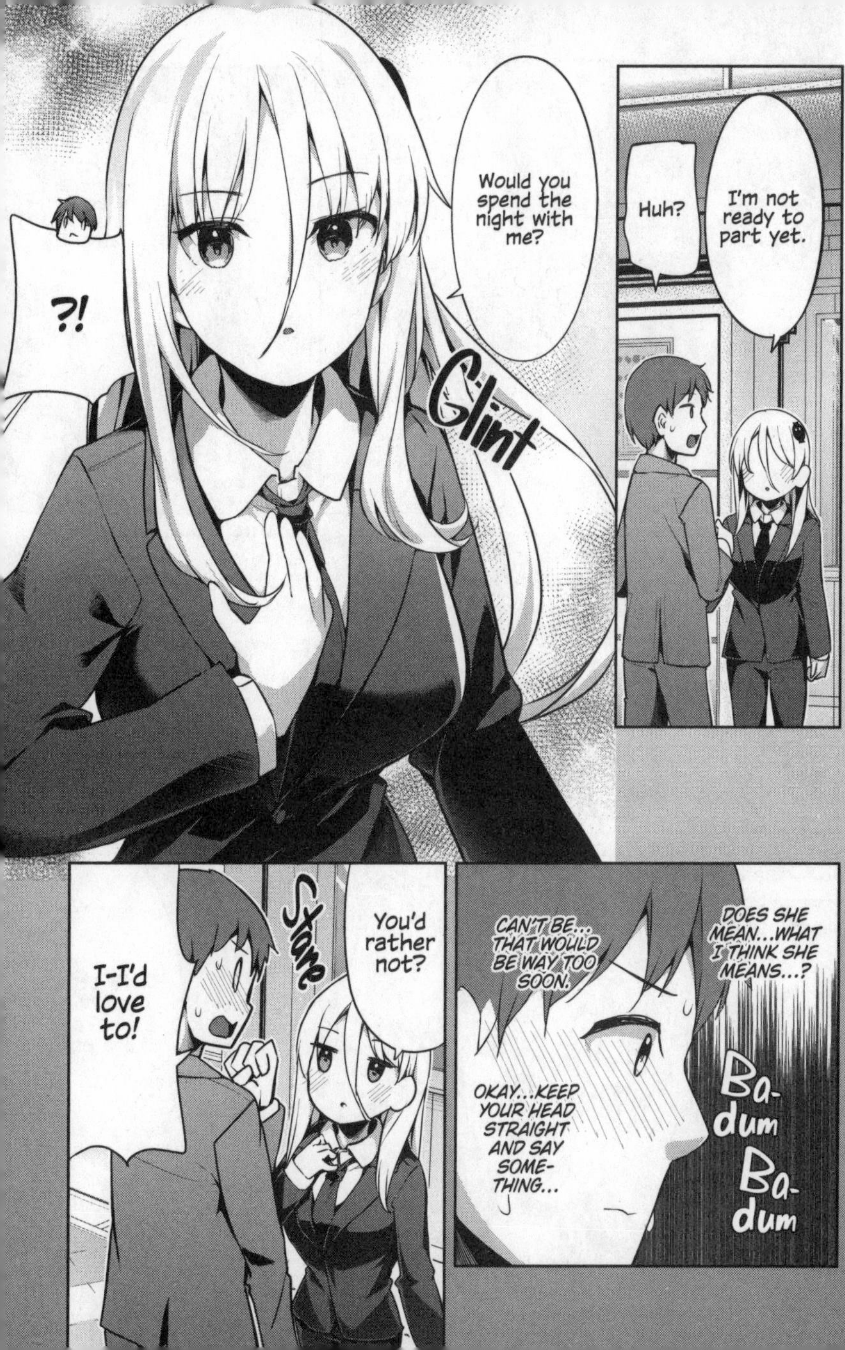

I'm not ready to part yet.
Huh?
Would you spend the night with me?
Glint
?!
DOES SHE MEAN...WHAT I THINK SHE MEANS...?
CAN'T BE... THAT WOULD BE WAY TOO SOON.
OKAY...KEEP YOUR HEAD STRAIGHT AND SAY SOME-THING...
Ba-dum Ba-dum
You'd rather not?
Stare
I-I'd love to!

BETTER IN THE DARK.

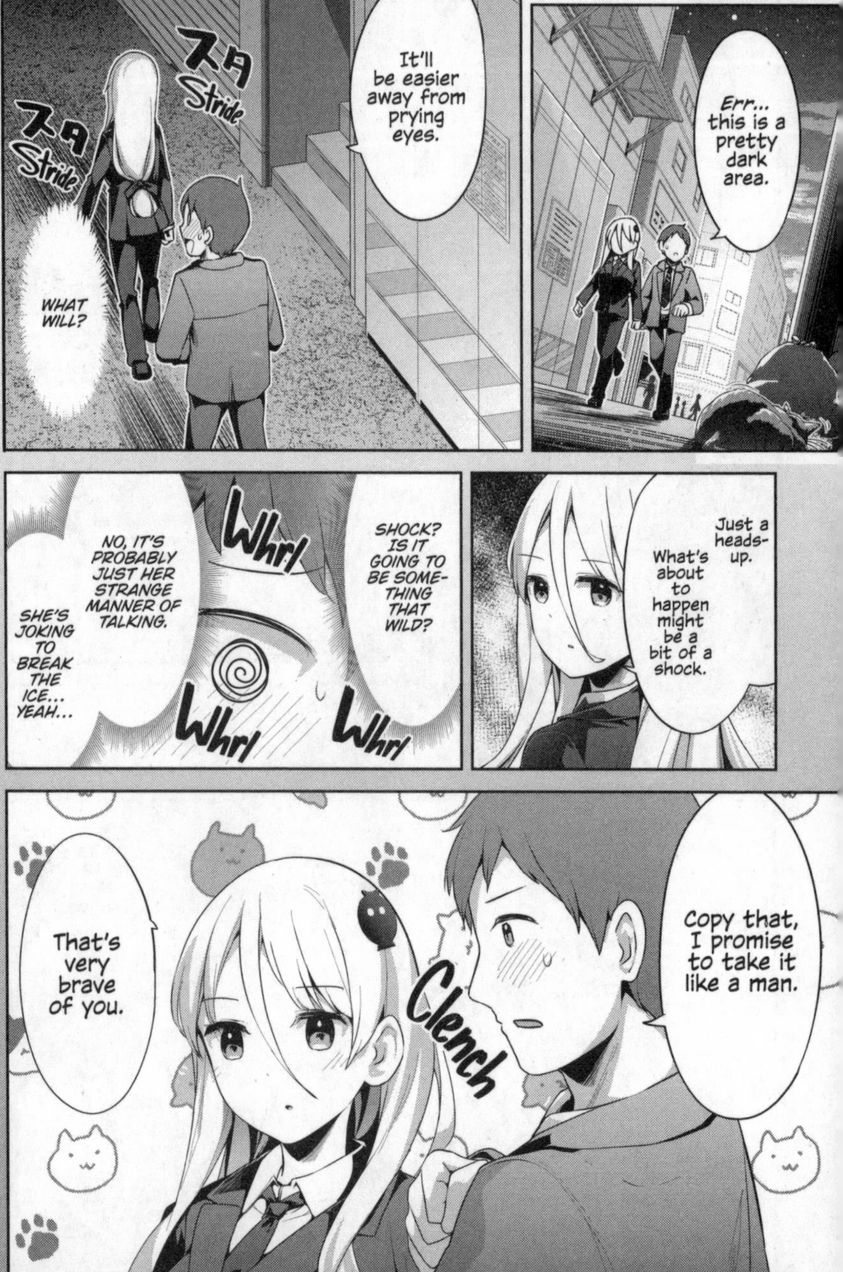

Err... this is a pretty dark area.
It'll be easier away from prying eyes.
スタ Stride
スタ Stride
WHAT WILL?
Just a heads-up.
What's about to happen might be a bit of a shock.
SHOCK? IS IT GOING TO BE SOME-THING THAT WILD?
Whrl
Whrl
Whrl
NO, IT'S PROBABLY JUST HER STRANGE MANNER OF TALKING.
SHE'S JOKING TO BREAK THE ICE... YEAH...
Copy that, I promise to take it like a man.
Clench
That's very brave of you.

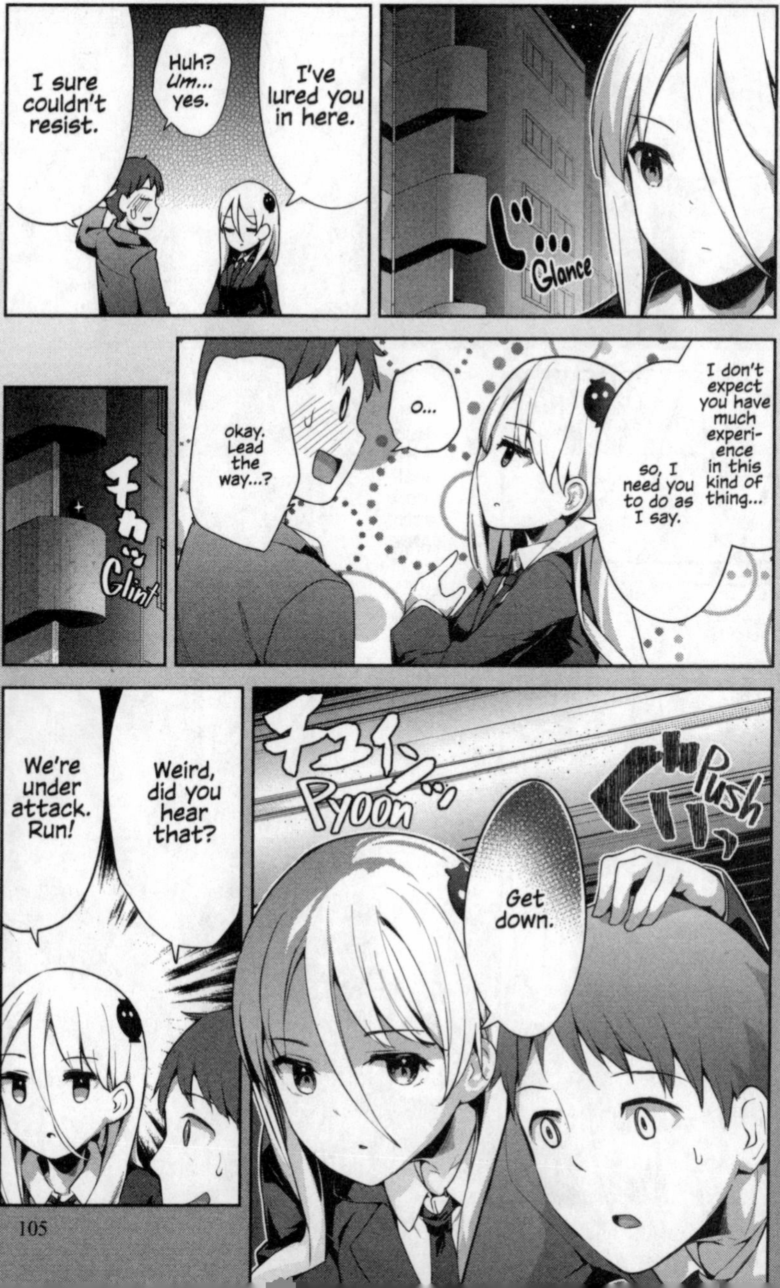
Glance
I've lured you in here.
Huh? Um... yes.
I sure couldn't resist.
I don't expect you have much experience in this kind of thing...
so, I need you to do as I say.
O...
okay. Lead the way...?
Clint
Push
Pyoon
Get down.
Weird, did you hear that?
We're under attack. Run!

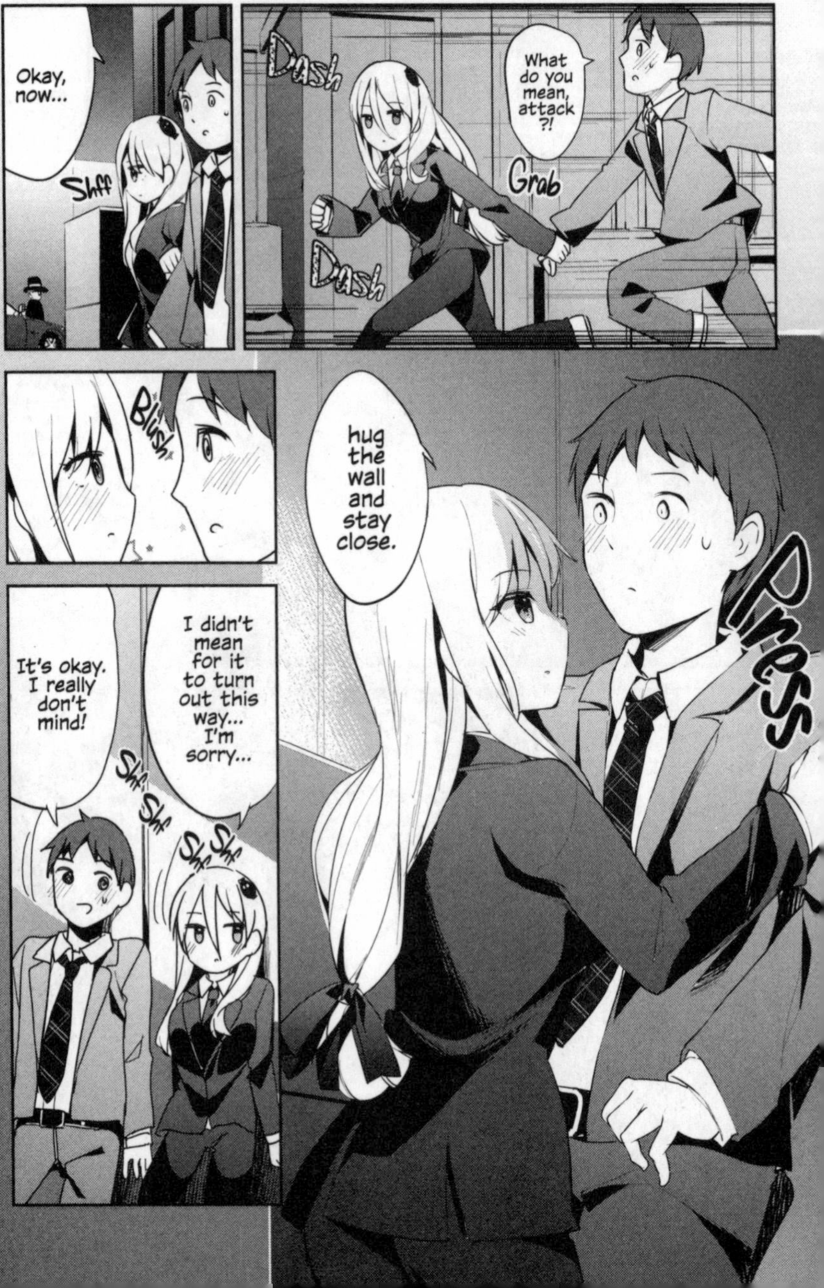
Dash
What do you mean, attack?!
Grab
Dash
Okay, now...
Shff
hug the wall and stay close.
Press
Blush
I didn't mean for it to turn out this way... I'm sorry...
It's okay. I really don't mind!
Shff
Shff
Shff
Shff

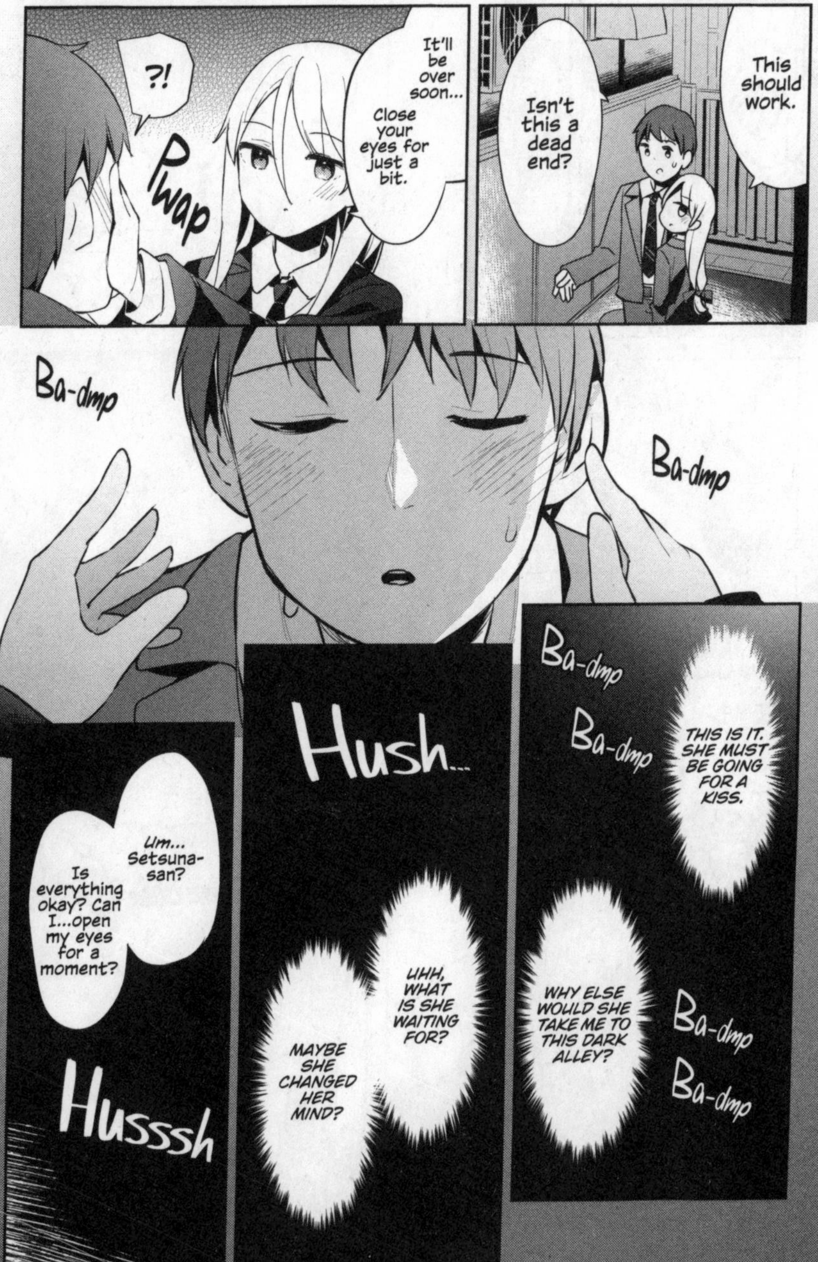
This should work.
Isn't this a dead end?
It'll be over soon...
Close your eyes for just a bit.
Pwap
?!
Ba-dmp
Ba-dmp
Ba-dmp
Ba-dmp
THIS IS IT. SHE MUST BE GOING FOR A KISS.
WHY ELSE WOULD SHE TAKE ME TO THIS DARK ALLEY?
Ba-dmp
Ba-dmp
Hush...
UHH, WHAT IS SHE WAITING FOR?
MAYBE SHE CHANGED HER MIND?
Um... Setsuna-san?
Is everything okay? Can I...open my eyes for a moment?
Husssh

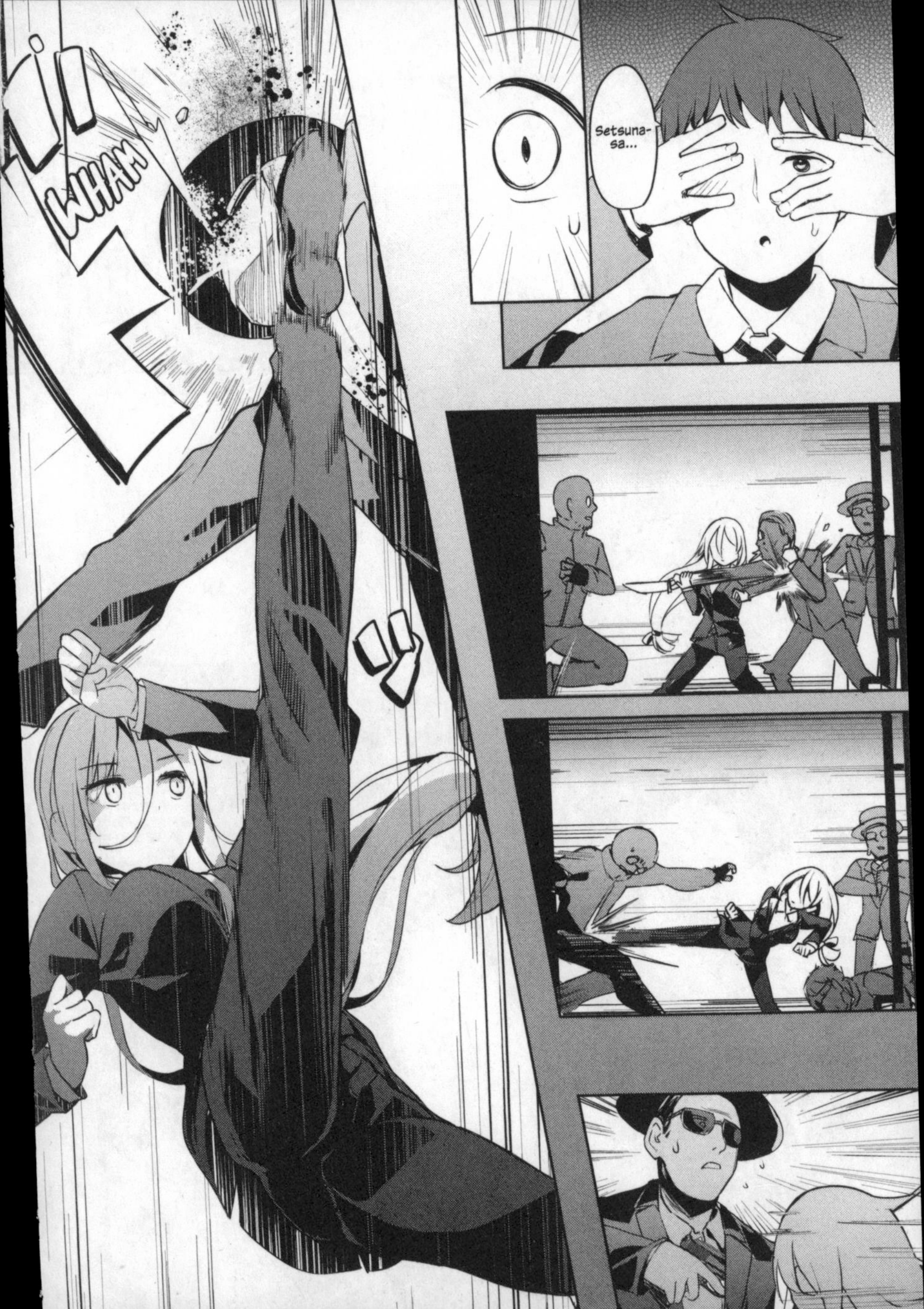
Setsuna-sa...
WHAM

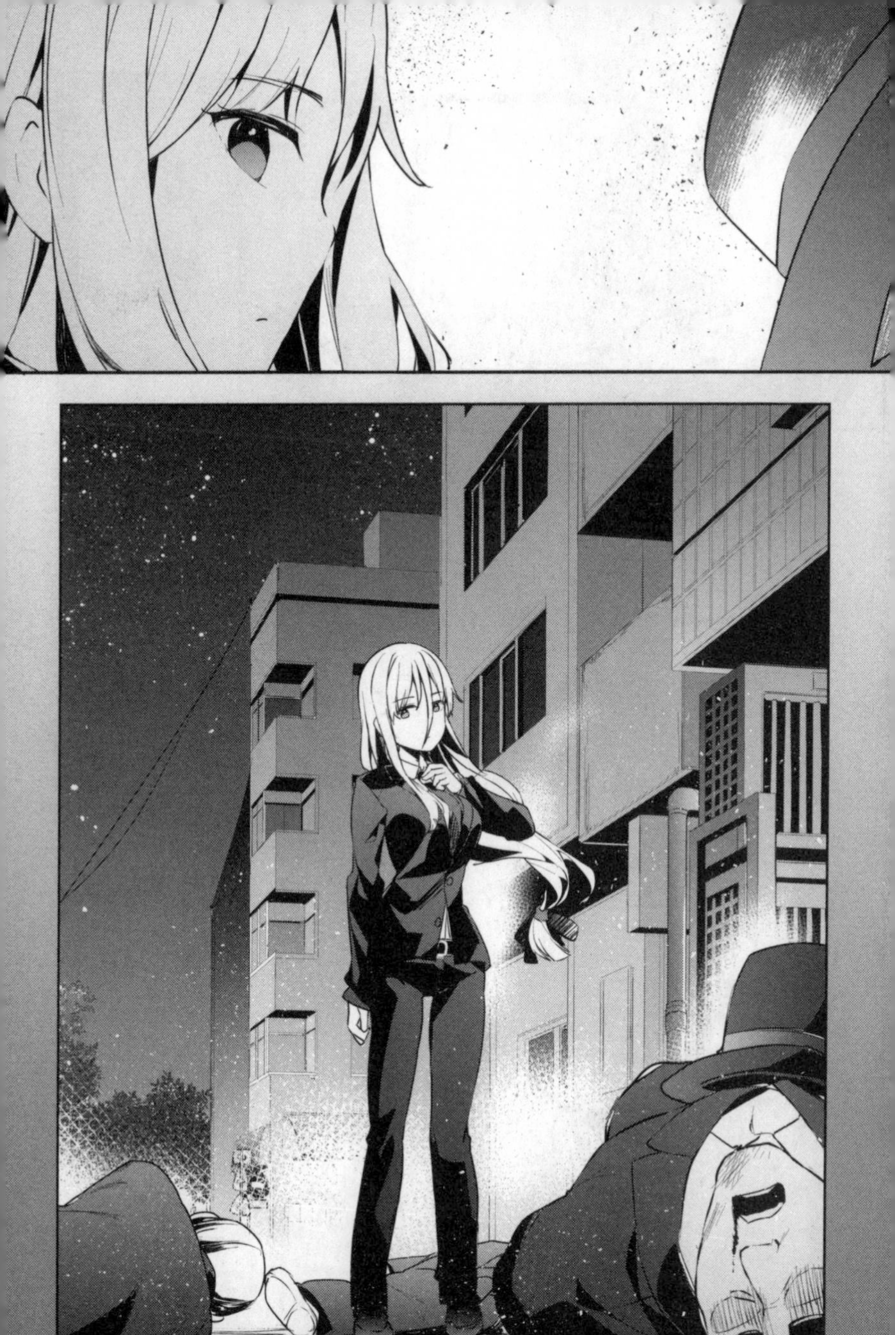

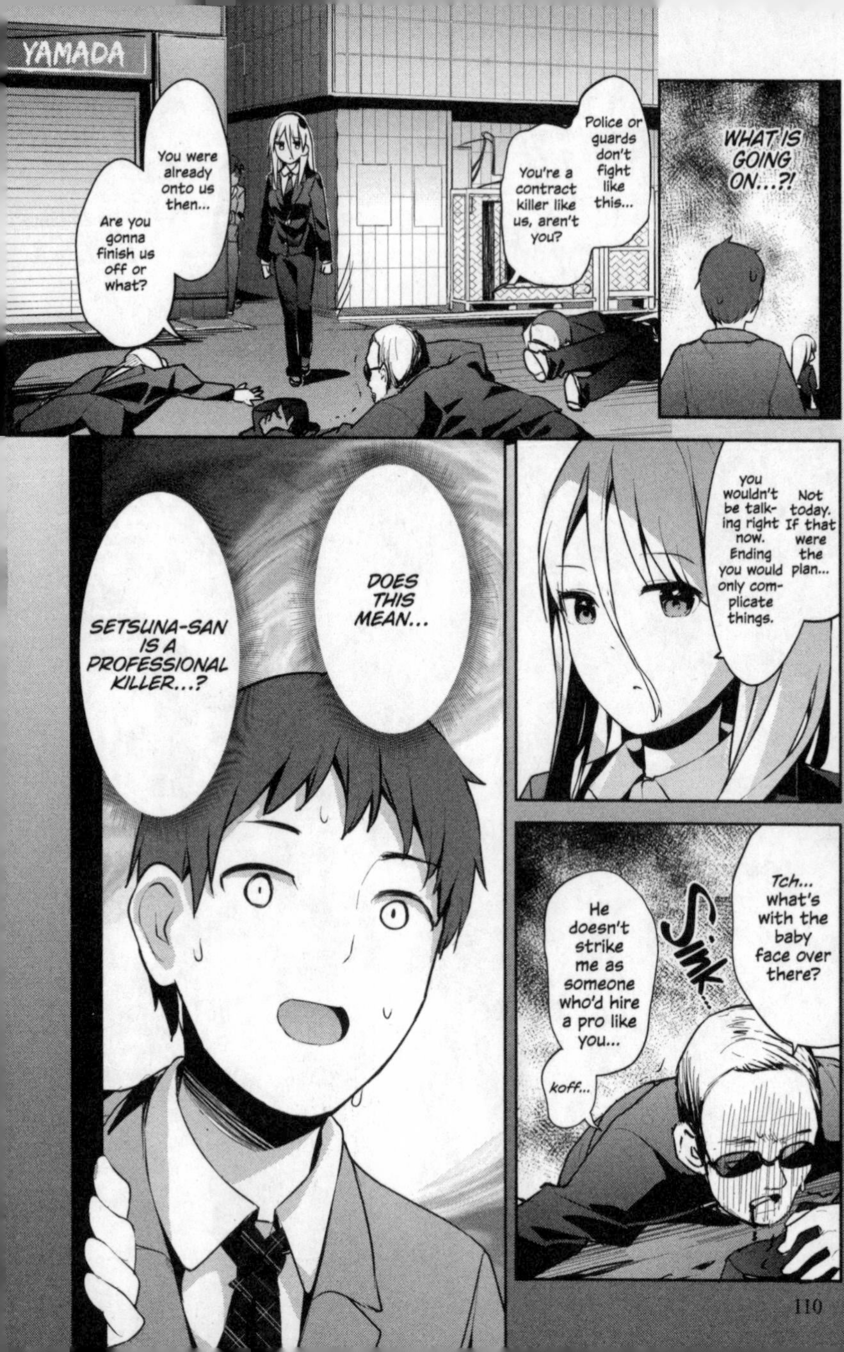

WHAT IS GOING ON...?!
Police or guards don't fight like this...
You're a contract killer like us, aren't you?
YAMADA
You were already onto us then...
Are you gonna finish us off or what?
Not today. If that were the plan...
you wouldn't be talking right now. Ending you would only complicate things.
Tch... what's with the baby face over there?
Sink...
He doesn't strike me as someone who'd hire a pro like you...
koff...
DOES THIS MEAN...
SETSUNA-SAN IS A PROFESSIONAL KILLER...?

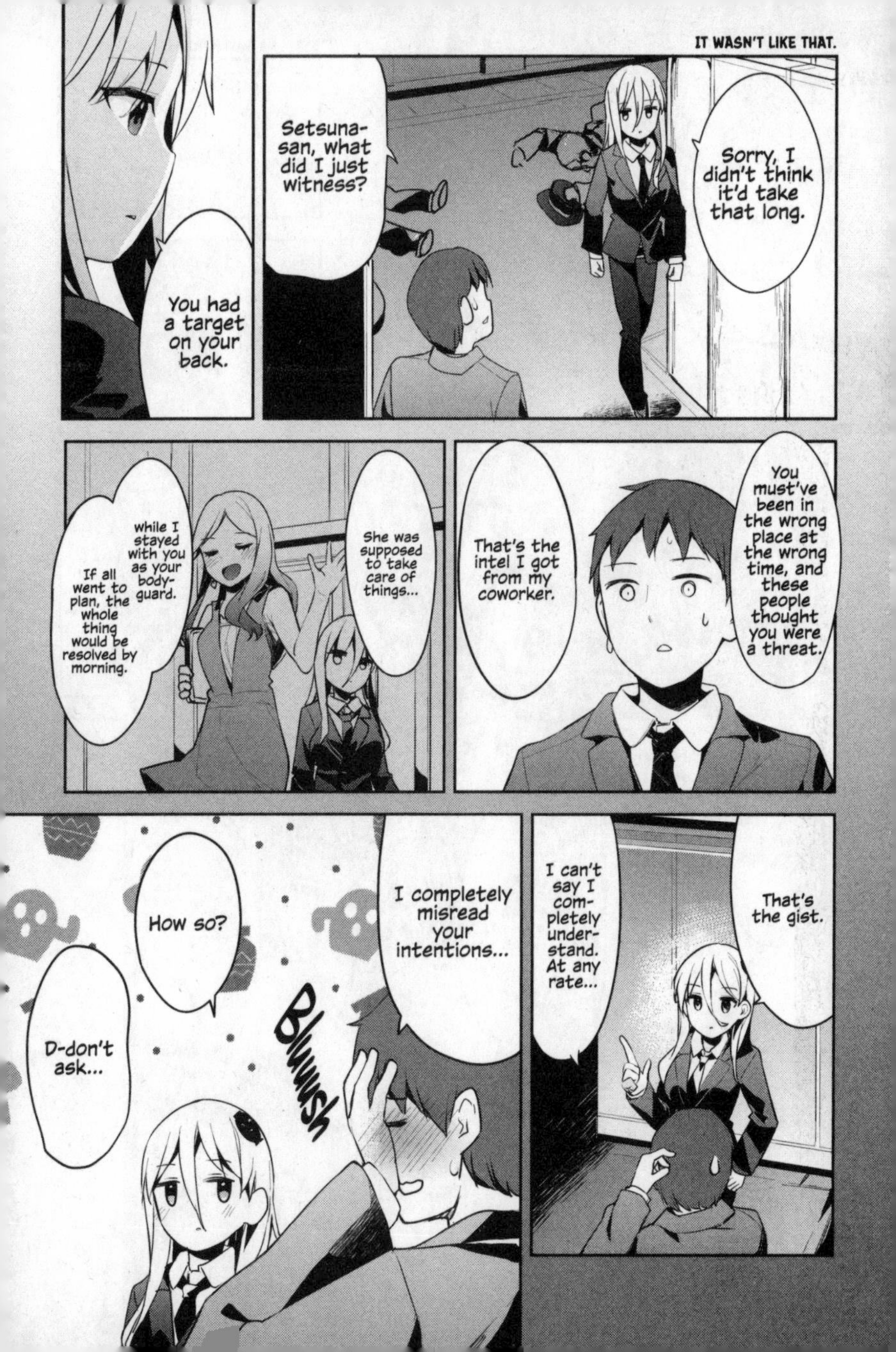
Sorry, I didn't think it'd take that long.
Setsuna-san, what did I just witness?
You had a target on your back.
You must've been in the wrong place at the wrong time, and these people thought you were a threat.
That's the intel I got from my coworker.
She was supposed to take care of things...
while I stayed with you as your bodyguard.
If all went to plan, the whole thing would be resolved by morning.
That's the gist.
I can't say I completely understand. At any rate...
I completely misread your intentions...
How so?
Bluush
D-don't ask...

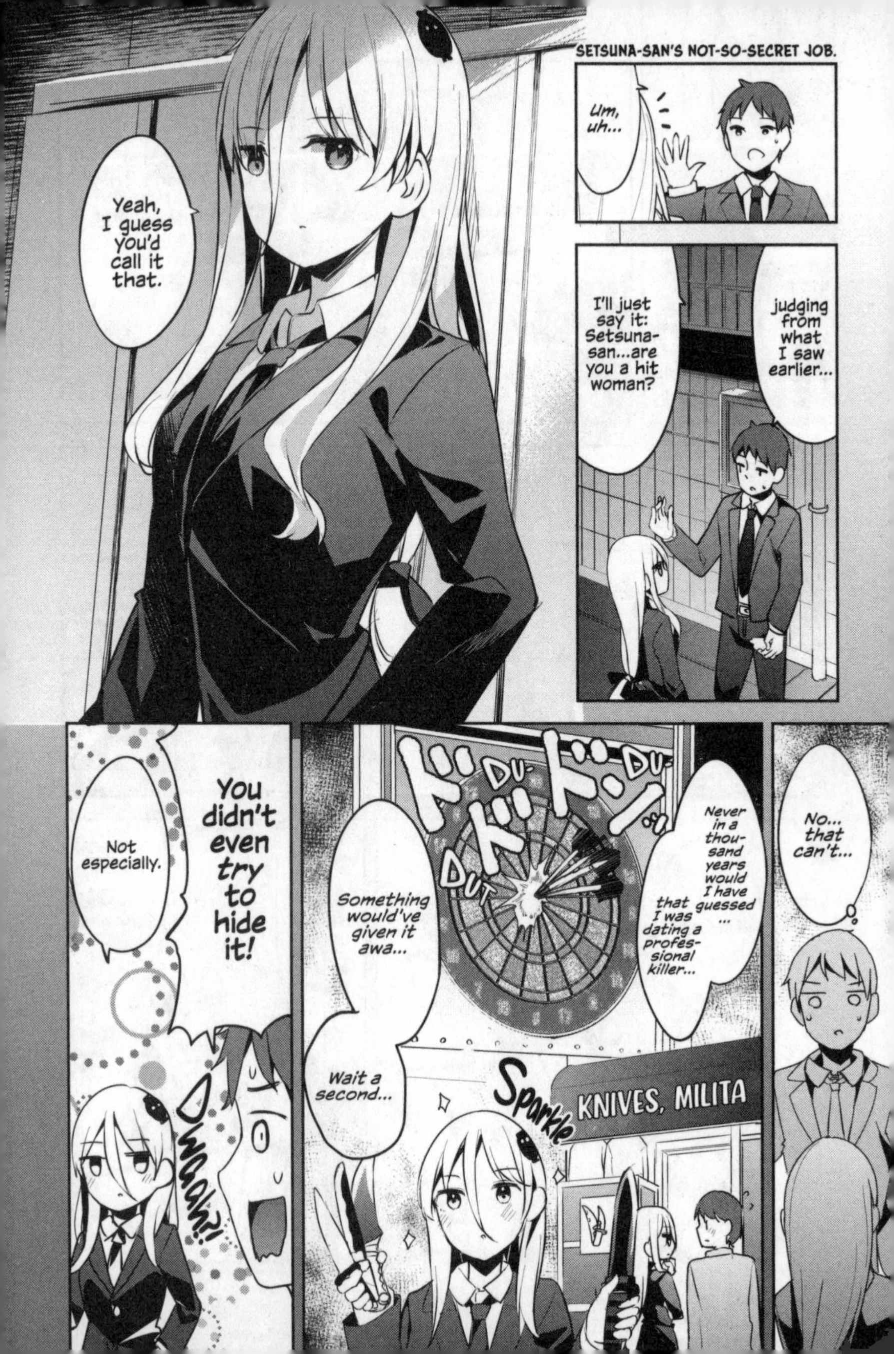
SETSUNA-SAN'S NOT-SO-SECRET JOB.
Um, uh...
judging from what I saw earlier...
I'll just say it: Setsuna-san...are you a hit woman?
Yeah, I guess you'd call it that.
No... that can't...
Never in a thousand years would I have guessed... that I was dating a professional killer...
DU- DU- DUT
Something would've given it awa...
Wait a second...
Sparkle
KNIVES, MILITA
You didn't even try to hide it!
Not especially.
Dwaah?!

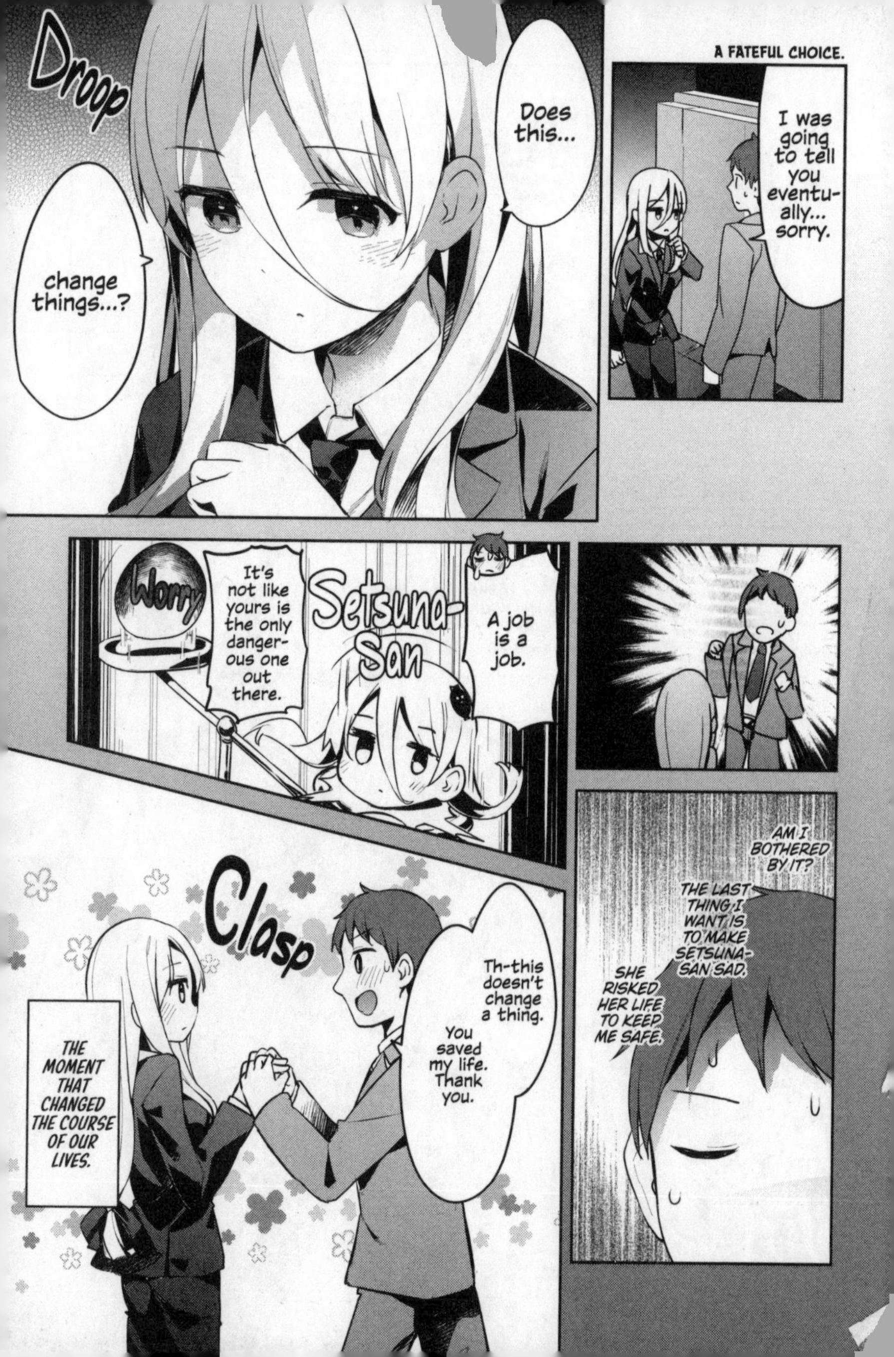
I was going to tell you eventually... sorry.
Droop
Does this...
change things...?
A job is a job.
Setsuna-San
It's not like yours is the only danger-ous one out there.
Worry
AM I BOTHERED BY IT?
THE LAST THING I WANT IS TO MAKE SETSUNA-SAN SAD.
SHE RISKED HER LIFE TO KEEP ME SAFE.
Clasp
Th-this doesn't change a thing.
You saved my life. Thank you.
THE MOMENT THAT CHANGED THE COURSE OF OUR LIVES.

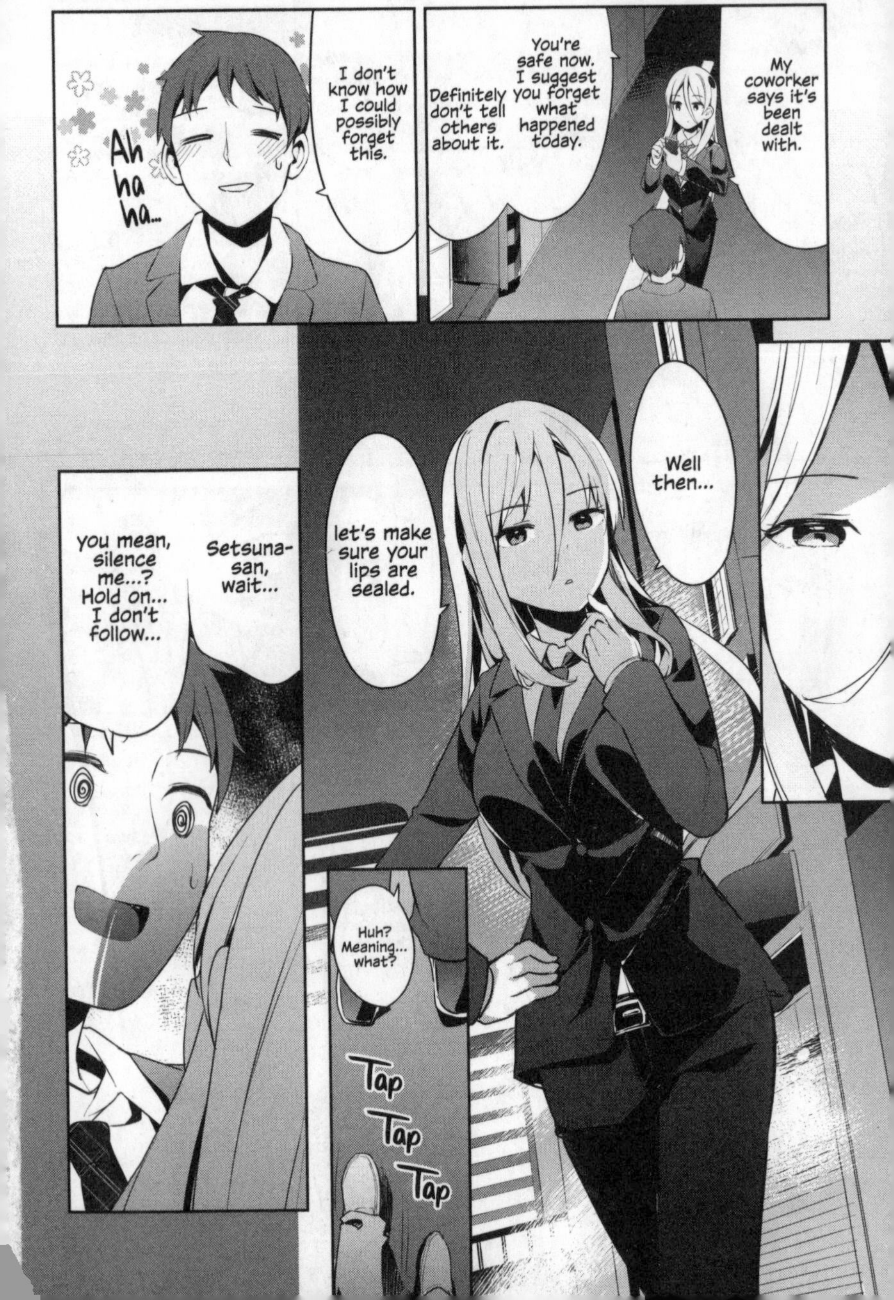
My coworker says it's been dealt with.
You're safe now. I suggest you forget what happened today.
Definitely don't tell others about it.
I don't know how I could possibly forget this.
Ah ha ha...
Well then...
let's make sure your lips are sealed.
Huh? Meaning... what?
Tap
Tap
Tap
Setsuna-san, wait...
you mean, silence me...? Hold on... I don't follow...

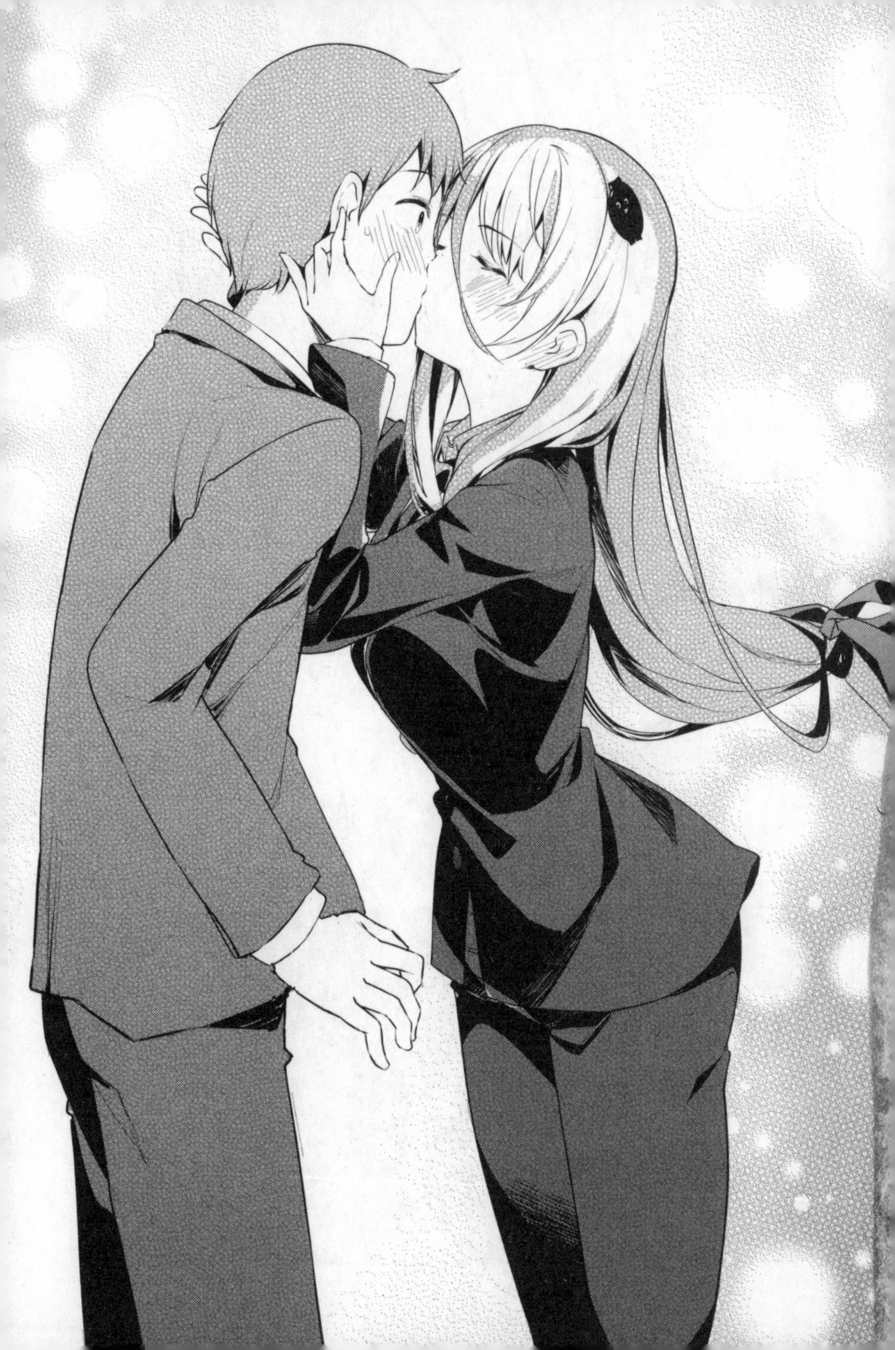

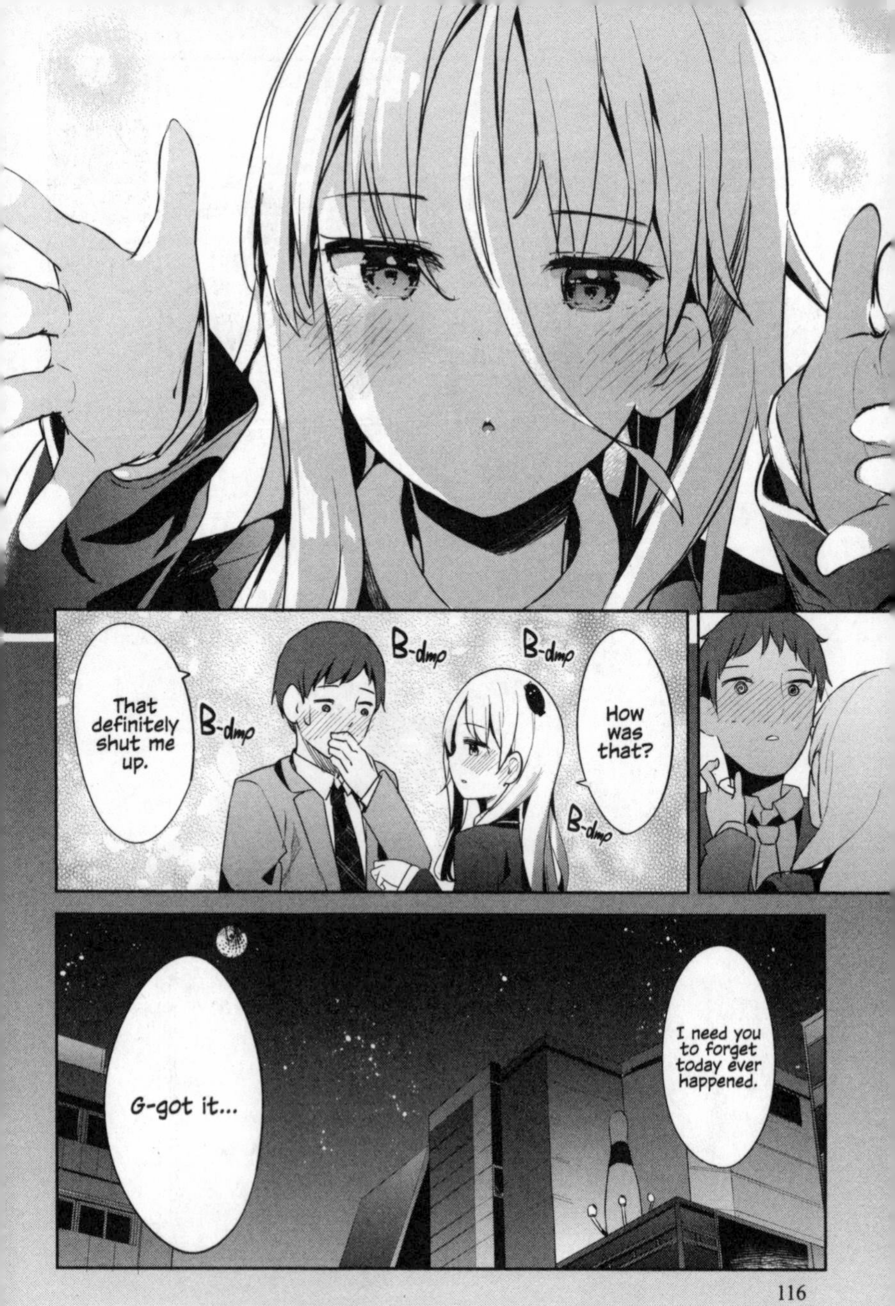
B-dmp
How was that?
B-dmp
B-dmp
That definitely shut me up.
B-dmp
I need you to forget today ever happened.
G-got it...

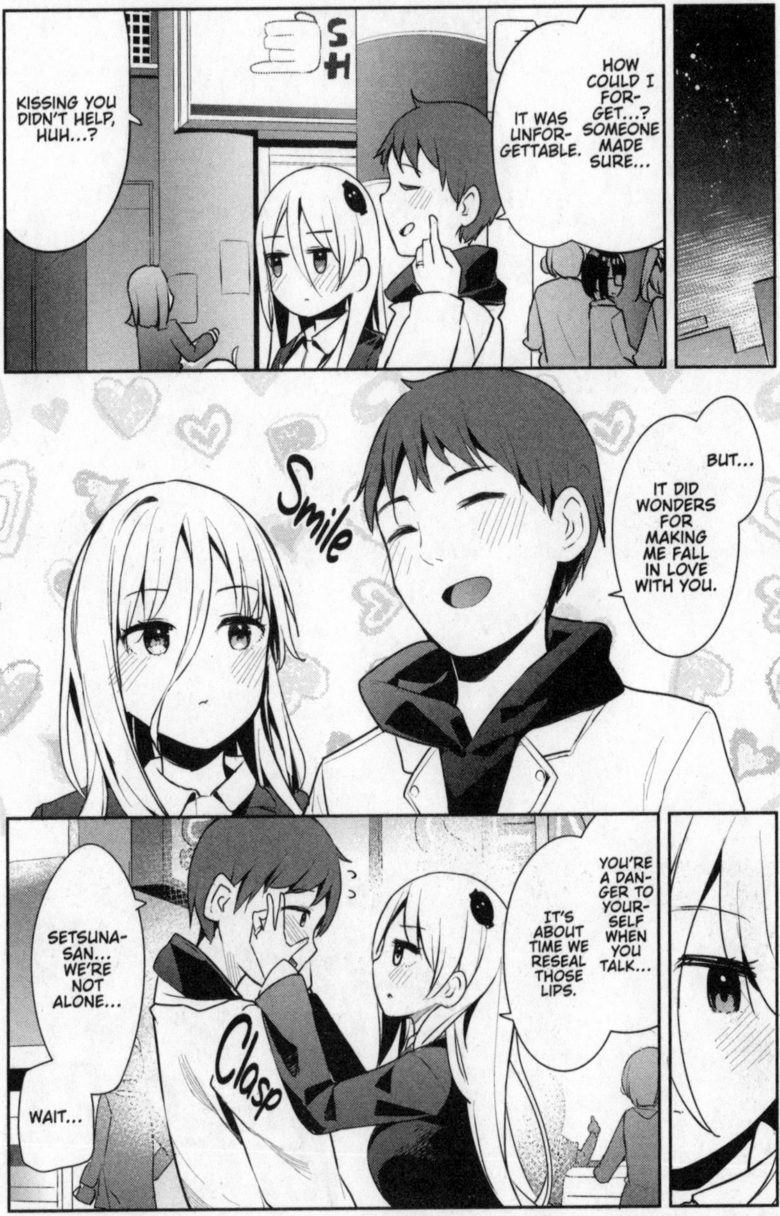
HOW COULD I FORGET...? SOMEONE MADE SURE...
IT WAS UNFORGETTABLE.
KISSING YOU DIDN'T HELP, HUH...?
BUT... IT DID WONDERS FOR MAKING ME FALL IN LOVE WITH YOU.
Smile
YOU'RE A DANGER TO YOURSELF WHEN YOU TALK...
IT'S ABOUT TIME WE RESEAL THOSE LIPS.
SETSUNA-SAN... WE'RE NOT ALONE...
Clasp
WAIT...

MY Lovey-Dovey Wife IS A STONE COLD KILLER

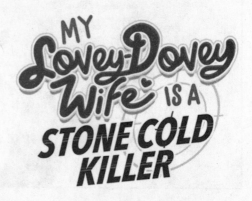

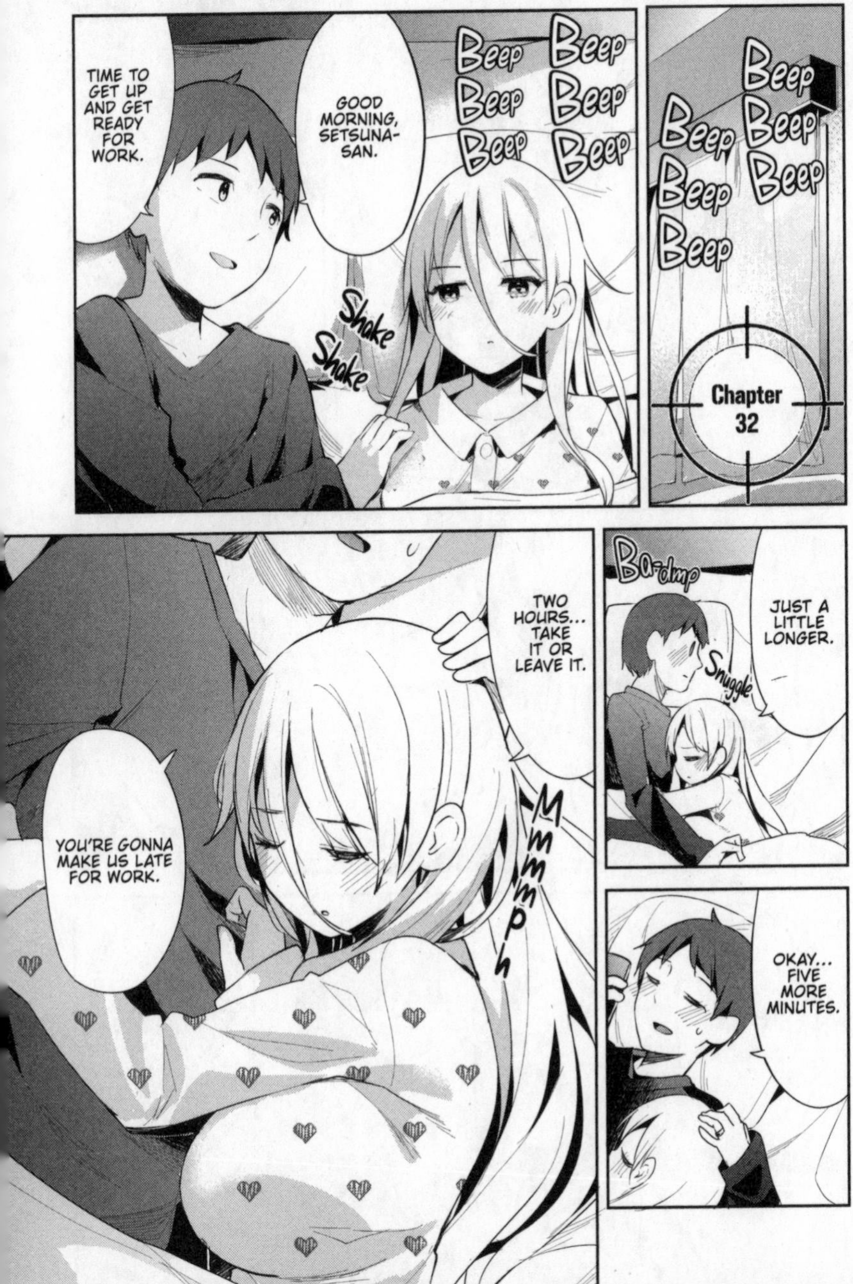
Beep Beep Beep Beep
Beep Beep Beep
Chapter 32
Beep Beep Beep
Beep Beep Beep
GOOD MORNING, SETSUNA-SAN.
TIME TO GET UP AND GET READY FOR WORK.
Shake Shake
Ba-dmp
JUST A LITTLE LONGER.
Snuggle
OKAY... FIVE MORE MINUTES.
TWO HOURS... TAKE IT OR LEAVE IT.
Mmmmph
YOU'RE GONNA MAKE US LATE FOR WORK.

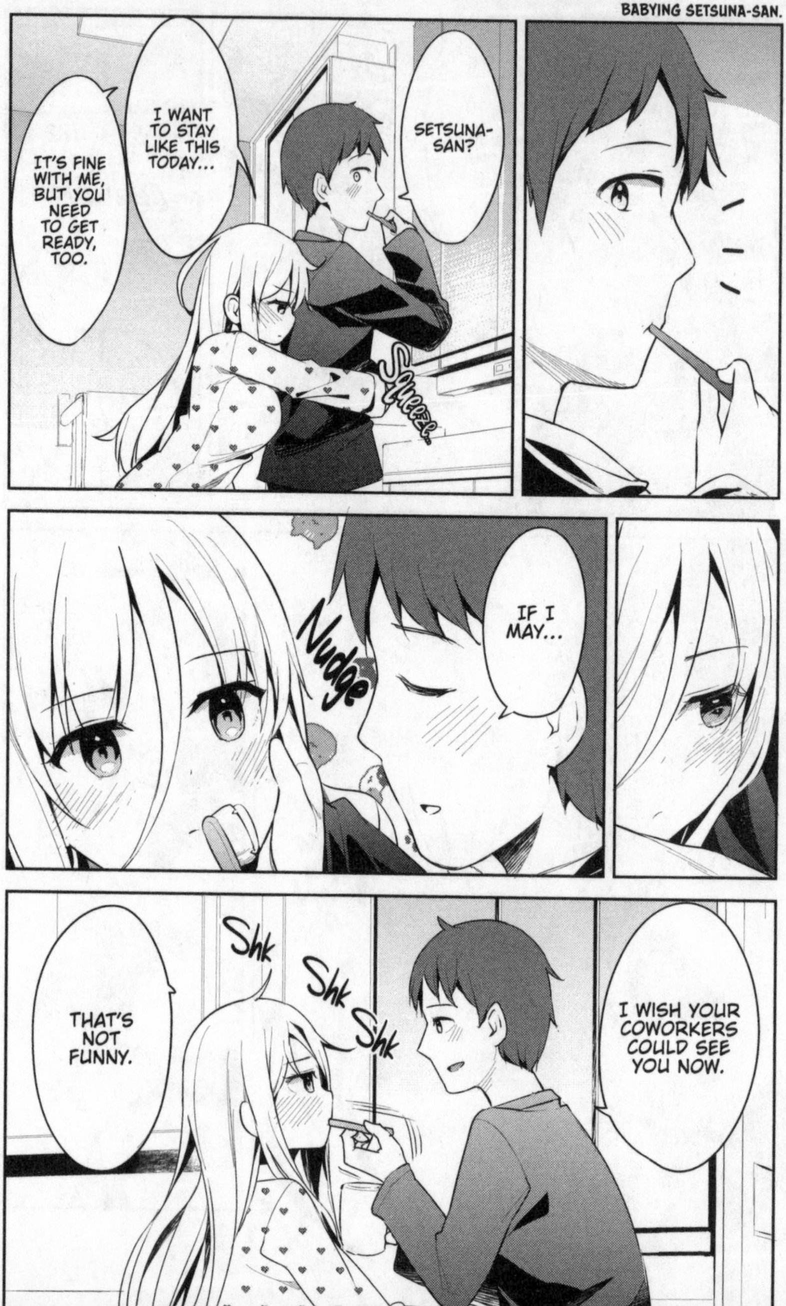
SETSUNA-SAN?
I WANT TO STAY LIKE THIS TODAY...
Squeeze
IT'S FINE WITH ME, BUT YOU NEED TO GET READY, TOO.
IF I MAY...
Nudge
I WISH YOUR COWORKERS COULD SEE YOU NOW.
Shk
Shk
Shk
THAT'S NOT FUNNY.

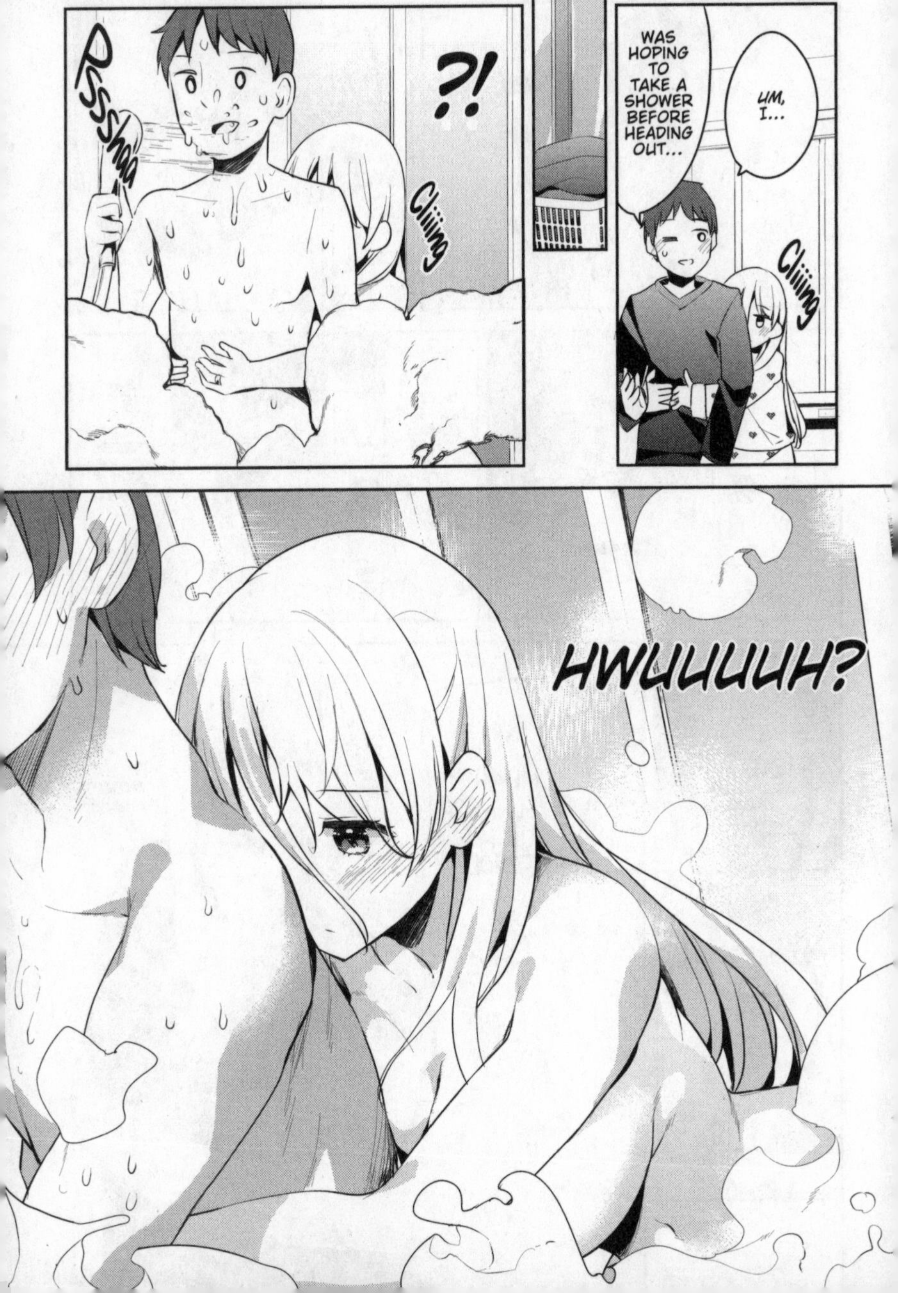
UM, I...
WAS HOPING TO TAKE A SHOWER BEFORE HEADING OUT...
Cliiing
Pssshaa
?!
Cliiing
HWUUUUH?

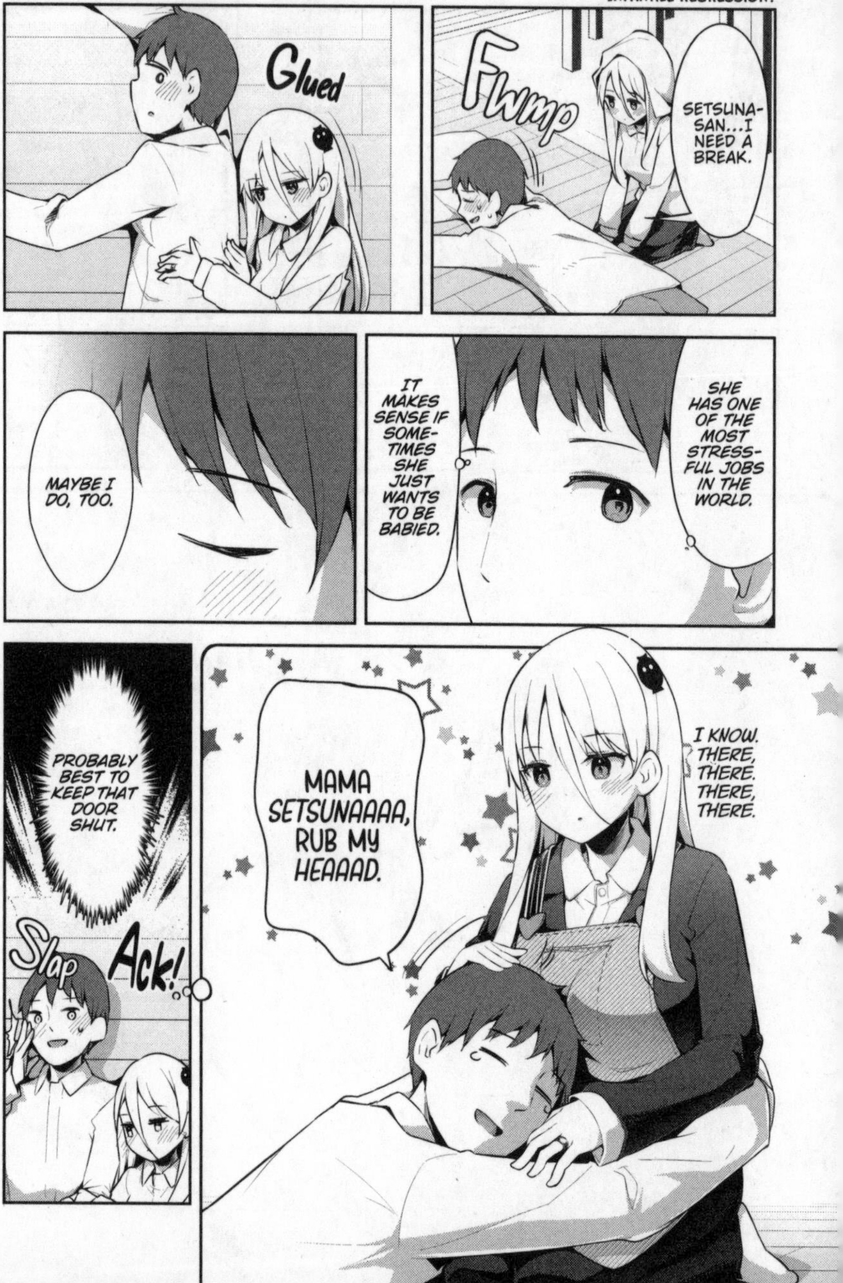
Fwmp
SETSUNA-SAN...I NEED A BREAK.
Glued
SHE HAS ONE OF THE MOST STRESSFUL JOBS IN THE WORLD.
IT MAKES SENSE IF SOMETIMES SHE JUST WANTS TO BE BABIED.
MAYBE I DO, TOO.
MAMA SETSUNAAAA, RUB MY HEAAAD.
I KNOW. THERE, THERE. THERE, THERE.
PROBABLY BEST TO KEEP THAT DOOR SHUT.
Slap
Ack!

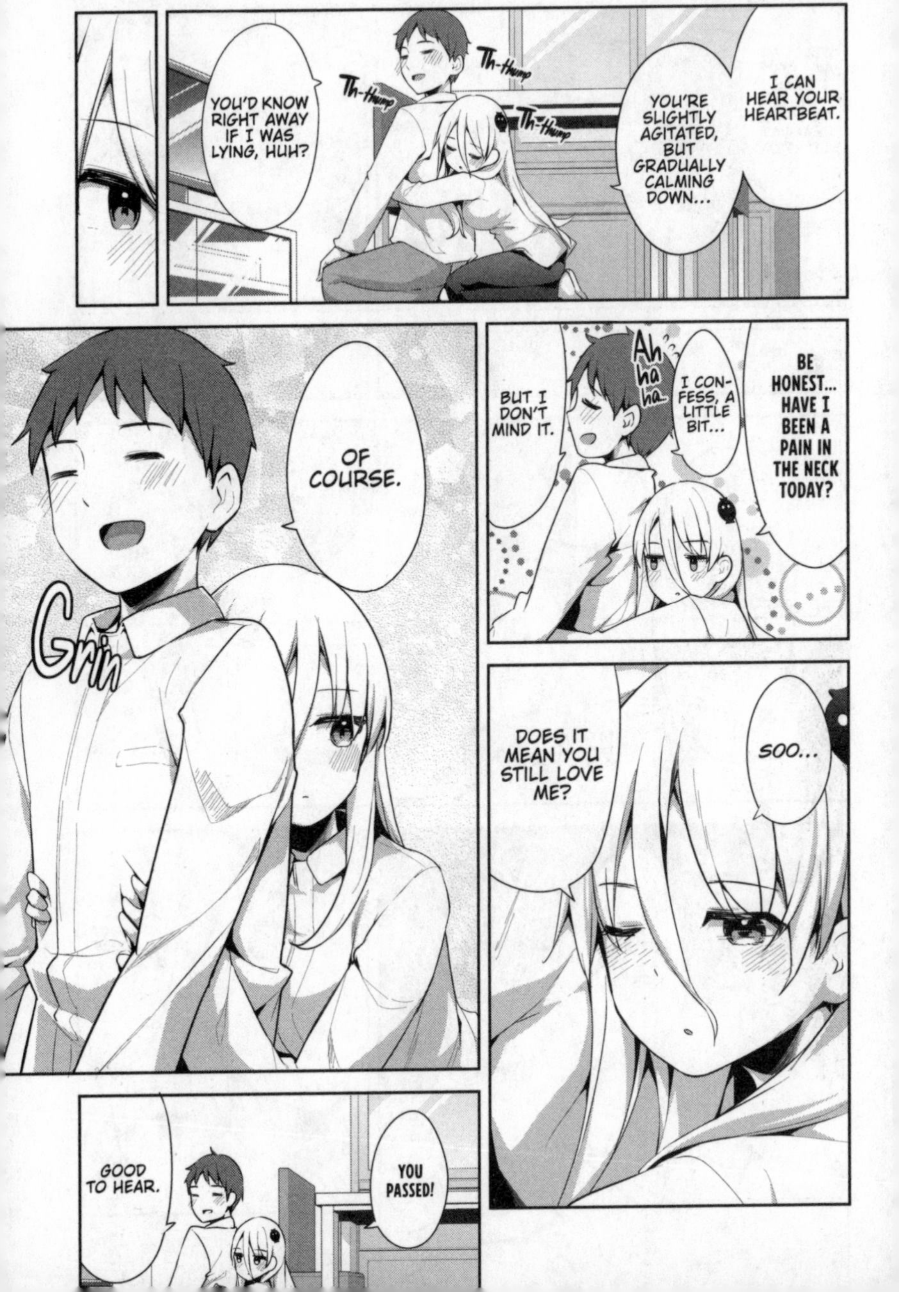
I CAN HEAR YOUR HEARTBEAT.
YOU'RE SLIGHTLY AGITATED, BUT GRADUALLY CALMING DOWN...
Th-thump
Th-thump
Th-thump
YOU'D KNOW RIGHT AWAY IF I WAS LYING, HUH?
BE HONEST... HAVE I BEEN A PAIN IN THE NECK TODAY?
I CON-FESS, A LITTLE BIT...
Ah ha ha
BUT I DON'T MIND IT.
SOO...
DOES IT MEAN YOU STILL LOVE ME?
OF COURSE.
Grin
YOU PASSED!
GOOD TO HEAR.

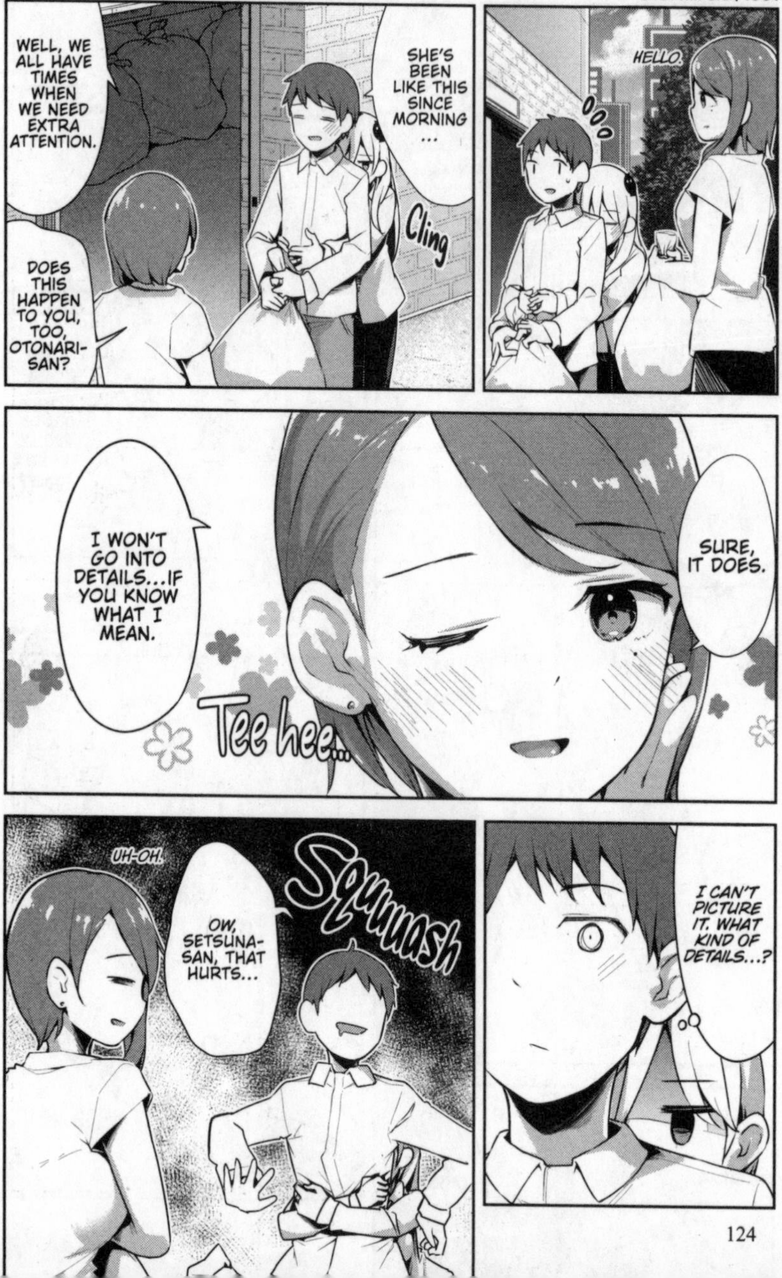
HELLO.
OOO
SHE'S BEEN LIKE THIS SINCE MORNING...
Cling
WELL, WE ALL HAVE TIMES WHEN WE NEED EXTRA ATTENTION.
DOES THIS HAPPEN TO YOU, TOO, OTONARI-SAN?
SURE, IT DOES.
I WON'T GO INTO DETAILS...IF YOU KNOW WHAT I MEAN.
Tee hee...
I CAN'T PICTURE IT. WHAT KIND OF DETAILS...?
Squuash
OW, SETSUNA-SAN, THAT HURTS...
UH-OH.

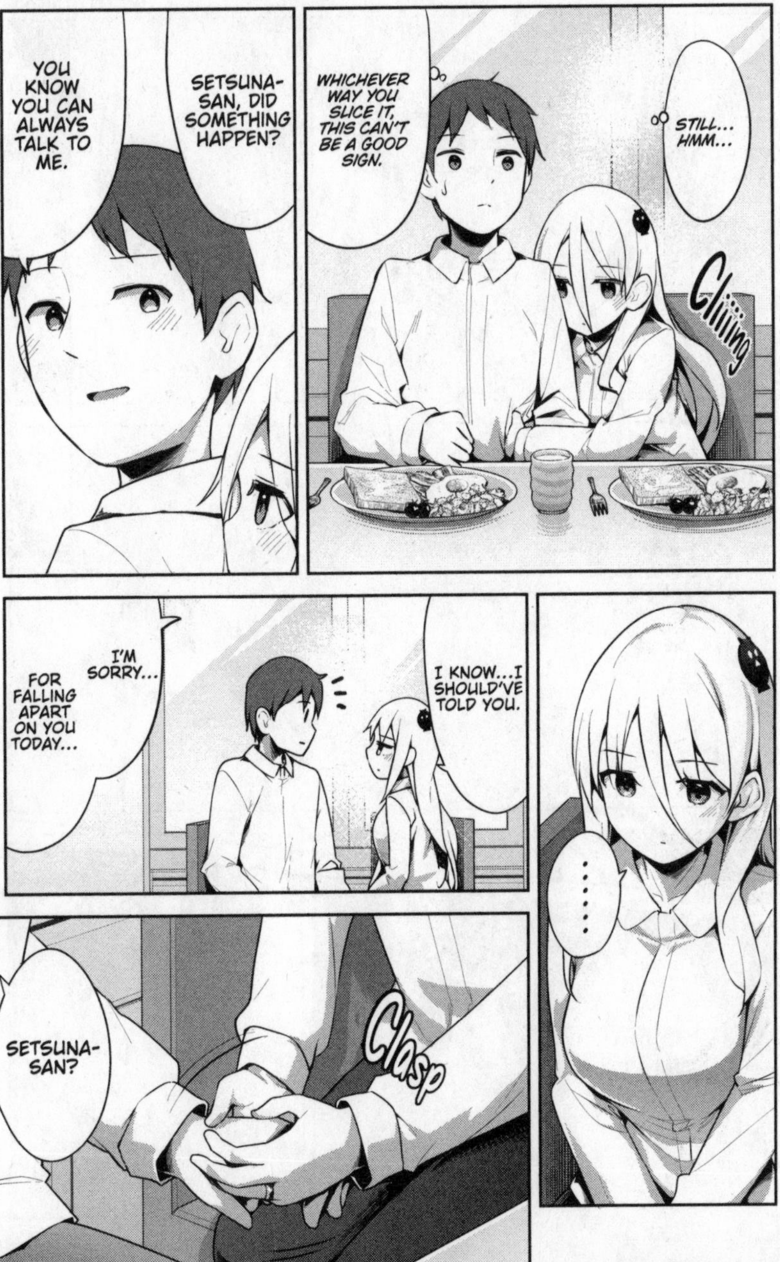

STILL... HMM...
WHICHEVER WAY YOU SLICE IT, THIS CAN'T BE A GOOD SIGN.
Cliiing
SETSUNA-SAN, DID SOMETHING HAPPEN?
YOU KNOW YOU CAN ALWAYS TALK TO ME.
......
I KNOW...I SHOULD'VE TOLD YOU.
I'M SORRY...
FOR FALLING APART ON YOU TODAY...
Clasp
SETSUNA-SAN?

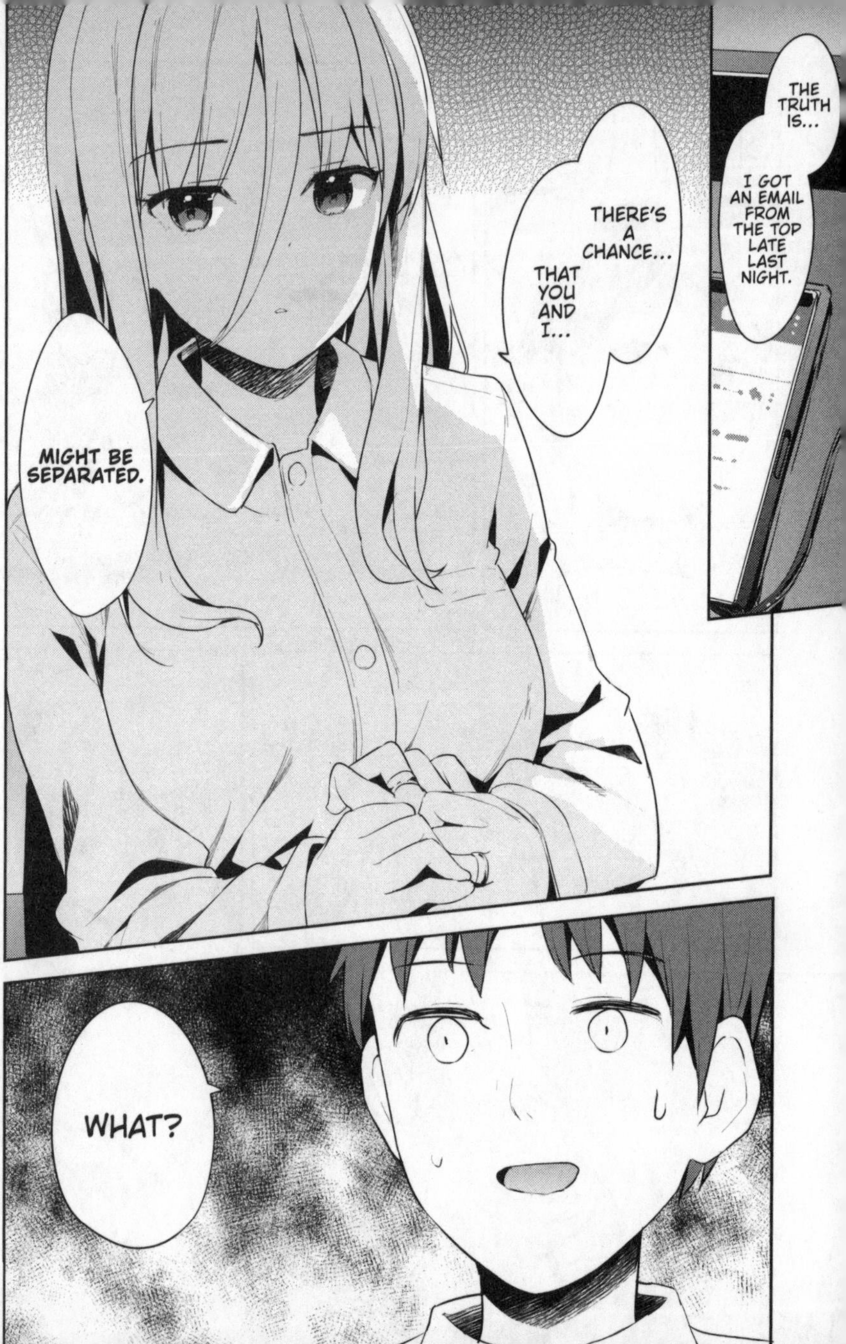
THE TRUTH IS...
I GOT AN EMAIL FROM THE TOP LATE LAST NIGHT.
THERE'S A CHANCE...
THAT YOU AND I...
MIGHT BE SEPARATED.
WHAT?

MY Lovey-Dovey Wife IS A STONE COLD KILLER

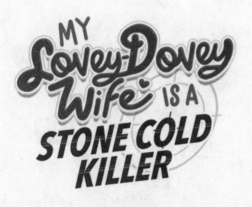

MY Lovey-Dovey Wife IS A STONE COLD KILLER

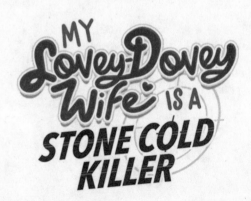

Afterword

So, volume 4 is here! Thank you for your support!

As winter gave way to spring in the story--the cherry trees blossoming and the ice between Setsuna-san and her mother thawing more--it coincided with real life, and I found myself working on this volume in spring.

The seasons in the manga used to be the same as the real world when the series just started, and I thought I could continue that.

But little by little, reality outpaced the story, and while the couple visited Setsuna-san's family in the country, the story started to lag behind by a whole year. Recently, it's fallen two years behind.

I think by the time this volume is published the seasons will be a bit off again.

Our couple's relationship remains new and exciting, so they share a lot of meaningful moments as they get to know each other. My wish for them is to take their time and continue to grow their connection at their own pace.

Now...you might be feeling alarmed by the ending.
Things did take a bit of an unsettling turn...

Worry not. Those of you with good intuition may have even figured it out. Something similar may or may not have happened in volume 2. I hope this gives you some peace of mind as you wait to see what happens. Stay tuned!

Donten Kosaka

FIND ME ONLINE!

Special Thanks

[Production]
dosiro-do-san
https://twitter.com/DosiroD

[Editor in Chief]
Yamamoto-san

[Designer]
Kusume-san

**Nagatsuki-san
Omegane-sensei
Kanae Kakitsubata-sensei**

And all of you readers!

About The Author

My Twitter

I might or might not post frequently...!

https://twitter.co m/higheast

Art Site

Support my work as a fan! My page on pixiv fanbox. Do I share original sketches of Setsuna-san and others? Maybe!

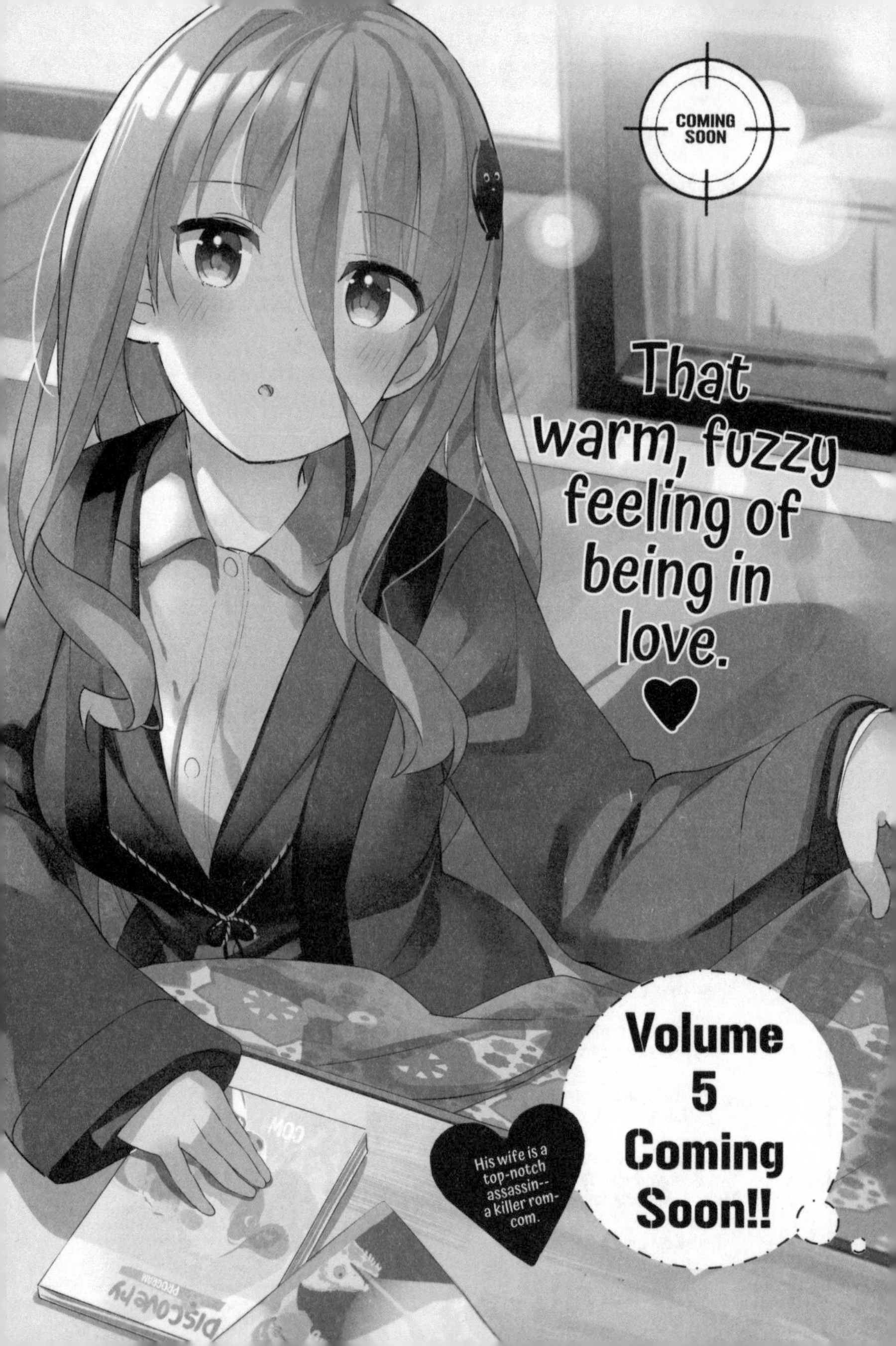
COMING SOON
That warm, fuzzy feeling of being in love.
Volume 5 Coming Soon!!
His wife is a top-notch assassin--a killer rom-com.

MY

Lovey-Dovey Wife IS A

STONE COLD KILLER

SEVEN SEAS ENTERTAINMENT PRESENTS

MY Lovey-Dovey WIFE IS A STONE COLD KILLER

story and art by DONTEN KOSAKA   VOLUME 4

TRANSLATION
Elena Kirillova

ADAPTATION
Tabby Wright

LETTERING
Mercedes McGarry

COVER DESIGN
H. Qi

LOGO DESIGN
Shi Briggs

PROOFREADER
James Rhoden

COPY EDITOR
B. Lillian Martin

EDITOR
Kristiina Korpus

PRODUCTION DESIGNER
Brennan Thome

PRODUCTION MANAGER
Lissa Pattillo

PREPRESS TECHNICIAN
Melanie Ujimori
Jules Valera

EDITOR-IN-CHIEF
Julie Davis

ASSOCIATE PUBLISHER
Adam Arnold

PUBLISHER
Jason DeAngelis

HAIKEI... KOROSHIYASAN TO KEKKONSHIMASHITA Vol.4
©Donten Kosaka 2022
First published in Japan in 2022 by KADOKAWA CORPORATION, Tokyo.
English translation rights arranged with KADOKAWA CORPORATION, Tokyo.

Seven Seas press and purchase enquiries can be sent to Marketing Manager Lianne Sentar at press@gomanga.com. Information regarding the distribution and purchase of digital editions is available from Digital Manager CK Russell at digital@gomanga.com.

Seven Seas and the Seven Seas logo are trademarks of Seven Seas Entertainment. All rights reserved.

ISBN: 978-1-63858-837-5
Printed in Canada
First Printing: April 2023
10 9 8 7 6 5 4 3 2 1

READING DIRECTIONS

This book reads from *right to left*, Japanese style. If this is your first time reading manga, you start reading from the top right panel on each page and take it from there. If you get lost, just follow the numbered diagram here. It may seem backwards at first, but you'll get the hang of it! Have fun!!

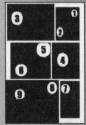

Follow us online: www.SevenSeasEntertainment.com